Le Montrachet

BERNARD GINESTET'S GUIDE
TO THE VINEYARDS OF FRANCE

Côte de Nuits

Extent of the AOC vineyards
(Grands Crus, Premiers Crus,
communal wines and others
with the Bourgogne appellation)

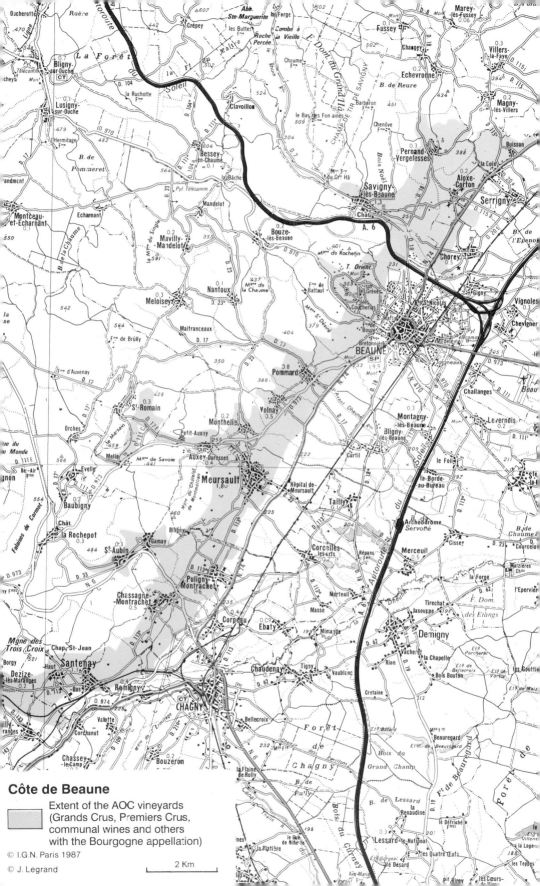

Côte de Beaune

Extent of the AOC vineyards
(Grands Crus, Premiers Crus,
communal wines and others
with the Bourgogne appellation)

© I.G.N. Paris 1987

© J. Legrand

2 Km

Jean-François Bazin

Foreword by Nicolas Faith

Le Montrachet

Translated by John Meredith

BERNARD GINESTET'S GUIDE
TO THE VINEYARDS OF FRANCE

Jacques Legrand

Originated and produced by:

Jacques Legrand SA

English version edited by:

Editor:	Nicholas Faith
Assistant editor:	Tamara Thorgevsky
Translator:	John L. Meredith
Copy editor:	Barbara Mellor
Editorial secretary:	Christine Fourton
Art director:	Henri Marganne
Layout:	Claire Forgeot

ISBN 0-582-07542-4 for Longman UK distribution
ISBN 2-905969-38-5 for the rest of the world

Printed in Belgium by Brepols, Turnhout

Foreword

At first it seems ridiculous to devote a whole book to a few acres of stony hillside, owned through the ages by an ever-changing, ever-squabbling gang of greedy rustics, producing a mere 30,000 bottles of wine a year. It is typical of rural France that even these tiny figures can be indefinitely divided and subdivided. We have Montrachet pure, one of those one-word signatures which carry an absolute authority (there aren't many, and most of the others are also in Burgundy). Then, in a hierarchy meticulously noted by Jean-François Bazin, come the lesser breeds from Puligny and Chassagne, the two villages which, like husbands marrying rich and noble wives, have increased their status – and their wealth – by joining their names to those of their spouses.

For the nobility is real. These slopes produce the subtlest, most elegant, simply and absolutely the best dry white wine in the world. Its fame was established centuries ago, and it has set a standard of excellence for more wine-makers, on at least three continents, than any other of France's fine wines (and that's saying a lot). Over the past twenty years in particular it has become clear that the chardonnay is a remarkably accommodating variety capable of producing fruity and drinkable wines from a wide range of soils and climates.

Montrachet's brother, Château d'Yquem, unquestionably the finest sweet white wine in the world, can rejoice in its own unique microclimate, an advantage denied to Montrachet; and Montrachet's neighbours have had a much easier task with their red wines, if only because the pinot noir is such an exacting grape that their own human inadequacies were less important. But the growers of Puligny and Montrachet cannot afford to rest on their laurels, for wine-makers in a dozen states in Australia and the United States in particular are snapping at their heels, conscious not only of the glory to be gained in any comparison with the original but also of the profit to be had.

No one has – as yet – got anywhere near Montrachet, but no one knows why. 'All the explanations are convincing, but none of them is adequate', says Mr Bazin. A local scholar, born amongst the vines, he has written a loving volume, a Burgundian book in that it displays the classic paranoia about the United States. But fortunately it does not display that Burgundian smugness, that assumption that all is for the best in the best of all possible worlds. Indeed he is not afraid of harsh judgements, all based on the sensible and understandable belief that anyone owning a plot, however tiny, in ground as sacred as Montrachet has a particular duty to ensure that his or her wine is worthy of the name.

Nicholas Faith

For Jacques,
this golden key...

I should like to thank most cordially everybody who has helped and advised me, in particular Mesdames Catherine Hernu, Agnès Livéra, Bernadette Nicot-Torgano and Marie-Pierre Romand; Mesdemoiselles Bernadette Blandin, Madeleine Blondel and Catherine Guyon; Canon Jean Marilier; Messieurs Benoît Chauvin, Gérard Curie, Raymond Dumay, Georges Renoy, Jules Tourmeau and Laurent Touvet; the bibliothèques municipales *of Autun, Beaune and Dijon; the* Archives départementales *of Côte-d'Or and Saône-et-Loire; the* Musée de la Vie bourguignonne *in Dijon and the* Musée du Vin *in Beaune; and the* Agence internationale d'urbanisme de l'agglomération dijonnaise *in Dijon.*

Contents

The enigma of Montrachet

What could be more ordinary than this meagre hillside? Nothing about it strikes the eye or captures the imagination. Barely differentiated from the plain, the tiny hill of Montrachet looks rather like a piece of Gruyère cheese on the landscape. It seems destined by nature to be left uncultivated, a land of bushes, scrubby grass and stones of interest only to goats. What crop would grow there? "Une peau de chagrin" (A reference to Balzac's philosophical novel. Editor's note), according to Pierre Poupon. Stendhal saw these slopes as a "small, unsightly arid mountain", although he added, "Are brilliant people ever ugly?" And brilliance is what it is all about, for this hill is clothed with vines: it wears the Golden Fleece.

Mont-Chauve

The Clos de Vougeot is an integral part of Cîteaux, its château and its Chevaliers du Tastevin. Majestically, its portals open wide to Eternity. There is nothing of the kind in Montrachet. The walls have only humble doors, symbolic and not even destined for carts. You might say that their dimensions are those of an angel with folded wings. This sublime modesty either reveals the ultimate in saintliness or disguises the most outrageous arrogance.

In the history of the *Grands Crus* Montrachet seems to be a late starter. But perhaps it wanted to appear last on the scene in order to mark its intention of taking the leading role. Pierre Larousse's *Grand Dictionnaire universel* of 1869 dedicated a lengthy article to the Clos de Vougeot and in 1874 gave only a single line to Montrachet, not even mentioning it in Chassagne, "where the most famous vineyards are Clos Saint-Jean and Clos Pitois". Straddling two villages, Chassagne and Puligny, Montrachet has a double, if not multiple history. For apart from these two villages, there are also hamlets here: Blagny, Morgeot, Mypont and others. Over the centuries, it has been linked now with the one, now with the other, with apparently no consistency.

◄ *Harvesting in Montrachet: bunches of pure gold*

A great number of Burgundy vineyards were known and appreciated as far back as the early Middle Ages: Clos du Roi at Chenôve, Clos de Bèze and Clos Saint-Jacques at Gevrey, Clos de Tart at Morey, La Romanée at Vosne, La Commaraine at Pommard and many others besides. Their exact outlines were established as early as the twelfth and thirteenth centuries. The Clos de Vougeot came into being in about 1110, and a hundred years later its walls went up, to stand till the present day.

Can history explain Montrachet? Before A.D. 1000, Chassagne reaped its one glory from the Clos Saint-Jean, a property belonging to the Abbey of Saint-Jean-le-Grand d'Autun. This was a Benedictine convent founded by Brunehaut in 589 and re-established by Charlemagne after the destruction caused by the Saracens. Thanks to the endeavours of Danielle Fèvre, a student from Dijon, we now know the history of the seigniory of Chassagne reasonably well. Its origins came about with the arrival of Guillaume Desrée in 1225. He already owned sizeable estates around Chalon and Chagny, where his family came from. In 1253 he purchased from the heirs of Arnauld de Corabeuf some eight and a half hectares of vines in Chassagne. With a high proportion of meadows, fields and woodland, the vines extended over this village, and also over the Saint-Aubin of today, Sampigny, Meursault, and on to the plain. At the time of what was known as the "tally of hearths" – the census of 1285 – this family were lords of the manor of half of Chassagne. The rest belonged to the Abbot of Maizières, the Abbess of Saint-Jean d'Autun, the Hospice of Bellecroix, Hugues de Barbirey, and so on.

At this time, the name of Montrachet did not figure in the prolific archives of the seigniory, preserved in Dijon. In the thirteenth century it was mentioned only once, in about 1275, in relation to an agreement between Pierre Desrée's widow and Hugues Corabeuf, settling their dispute about rights of pasture at Ouroux and Gamay, two neighbouring hamlets: Symone was allowed to take stones from the quarry at Montrachet. At that time the hill was probably covered with bushes and scrub and scarred with quarries, as is the case all over the Côte. There were doubtless a few vines here but there is nothing to indicate their name or reputation.

Montrachet? *Mons Rachicensis*, wrote the priest Claude Courtépée in the eighteenth century: "an uncultivated hill". And among the deeds of the Abbey of Maizières we find "Mont Rachaz" (1252), "Mont Raschat" (1286-1287), "Mon Rachat" (1380), "Mont Rachat" (1472) and "Montrachat" (1473). Generally speaking these are references to vines situated "beneath" this little locality, meaning halfway down the slope or even lower. Does this imply the most generally accepted etymology: "Mont-Chauve" (the Bald Mount)? Such a denuded hillside in the middle of the landscape could well have inspired this name. The old French word for ringworm was "rache": could the name mean a mount which was shorn and suffering from "rache", with its slabs of rock and its *murgers* creating the impression of baldness? Gérard Taverdet has suggested "the Mount of the Bird of Prey" ("rachet" in old French being a bird of prey). Obviously this is more flattering. And do there not exist the names Montfaucon (Falcon's Mount), Montmeilland (Kite's Mount) and others? Without fear of contradiction, we can state categorically that Montrachet owes its name to this hill. For many years, right up to the nineteenth century, people spoke of Mont-Rachet, Mont-Rachat or Morachet. Moreover, there are parallel examples in many villages and crus: Voullenaye for Volnay, Mursault for Meursault, and so on.

Whatever the case, neither "t" should be pronounced. The first mute "t" comes about from the name Mont-Rachet, still common up to the end of the nineteenth century. We should not forget that the people of Burgundy soften all their words, especially where there is the letter "x" (Fixin is pronounced Fissin, Auxey becomes Aussey, etc.). As for the people of the cru, they have always said "Morachet". This pronunciation even features in a debate in the Chassagne town council at the end of the nineteenth century.

After this, the history of the seigniory of Chassagne is more confused. The relatively sparse documentary evidence does not enable us to piece together the chain of events with any precision. The Crux family is mentioned, and from 1438 the Oizelet family took control of the village for sixty years, along with several other lords (Damas, Pitois and others).

Apart from the Clos Saint-Jean d'Autun, whose fame was well established, no one here in the fourteenth and fifteenth centuries was tempted to purchase any vines with a view to developing them in order to create a vineyard and a cru. The name Montrachet still remains inconspicuous in the archives. Can such timidity to be explained? The majority of the Grands Crus owe their initial existence and development to religious communities (Cîteaux, Cluny, Bèze, innumerable monasteries and canonic colleges), to a ducal or royal estate, or to great families. The lords of Chassagne were certainly of a modest lineage and were not driven by ambition to create immortal works. On the other hand, Chassagne lies at the far end of the Côte. Up to 1275, the village belonged to the seigniory of Chagny, so being dependent on that château. Chagny's own measure was used to calculate the quantities of wine to be delivered to the lord. Soon after, noblesse oblige, it was the measure used in Beaune which gradually took precedence. Dependent on the bailiwick of Dijon, itself responsible for Beaune, Chassagne increasingly attracted the attention of the capital of Burgundy. This was the way the balance was tilting and, taking the line of least resistance, the flow caused this wine increasingly to be associated with Beaune. But all this did not take place in a day, nor even a century: it was when Chassagne was entirely in Beaune's orbit that its wines began to achieve fame.

This barren, rock-strewn and unimpressive hillside is none other than the celebrated Montrachet. Its sparse grass would not feed a goat. And yet this is the cradle of a wine sought after by all true wine lovers. ▶

Moreover Chassagne is not large, and on top of that it is divided into the two hamlets of Chassagne-les-Hautes and Chassagnes-les-Basses, or Chassagnes-les-Grandes and Chassagnes-les-Petites. Although it has a superb aspect, this little village has had great difficulty in finding itself a place in the sun. Over the years, wars and turmoil have varied its population from a few dozen to a few hundred. For a long time it did not have its own church, sometimes using that of Saint-Aubin, sometimes that of Puligny. The right to build a chapel, achieved after a mighty struggle in 1462, well illustrates this difficult battle for emancipation. The authorization, covering pages upon pages, stipulates that this modest church may not have either baptistry or a surrounding cemetery, nor even a collecting-box: in other words, it was forbidden anything which might reduce the income of the clergy round about. However, a dispensation of 1486 freed the inhabitants of Chassagne from the obligation of giving Puligny bread which had been blessed.

At the end of the fifteenth century, in 1480, the seigniory became the property of one family, that of François de Ferrières. As the lord of Saffres and now of Chassagne, he was *maître d'hôtel* (an honorary title) to Philippe de Hocberg, Comte de Neuchâtel, Maréchal de Bourgogne and, most notably, *seigneur* of Chagny. He was also one of the king's aides-de-camp. He owned vast estates, yielding a considerable income, right up to Mâcon and Salins. A *rentier* dated 1483 and listing his income indicates that François de Ferrières was the direct owner of 7 hectares 44 ares (18.4 acres) of vines at Chassagne and that he also rented out some 22 hectares 25 ares (55 acres) of vines. This document is especially interesting in that it indicates the precise extent of the viticultural estate in relation to the size of the village (some thirty hectares) and also mentions the role of vignerons. He kept under his own management as many of his fields as he put out to rent. As for the vineyards, he worked only a third of them. Because it needs careful and vigilant attention, a vineyard is better cultivated by a tenant-farmer who becomes more or less its owner rather than by workers or casual labourers who have no interest in the fruits of their labours. The seigniorial rights were no different from the usual ones, preventing the villagers from selling their wine to others, for instance, or requiring a proclamation of the harvest allowing the lord to harvest two clear days before everybody else. This ensured that he had the necessary labour-force and accordingly it enabled him to supervise harvesting by other people.

What did the village of Chassagne look like at this time? On the hilltop, woodland (Chassagne comes from the French "chêne", meaning oak tree), then further down scrub, uncultivated land and bushes, holes left by quarrying, and lastly vines interspersed with meadows, fields, patches of gardens and houses. Since the thirteenth century the landscape has changed a lot. In those days tithes were paid mostly in oats and wheat. Since then, the vineyards have gained considerable ground both above the village and below as far as the path to Couches.

Gradually the wine of Chassagne lost its anonymity. In 1383 for example, the lord decided to extend his vineyards here. He indicated that they were to be planted with "noyriens" (the pinot noir) and "saulvoigniens" (sauvignon? the savagnin of the Jura? a white variety?). Whatever, this was a case of choosing for the best, for the gamay came into use everywhere during the fourteenth century. Philip the Bold banished this stock in 1395.

The *rentier* of 1483 from the archives of the seigniory of Chassagne is the first document to indicate the existence of Montrachet, mentioned particularly for its 21 ares 40 centiares (0.5 acres) of vines. As there is mention of other vines surrounding this parcel, the presence of this *climat* is certain. Montrachet doubtless emerged gradually over the fifteenth century. And the wine was already white, for in referring to this parcel, the text speaks of "the lord's white vines". Montrachet does not yet have a separate place in this list of assets, which lays special stress on 1 hectare 71 ares (4.2 acres) at the Bergerie, 1 hectare 71 ares (4.2 acres) at the Cloux Devant and 3 hectares 42 ares (8.5 acres) in one stretch at the side of the old château which later absorbed part of this vineyard.

The religious estates remained very large: there were still the monks of Sainte-Marie de Maizières, the nuns of Saint-Jean d'Autun, the Priory of Corpeau, and the churches of Saint-Aubin, Puligny, Chagny, and so on. A few secular estates were also included, such as that of Philippe Martin, lord of Bretennières and mayor of Dijon. The lord owned only a small part of all the land. By the side of these great proprietors, the inhabitants owned a few plots here and there, generally between 4 and 8 ares (0.1 and 0.2 acres). The man with the largest of the lord's tenancies had 1 hectare 32 ares (3.3 acres) of vines, and only one parcel belonging to the villagers was as large as one hectare. The majority of today's *climats* already featured in fifteenth century texts: la Bergerie, le Clos Devant, l'Orme Goudart, au Criot, le Clos Saint-Jean, en Champguin, au Blanchot. The vine was the only plant in the *climats* of Blanchot, Parquelot, en Coullontet and Es Ourlières, and it occupied most of Voisenot.

The Cistercians of Maizières

The dominant presence of the Cistercians exercised a determining influence on the majority of the *Grands Crus* of Burgundy. The parent foundation was the Abbey of Cîteaux, the first to be established, which created its viticultural estate at the very beginning of the twelfth century. Situated in Côte de Nuits, it developed the vineyards there. The vines hardly went beyond Meursault.

The daughter establishment to La Ferté, itself the daughter of Cîteaux, the Abbey of Maizières was founded in 1132. Close to Saint-Loup-de-la-Selle (Saône-et-Loire), between Beaune and Verdun-sur-le-Doubs, Maizières, like Cîteaux, is on the plain. Its relationship to Montrachet is exactly the same as that of Cîteaux to the Clos de Vougeot. Its estates spread out over

today's *départements* of Saône-et-Loire and Côte-d'Or, with cultivated land and forestry, windmills, lakes, a tile-works, an iron foundry and a glassworks. Its numerous vineyards covered the hillsides of Beaune, Pommard, Saint-Aubin, Puligny, Blagny... and Montrachet? That goes without saying. But unlike those of Cîteaux at the Clos de Vougeot, the monks of Maizières were not driven by any ambition to undertake extensive reorganization of land in order to establish an immortal plot.

In 1200 Guy de Saint-Sernin renounced half of the tithes of Puligny at Blagny in favour of Maizières. Presented as a gift by the Bishop of Langres in 1184, the land at Blagny appears to have been the abbey's first parcel of vines. In May 1252 the brothers Pierre and Arnolet de Puligny made several donations to Maizières, including some land under vines in "Mont Rachaz" or "Montrachaz". In 1286-87, Gui Berrier of Chagny gave Maizières a parcel of a vineyard together with other land and outhouses, situated in "Mont Raschat" between the land owned by the church of Puligny and the vines owned by the heirs of Croichon de Gamay.

There was also a legal case between Etienne Chapuis, the priest of Puligny, and the Abbess of Saint-Jean-le-Grand d'Autun concerning one fifth of an acre at "Mont Rachat" next to the vines given to the church of that parish by Clément de Puligny, the former priest (1472). The following year, there was a matter of a third of an acre of vines on the "Mountain of Montrachat", which

---

▲ *Between Beaune and Verdun-sur-le-Doubs lies the former Abbey of Maizières whose Cistercian monks developed Montrachet, rather like Cîteaux at the Clos de Vougeot.*

had been planted on uncultivated land eighteen years previously. In 1725, the Chartreux of Beaune refused the Abbey of Maizières the tithes on their vines at Montrachet because of the privileges granted to their Order. The Abbey owned cellars, presses and vats in abundance. Its wines had a good reputation. Soon after, it acquired a house in Beaune, Petit-Maizières, and in 1304, it obtained "free entry" into the town for its wines in exchange for the gift of a tower in which the great clock of Beaune was to be installed.

It is clear that the Cistercians of Maizières also contributed in large part to the formation of the viti-vinicultural entity of Montrachet as well as the fame of this *cru*, but monastic prestige did not reflect on all wines in the same way. Maizières was not Cîteaux. So Montrachet could not pretend to be the equal of the Clos de Vougeot. Doubtless the property was too scattered for its name to gain any reputation. On the other hand, Maizières had a great quantity of grapes to be pressed. In 1789, its viticultural assets spread over 18 hectares at Blagny and Puligny, 5 hectares at Beaune, slightly more at Savigny, 10 hectares at Meursault, 2.5 hectares at Volnay, nearly 8 hectares at Pommard: in all, around 50 hectares of vines among the best *climats* of the Côte de Beaune, Montrachet representing the largest part. Here the monks had a chapel and a house. But all this was to disappear under the Revolution.

And what about Puligny? This village has been the subject of research by Jean-Louis Alexandre, a local bookbinder. Its church was given to Cluny in 1095. The seigniory belonged to the Mypont family, then after a short spell to a duke at the time of Philip the Bold, to the Jaquots (of the Burgundy Parlement), and to the Marquis d'Agrain. As for the seigniory of Chassagne, François de Ferrière's descendants sold it in 1577 to the La Boutière family. Originating from the Charolais region, this family had settled in Autun before buying the land of Chassagne and the Château des Prés in Chagny from the Duc de Nemours. Enterprising and generous, the barons of La Boutière stand out as "good lords". They rebuilt the church and the presbytery of Chassagne, put to the flame under Louis XI. They encouraged the repopulation of the village, which had been decimated by plague and deprived of water. To "foreigners" who were willing to settle there, they offered considerable financial assistance. So Chassagne was reborn. But at the beginning of the seventeenth century, it was still in a bad way. Courtépée records a purchase of land in Montrachet at a pretty low price. In 1706 Charles de La Boutière married his only daughter to Jean-François-Antoine de Clermont-Montoison. Four years later, just before his death, he made his son-in-law the residuary legatee of his assets. Montrachet, Chassagne and Chagny thus became Clermont-Montoison, and finally stepped into the pages of History.

"To the rescue, Montoison!"

When he made this appeal in the thick of the battle, Charles VIII gave the Clermont-Montoison family a war-cry. "To the rescue, Montoison!" could

equally as well have been the motto of Montrachet, so closely did the name
of this family accompany the wine as it gradually rose to the very pinnacle of
fame. The Clermont-Montoisons were a branch of the Clermont-Tonnerre
family. In the middle of the fifteenth century the founder of this youngest
branch, Claude de Clermont, became Lord of Montoison on the death of
his aunt, the wife of Robert de Seyssel. His son Philibert, known as "Bold
Montoison", covered himself with glory at Fornoue. His other son Antoine,
Baron de Montoison, continued the line into the sixteenth century.

The new lord of the region, Jean-Baptiste de Clermont's son, was associated with the vineyard until 1741, when he died in his château at Chagny,
as did his son, Louis-Claude. In 1776 one of his daughters married Charles
de La Guiche, from a family which today still features in the Who's Who
of great wines thanks to the vines it owns at Montrachet. Louis-Claude died

in 1787 and so did not see the outbreak of the Revolution. The family went into exile and its assets were seized by the nation and sold at auction. His son-in-law Charles de La Guiche was condemned to death and perished on the scaffold in 1794. The family name died out with the death of Charles, Marquis de Clermont-Montoison (1773-1856).

At Chassagne the Clermonts developed a policy of buying up and reorganizing land. In 1749, forty years after taking possession of their estate, the vines they rented out (often for half the harvest) already covered over 31 hectares 25 ares (77.2 acres). In about 1780 Claude Courtépée noted that out of the 7 hectares 70 ares (19 acres) at Montrachet, just over 4 hectares 28 ares (10.6 acres) belonged to the lord. Among other proprietors were the Comte de Sassenay in Saint-Aubin, a Monsieur Bonnard in Arnay-le-Duc and a Monsieur Boiveau. In the town hall at Puligny is preserved a marvellous *terrier* (register of landed property), drawn up in about 1740 and discovered much later on a bookseller's stall on the banks of the Seine in Paris. It shows the fine quadrilateral formed by the Montrachet estate belonging to the lord of Chassagne, the other proprietors (Chartreux de Beaune, André, etc.) owning vertical strips above this large parcel. At this time, part of the vineyard was held on lease by wine-merchants and by the family La Tour (or Latour). Marketing was often looked after by the producers, whether religious orders or great landowners. There were also a few merchants or their agents who sold Burgundy wine in Paris, as the establishment of glassworks such as the one at Epinac promoted the selling of wine in the bottle, by "baskets" of 24 to 60 bottles. In his little book on the wines of Burgundy, published in London in 1728, the priest Arnoux describes this white wine as "the most curious and the most delicate in France". "A wine whose finesse can be adequately expressed by neither the Latin nor the French tongue."

From Jefferson's travel notes

So the wine finally achieved its due and glorious renown, and on this point we have a first-hand witness. He was not a Burgundian boasting about his origins and so putting his objectivity in doubt. The visitor was a foreigner and, what is more, a citizen of the United States. He has handed on to us a simple account of his impressions on his voyage. Here is what Thomas Jefferson wrote in his travel notes on March 8, 1787: *"Aussay. Paid Monsieur Parent, guide to this place which is the depot of the wines of Montrachet 6 f."*

◄ *Contrary to local tradition, this portrait is not of Jean-François de Clermont-Montoison, but probably depicts Louis-Claude de Clermont-Montoison, the largest landowner in Montrachet in the mid-eighteenth century. Pastel drawing by Allais dated 1747. Hôpital de Chagny.*

Land Register of Puligny drawn up by Jean-Baptiste Rigoley, the lord of the manor. Discovered at the stall of a bouquiniste *in Paris, it is now preserved in Puligny town hall.* ►

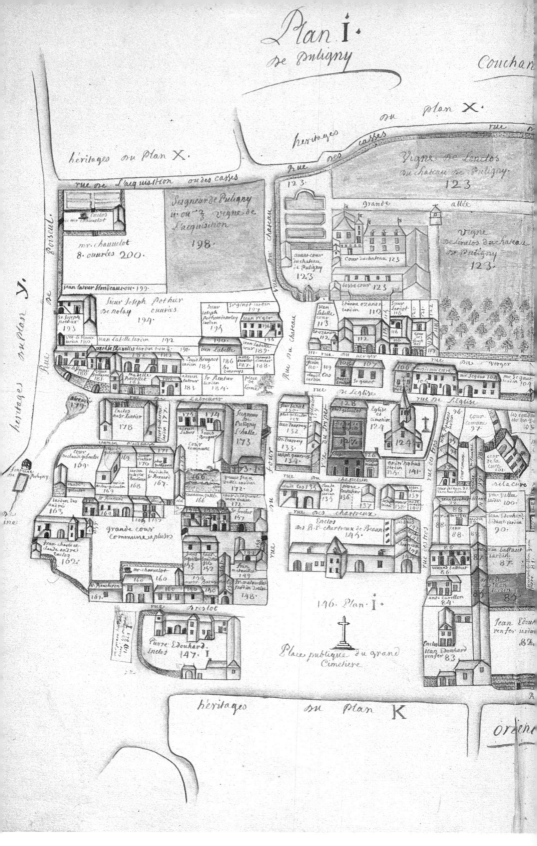

heritages au plan N.

heritages au plan M.

Pasquier de Proste 220.

Pasquier au Proste L.

Pasquier derrier la Velle 30.

Les veu viuand Battaut 1. ou ½ meix pelletier 3.

Suur lardot 1 ou 4.

6.

Estienne ozanon et Jean Labelle 4. ouuréez meix Pelletier 7.

Suur Joseph Pothier de nolay 3. ouuréez meix pelletier 8.

9.

10.

6.

11.

Venne viuand Battaut 1. ou meix pelletier 12.

pierre Bouchard et Joseph musard laine es Jeune 13.

pierre Bouchard 1. ou meix pelletier 15.

Suur Belin 1. ou meix pelletier 16.

monsr Bessenard 2. ouuréez meix Pelletier 18.

les 3. ou meix Pelletier 19.

er de nolay 1. ou de la chapelle 20. I.

antoine deschaux 1. ou de la chapelle meix pelletier 21. I.

deschaux 1. ou ½ meix Pelletier 22.

claude Girardin 1. ou meix pelletier 23.

meix pelletier 1. ou 24.

norman blard 1. ou 26.

Suur lardot 1. ou 27.

Sauuanecat masson 1. ou ½ Meix Pelletier 28.

Rue moin.

Suur Loppin pothier 1. ou ½ derrier la velle 31.

Les chartreux de Beaune 4. ouuréez derrier la velle 32.

Suur chauansot 3. ou ½ dont 1 ou es Jaune derrier la velle 33.

Suur chauansot 3. ou ½ derrier la velle 34.

madelle Barollet 4. ouuréez et ½ derrier la velle 35.

monsr Chauuelot 8. ou ½ derrier la velle 36.

Suur Loppin Pothier 1. ou ½ derrier la velle 37.

Jean Polot 4. ouuréez derrier la velle 38.

Les chartreux de Beaune 3. ou ½ derrier la velle 39.

Etienne ozanon 3. ouuréez et ½ derrier la velle 40.

mr Segau 2. ou derrier la velle 41.

mr Butrignot 2. ou derrier la velle 42.

Suur marten 1. ou et ½ derrier la velle 43.

mr Loppin de masse 3. ou ½ derrier la velle 44.

Suur Joseph Pothier de nolay 2. ou derrier la velle 45.

melle Barolles 1. ou es ½ derrier la velle 46.

Jean Labelle 1. ou es ½ derrier la velle 47.

Venne viuand Battaut 1. ou derrier la velle 48.

Suur Martin 1. ou 49.

fran corrot 1. ou 50.

claude cas 1. ou ½ derrier la velle 51.

claude cas ½ ou 52.

claude andré 1. ou en Jaune 1. ou es ½ en blanc derrier la velle 53.

Venne viuand Battaut 1. ou derrier la velle 54.

Mr Loppin Pothier 4. ou derrier la velle 55.

monsr Chauuelot 1. ou derrier la velle 56.

Jean Latour Blondeau 1. ou derrier la velle 57.

madelle Barollet 1. ou es ½ 72.

1. ou ½ 71.

Pierre Bouchard 1. ou es ½ 70.

68.

69.

Suur Bartelin 3. ouuréez 3. derrier la velle 76.

Sauuanecat masson 4. ou ½ derrier la velle 69.

La chapelle de Puligny 6. ouuréez derrier la velle 67. I.

monsr Chauuelot 3. ou et ½ derrier la velle 66.

Suur Loppin de masse 1. ou derrier la velle 65.

La chapelle de Puligny 8. ou derrier la velle 63. I.

64.

62.

61.

60.

Les chartreux de Beaune 2. ou ½ derrier la velle 59.

Meurtaux et a Beaune

heritages au Proste

203. 204. 205. 206. 207. 208. 209. 210. 211. 212. 213. 214. 215. 216. 217. 218. 219.

27

The United States' Ambassador to the Court of King Louis XVI, Thomas Jefferson was to become President of the United States several years later. The author of the Declaration of Independence, this Virginian was one of the founders of American democracy. A free-thinker, he was interested in everything: science, the arts and, naturally, wine, which he knew wonderfully well. When he broke his wrist, he was advised to take the waters at Aix-en-Provence. He planned to go there in the spring of 1787, but his journey turned into a voyage round the vineyards of France over several months. Jefferson was not only the first American tourist in Burgundy; he was the first American to fall in love with its wines.

He had an entirely precise and astonishingly up-to-date idea of the different terrains and *crus*, of the quality and influence of the year of the vintage, of the concept of proprietor, manager and merchant-vintner, and of prices. His travel notes (no similar French document exists at this time) tell us what was being said at Court and in Parisian high society on the eve of the Revolution. They also record his own reflections as a cultivated and perspicacious visitor. Also we find the correspondence he conducted with the cooper from Beaune, who was his guide in Burgundy and later his supplier.

In Jefferson's hand were four aces: Chambertin, Romanée, Clos de Vougeot and Montrachet. Curiously enough, he observed that the best red and white wines, Chambertin and Montrachet, were at the two extremities of the Côte. He wrote: "It is claimed that the neighbouring vineyards produce wines of the same quality, but because they belong to individuals, they have not been able to establish a name for themselves and so are sold just like any other wine." He notes that Montrachet sold at 1,200 livres per *queue* (two *pièces* of 228 litres) or 48 sous per bottle, whereas the Meursault-Goutte d'or fetched 300 livres per *queue*. The prices of Montrachet were the same as those for Chambertin, the Clos de Vougeot and La Romanée but the Volnay fell to 300 livres per *queue*. The reds were dearer than the whites; only the Montrachet among the white wines rose to the level of the *Grands Crus* of the Côte de Nuits. Jefferson doubtless preferred the Meursault-Goutte d'or, and from 1803 he stocked Chambertin in the cellars of the White House after his election as President of the United States. But his letters show that he did not remain unmoved by his visit to Monsieur de La Tour's cellars in "Aussay" (Auxey). "Would you be kind enough to let me know if Monsieur de La Tour still has any of those 4 casks of Montrachet 1784 I saw in his cellar and of which I bought one?" (Paris, December 17, 1787). Etienne Parent replied that he had made immediate contact with Monsieur Latour, but that he no longer had any Montrachet 84, proposing instead the 85 at 300 livres per cask. In Chagny there were still 6 casks of 84 and at the same price. "I think this wine is better than the Latour, but I await your orders," Parent wrote.

Even more interestingly Thomas Jefferson pestered his Beaune correspondent with the request that he obtain for him not only some baskets of bottles but also vines, which he certainly wanted to plant. In Paris? Or in Virginia, since he tried several times in the course of his life to create a vineyard in his own country? And he did not want just any old vines. He asked for Chambertin, Clos-Vougeot, Romanée and Montrachet. On February 3, 1788, Etienne Parent obtained 12 vines from Montrachet (of which six were from Monsieur Clermont), 10 from Clos-Vougeot, 9 from Chambertin and 8 from Romanée. On February 20, 1788, Thomas Jefferson wrote announcing that the wine and the vines had arrived safely. At Monticello, Jefferson then tried to establish a vineyard with Burgundy sets which died after being attacked by phylloxera, though he was unable to understand the reason. However, he noted that the soil of Virginia is often "very similar to that of Chambertin and Montrachet which produce the very famous wines of Burgundy. It is pebbly, red and lacking in sand". A good reference!

The nobility had "launched" the wine of Montrachet: the Revolution could now come. This is not a unique example in Burgundy: the Croonenbourg family and after them the Contis gave all their attention to the Romanée and the *noblesse de robe* of Dijon formed an ardent attachment to the *Grands Crus*. However, this was not always the case. The reputation of other *crus* was still being developed by the abbeys (Clos de Vougeot) or by the emerging merchant class (Claude Jobert in Chambertin). Contrary to the majority of the other vineyards, Montrachet has never been a monopoly. This is not therefore the initial and essential element of a *Grand Cru*. Moreover, its fame is not simply the result of man's work.

The diary of Paquelin, a vigneron

Then came the Revolution. The sale of properties sequestered by the Revolutionary government from the aristocracy who had emigrated and from the religious communities brought about the collapse of several estates, though this little benefited the local people. The 4 hectares 28 ares (10.6 acres) of the Clermont-Montoisons in Montrachet are said to have been sold on the second day of the month Germinal in Year II of the Republic (March 22, 1794) in two lots to Henri Pourtalès (35,000 livres and 37,100 livres plus fees). The nation also appropriated Claude-Henri de Sassenay's Montrachet (1 hectare 37 ares, or 3.4 acres, sold in four lots), along with other vines belonging to the Chartreux of Beaune (1 hectare or 2.5 acres), the Abbey of Maizières (42 ares 80 centiares or 1.1 acre), the Bâtard of Charles Perreney de Baleure (26 ares or 0.63 acres), the benefice of Chassagne (30 ares or 0.74 acres), and the Chevalier of the Rigoley family from Puligny (26 ares or 0.63 acres).

Contrary to what took place with the majority of the *Grands Crus*, Montrachet was barely affected. It was already very much divided up between numerous owners, who lost nothing with the coming of the Revolution. The situation was in fact extremely complicated. Three vignerons from Chassagne received vines in Montrachet on *métayage* which had belonged to people who had emigrated (1793), but the Republic was quick to react. The

CÔTE DE NUITS.

RÉCOLTE de 1803.

	la pièce.	
Chambolle, Morey.	160	170
Nuits, Vosne, cuvées bourgeoises.	200 210	220
Idem, têtes de cuvées.	250	—
...hebourg, St.-George, Chambertin.	350	400
...che, Romanée, Clos de Tare.	450	—

RÉCOLTE de 1802.

	la pièce.	
Chambolle, Morey.	290	310
Nuits, Vosne, cuvées bourgeoises.	390	415
Idem, têtes de cuvées.	500	—
Richebourg, St.-George.	550	600
Tache, Romanée, Clos de Tare, Chambertin.	700	—

VINS VIEUX.

	la pièce.			la bouteill.
	1795	1798	1800	
Chambolle, Morey.	460	450	280	2.10 2.
Nuits, Vosne, 1.ᵉ qualité.	600	580	400	2.5 2.8
Idem, 2.ᵉ qualité.	550	540	360	2. 2.5
Richebourg, St.-George, Romanée, etc.	750	740	—	3.15
	1000	950	—	4.10 —

Nota. La pièce contient 250 bouteilles; elle se divise en deux feuillettes.

CÔTE DE BEAUNE.

RÉCOLTE de 1803.

	la pièce.	
Savigny, Aloxe.	150	160
Beaune, Chassagne.	165 170	175
Pommard, Vollenay.	180 185	195

RÉCOLTE de 1802.

	la pièce.	
Savigny, Aloxe.	290	300
Beaune, Chassagne.	330	350
Pommard, Vollenay.	360	380

VINS VIEUX.

	la pièce.			la bouteill.
	1796	1798	1800	
Beaune, 1.ᵉ qualité.	520	580	350	2.75 2.5
Idem, 2.ᵉ qualité.	480	470	300	2.10 2.
Pommard.	540	530	360	2.15 2.5
Vollenay.	560	540	370	2. 2.5
BLANCS.				
Meursault.	520	500	—	2.15 —
Bâtard-Montrachet.	550	540	—	3.
Montrachet.	800	750	—	4.

GRANDS ORDINAIRES.

		la pièce.	
	1.ᵉ qualité.	100	110
NOUVEAUX.	2.ᵉ qualité.	80	90
	Communs.	50	60
VIEUX.	1.ᵉ qualité.	160	175
	2.ᵉ qualité.	120	130

administrator of the district of Beaune ordered the municipality to have the 5 hectares (not 4 hectares 28 ares – or 10.6 acres – now, but 5 hectares) of Clermont-Montoison vines cultivated correctly, as well as Prodin-Rigoley's 34 ares (0.8 acres) in Chevalier-Montrachet which had remained untended. It was further decided that three vignerons would tend these vines for half their yield, the harvest being mixed together in the vat. "Obviously, half of the wine belongs to the Republic", stipulates the resolution. "Vignerons must pay their taxes on the land and not plant vegetables there". So there were to be neither lettuces nor leeks in Montrachet! Moreover, the Pourtalès sale lay in question. Had it been ratified? In fact the Laguiche family (from now on no longer the "de La Guiche" family) came into possession of these vines just after the Revolution. A document enables us to share the state of mind of the inhabitants of the region during these years. It is the *Quaier de Mémoires*, written between 1753 and 1806 by Charles Paquelin, a vigneron from Chassagne (published in part in the *Revue de Bourgogne*, 1914). The owner of a small fortune, Charles Paquelin came from one of the oldest families in Chassagne. In his diary he chronicles every year the Good Lord sends. He records the events which interest him, the good and the bad weather, the quality of the harvest and the wine. He saw 1789 as the most unhappy year of the century. Events at Versailles and in Paris caused him considerable anxiety. "We made scarcely any wine and it had the palest colour imaginable," he noted sadly. But Charles Paquelin thought that the king and the nation would come to a compromise. As time went by, he regretted the insults heaped on his old religion and on the priests. Although he had never been in favour of the overthrow of tradition, he was to expand his ideas politically, rejecting the monarchy and applauding Bonaparte. In 1792, the "fourth year of Liberty", he wrote: "People of ill intent have arrived in Chassagne, destroying everything belonging to those who have emigrated, taking away barrels, opening them and drinking the wine; this went on for three days..." In 1793 he jumps straight from the death of "Louis Capet" to this comment: "The little white wine is selling at fifteen sous in the bars."

Famine, worthless *assignats* (Revolutionary bank notes), this diary of a simple man gives us a clear picture of how the Revolution was viewed by the world of growers – with fear, but with a certain sympathy. Charles Paquelin was attached to his church in Chassagne and he did not align himself with measures taken against the Church. On the other hand, he gradually became hostile to the "aristocrats", though he saw no way of achieving better conditions by the sale of their assets. The now wealthier upper middle-class took the place of monks and nobles and the people were unable to interpose their will. In this diary there was never any question of Montrachet or the *crus*, but simply of red wine and, in the case of white, what he calls the "little wine". A never-ending list of woes: "It is a good wine this year with a fine colour, but it is selling cheap... No one wants the poor little wines of last year; they are not well thought of." The diary finishes with these lines in 1806.

The most precious asset

If the fame of Montrachet does not result simply from man, what is its cause? It is sufficient to study a map or look at the landscape to understand to what

---

◀ *A list of eighteenth-century wine prices. Musée du Vin, Beaune.*

extent the Côte is indivisible. If the Revolution's scissors had cut up the Côte-d'Or differently, to include for example Rully and Mercurey, these vineyards would logically be attached to the Côte de Beaune today. However, unity does not rule out diversity. So Montrachet marks a transition between the "Good Côte" (as it was formerly known) and the Côte of Chalon, between the sway of Cîteaux and that of Cluny. From Dijon to Meursault, the Côte lies more or less in a straight line, indented by combs hacked into its sides. Sombre, sometimes austere, often impoverished, such was the order founded by Saint Bernard. At Chassagne and Puligny, however, the Côte casts off its hair shirt and assumes freedom of movement. It ripples; the slopes of hills and valleys follow gentler lines. Meadows, fields and thickets soon intermingle with the vines. Very gradually, the general impression changes. The landscape has already come under the influence of Cluny. We have one foot in the north, the other in the south; it is a sort of watershed for vines.

Arriving from Lyons, the hill of Montrachet looks like the first step on a huge stairway leading to the palace. If we come from Dijon, the impression is the other way round. This hill resembles a final wave rolling along the plain, giving a last sigh from the depths of its soul. The Côte-d'Or has only one word more to say: Montrachet. It gathers all its strength, all its memories and all its virtues to express the best of itself here. Is the secret in the soil? The Ancients were convinced of it. If we are to believe the priest Arnoux (1728), the well-nigh miraculous good fortune of Montrachet is due to having "a vein of earth which makes this terrain the only one of its kind": a sort of seam. "The soil in this canton is thin, light and very permeable to the action of the air," writes Doctor Denis Morelot (1831). "It is made up of an admirable mixture of clay, calcium carbonate, iron tetroxide and the remains of vegetable matter." Such soil is rare. So rare that, according to one tradition, when people were digging there, they scraped the earth off their clogs before leaving, so as not to lose a single ounce of such a precious soil when they walked on the roads. In the same way, gold polishers and diamond cutters used to comb their hair and clean their ears and finger-nails before leaving their work. So rare was this soil that sometimes earth had to be taken from the upper part of the slope to enable the higher rocky area of Montrachet to be cultivated. Chevalier-Montrachet no longer has much of its original earth. It too, in its turn, has been replenished. But we should not be too shocked by this. Large quantities of earth from the *département* of Saône were brought into Romanée-Conti in the middle of the eighteenth century and it is no worse for that. The essential thing is to know the origin of this soil which, moreover, as the years pass by is gradually washed down the slopes by storms. At one time it was taken back up again in winter in baskets. "If this had been the valley of the Douro", Alexis Lichine remarks, "terraces would have been made."

At this southern limit of the Côte there is a difference of nearly 200 metres in height between the plain and the plateau. At the top there are sheer

cliffs of Rauracian limestone, then a deposit 'talus' with frequent outcrops of Callovian limestone together with Argovian marl forming a shoulder. Further down, the steep lower slope is cut from Bathonian limestone. There are many *murgers* among these rocky outcrops: these are huge piles of stones thrown up from the soil over the centuries; bushes cling to them and snakes thrive happily among them. These *murgers* show that the land under vines has resulted from a long struggle against the stones, the red lava-like flows which have turned grey with the passing of time.

However, various geological factors complicate this structure. Marked by a fault, the lower slope of the Puligny talus reveals Bajocian marls and limestone of crystalline appearance formed by crinoidea. This is the upper part of Chevalier-Montrachet. Mingled with scree, the Bathonian limestone forms

▲ *A simple shelter among the vines has been made from a* murger, *originally built to store tools or to give shelter.*

33

the bedrock beneath Montrachet and part of Bâtard-Montrachet. The Montrachet slope is composed of the edge of a plateau with practically no soil, or covered with skeletal brown earth over very hard Bathonian limestone. The vine-growing slope begins at the highest part, with light rendzines formed over the Bathonian marls and marly limestone (upper part of Chevalier-Montrachet). Rather unstable, these were the soils which were "raked off" in the past to reinforce the soil of Montrachet. Normal rendzines make up the lower part of Chevalier-Montrachet (Bajocian and Upper Bajocian limestone). This is a brown chalky soil which is very chloritic, notably in the upper third of the vineyards, where a bed of red marl – the priest Arnoux was right – has a carbonate content of 13%. This is the highest found in Burgundy. The alluvial glacis is covered with brown chalky clayey soil whose pebble content rapidly decreases as the incline of the slope becomes less severe. These ancient alluvial deposits cover Pliocene or Quaternary deposits of the Bressan basin. This is the situation at Bâtard-Montrachet, at the bottom of the slope. The soil on the south part of Montrachet is made up of stony clays and silts.

This geological glimpse tells us much about the natural potential of the vineyards. The limestone scree, gravelly and with a high proportion of pebbles, and the marl, rich in limestone fragments on well-exposed slopes, give the best white wines. Moreover the growers endorse these observations which they have confirmed at first hand. Yes, this brown red band crossing the middle of Montrachet really exists. "But", they say, "be careful. It should not be disturbed too much. If we dig too deeply into it, we shall no longer find good soil and the vines will not grow well." In saying this we have said next to nothing, for indeed the complexity of the *Grands Crus* does not cause despair only among American investigators. Rolande Gadille devoted her doctoral thesis to a microscopic study of the vineyards in Burgundy. In an endeavour to learn what is responsible for the majesty of these *crus*, she studied each in turn from Chenôve to Puligny.

Altitude: at a height of 250–270 metres, Montrachet is among the lowest of the *Grands Crus* (like Musigny and La Romanée-Conti). Chevalier-Montrachet, rather higher (265–290), lies at the height of the majority of the *Grands Crus*. On the other hand, Bâtard-Montrachet (240–250) has only the Clos de Vougeot at the same height. The general opinion is that the vines flourish best halfway up the slope, a position which enables them to support dry or wet years without trouble. From the evidence, Puligny and Chassagne only partly confirm this truth. As for the slope, it is moderate at Montrachet (10%), steep in Chevalier-Montrachet (20%) and very slight or even non-existent further down.

Chassagne stone: one of its most notable recent uses has been for refurbishing of the Louvre Museum in Paris. ▶

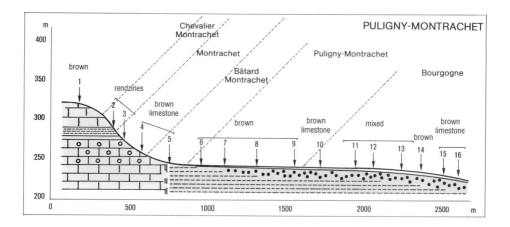

Mineral resources: there is nothing particularly interesting as regards organic nitrogen. Phosphoric acid: not much (its influence seems more important for red wines). Carbonate content: exceeds 11% in Upper Montrachet and falls to 1.5% in Bâtard-Montrachet. But Musigny has even less: try to draw conclusions if you can! Potassium, magnesium: no observations to be made. One thing should be noted however: an astonishing concentration of sodium on the slopes of the great white wines (Montrachet, Meursault-Perrières).

Whether we are speaking of body or finesse, it is beyond doubt that all these elements influence the quality of the wine. But in what way and in what proportion? Our knowledge is still rather vague. The same is true for trace elements. In particular, it is claimed that chromium promotes fertilization, that zinc reduces acidity and develops a richness in sugar, that cobalt cuts short the length of time for ripening, etc. Is anyone aware that a bottle of Montrachet contains magnesium, copper, strontium, titanium, lead, tin, gallium, beryllium, molybdenum, vanadium, nickel, chromium, zinc and even silver? Only gold is lacking, but poets have added that to the list. A study has been made of the amount of trace elements present in Montrachet's soil, in samples of vine-leaves taken from here and in the wine produced in this *climat*. What were the findings? A preponderance of magnesium was observed, an exceptionally high level of lead and the presence of gallium and beryllium. The quantities which can be assimilated by the wine are, however, very variable: Montrachet for example is very low in vanadium but high in copper.

As for stones, they warm the soil, retard erosion and protect the vines. Their influence is particularly marked on the alluvial lower slopes. So Bâtard-Montrachet has 10% stones, whereas the nearest vines on the plain have only 5%. But this is only a small proportion, for many *Grands Crus* have 30% stones in their soil.

And clay? If the great reds often have large amounts of clay (30% to 40% in Chambertin), the level is rather lower in the great whites (32% to 36% in Montrachet). However the percentage rises at Bâtard-Montrachet, where it reaches 50%. From this we can see the importance of stones in ensuring porous and permeable soil.

Like Rolande Gadille, whose humility cannot but be admired, let us admit that these mysteries defeat us and that it is pointless to attempt to explain the quality of Montrachet's wine on the basis of an analysis of the soil and subsoil. Of course, this aspect will enter into the final equation, but it would be presumptuous to claim to discover the *Grand Crus'* secret merely from their geology. Moreover some people are of the opinion that the water-table and the flow of water through the subsoil are the determining factors. For in Puligny we have our feet practically in the water.

Feasting on the sun

Doctor Jules Lavalle (1855) makes a distinction betweeen "the part whose exposure is almost directly south-east, in the region of Puligny, and that which is almost completely south-east in the commune of Chassagne". He concludes: "It is in the part which faces only south-east that Montrachet wine is produced in all its exquisite finesse and divine perfection." This comment reminds one of the "three Clos de Vougeots": from the top, middle and bottom. So could "two Montrachets" be said to exist, one to the south-east and the other to the south-south-east? Puligny or Chassagne? The distinction is not so clear-cut. Moreover, we need to look at the vines in order to understand. In Chassagne, some rows face south-east, or even directly south. In Chassagne and Puligny, other rows follow a line along the south-eastern slope. Relatively rare in a *Grand Cru* (though it exists in Chambertin), this different orientation of the vines has existed for no more than a century. Up to the phylloxera crisis, vineyards were planted "willy-nilly", with no overall plan. A rational approach only really first started in Burgundy at the end of the nineteenth century. Before Doctor Jules Lavalle, Doctor Denis Morelot (1831) considered that the sun and soil together played their role in this success referring to "the felicitous combination of a good exposure and suitable soil", and stressing what appears to him to be essential: "The wine of Montrachet is of superior quality because of its south-eastern exposure." According to "reputable authors", we ought to be able to distinguish two different types of wine from Montrachet. Yet the vineyard is small, and no one could deny that it is a single entity. In any case, tastings do not confirm these supposed differences.

◄ *The soil at Puligny-Montrachet: several layers of limestone intersected by a bed of marl at the top of Le Montrachet. Marl is found on the alluvial glacis, then limestone fragments. Taken from "La Côte viticole, ses sols et ses crus" by S. Mériaux, J. Chrétien, P. Vermi, N. Leneuf,* Bulletin scientifique de Bourgogne, *1981, t. 34.*

The vines cling to a poor thin soil here.   ▶

It has always been said that Montrachet "feasts on the sun". And nothing could be more favourable than a south-south-east exposure, which captures the sun's rays from dawn to dusk. It soaks up the sun like Corton, Saint-Georges, La Tâche, La Romanée-Conti and Chambertin, but even more so because its feet face south. Furthermore the inhabitants of the village practically believe that they live in paradise. "The soil of Chassagne is very hot and very light", we read in the *Manuel des vignerons-associés de Chassagne* (1844). "This *climat* is so situated that it receives the sun's rays the whole day through. The rocks around it reflect the sun on to the plain. These are vital factors in maintaining the high temperature to which we owe the excellence of our wine." One local story has it that in the middle of the Creation, the Almighty agreed to take a short rest only after creating Montrachet. This terrain seems to retain more heat than neighbouring vineyards, giving back in the bottle a hundred times over this intense inner fire. "You

would think that it has absorbed more sun than all the others", wrote Maurice des Ombiaux, the Belgian poet. I discussed this point with Michel Vieira, who has been working in these vineyards for more than twenty-five years. Poetic overstatement? Not in the least. "The first and last of the sun's rays caress Montrachet", he told me, adding "Moreover the snow always melts here first." And it is true, just as it is true that fogs are rare in Montrachet.

Old vignerons' tales? I wanted to be sure about all this, so I consulted Roger Dubrion, headmaster of a school in Beaune and author of a thesis on the Mediterranean plants to be found in eastern Burgundy. Accordingly, he speaks of the *climat* of Chassagne-Montrachet and in particular of the hill of Montrachet. "Numerous Mediterranean species are to be found here, demonstrating the very dry and hot ecological conditions", he told me. The soil is like a slow combustion stove, maintaining the heat of the vineyards during the night and throughout the autumn. The air circulating on the slopes also diminishes the risk of frost. Moreover one little spot is known as Petit-Nice and another as Beau-Soleil (splendid sun). "From the point of view of the climate", says Roger Dubrion, "Montrachet is a sub-Mediterranean 'sun-resort' which from April to October, particularly in its maximum temperatures, is like a resort in the Rhône valley such as Montélimar. These higher temperatures seem to be the result of the influence of the limestone. Acting as a filter, it creates a dry zone, reflecting during the night and throughout autumn the heat it has absorbed in the daytime or during the summer. They are also the result of the southerly and south-easterly exposures, the existence of a hot belt on the slopes with high turbulence, and a very slow drop in temperature which prolonges the favourable warm conditions."

This then explains the profusion of Mediterranean plants in this part of Burgundy. Their existence will doubtless throw new light on the exceptional microclimate of Montrachet. One could say that it has the lilting accent of the Midi.

There is indeed a microclimate. The little village of Chassagne-Montrachet has no fewer than six different climates, half of them with several underlying nuances of their own. Bâtard has that characteristic which predominates in Saône, a transitional climate between the plain and the Côte (hot, well-exposed, moderately dry). The soil there is more aerated and less heavy than on the plain. The gentle slope favours drainage but the water remains close to the surface. Then in Montrachet and Chevalier-Montrachet, sheltered from the west winds, the weather is drier, less subject to rain from the coast and, being on a soil of limestone and fragmented stones, well drained. The cold of winter is less harsh; the morning frosts are less severe and do not go on so late into April and May; and the weather is warmer right from the start of spring. Between the plain and the butte of Montrachet, the differences in temperature can occasionally reach 8° to 10° C (46° to 50° F) in spring and autumn, much to the advantage of the *Grands Crus*. One part of the hillside has a climate which is particularly favourable to the vines: Dents de Chien, whose few parcels have been assimilated into Montrachet. If it was not planted with vines, it was because there was no soil. A few Scots and Austrian pines rise above an area of dry grass. Box trees, small white oaks and almond trees bear witness to the Mediterranean climate. The tall violet spires of viper's bugloss and the purplish stems of brome, an oat-like grass, mingle with Cantabrian convolvulus, a species found in hot dry regions and which reaches here its northern limit in France. Elegant cedars cast their welcome shade over the well-to-do gardens of Puligny, and cicadas sing throughout the summer.

Many other mysteries have also been looked into. Do the forests which cover a part of the Côte play a role in the development of the *crus*? The Vicomte de Vergnette-Lamotte considered this in 1864, but confessed that it was impossible to produce a serious thesis because of the bareness of the hill of Montrachet.

The King of Vines

Does the secret then lie in the vines? Undoubtedly. We have seen that in the fourteenth century the lord of Chassagne chose the pinot noir or the "saulvoignien", a puzzling stock which can certainly be included in the family of whites. Whites and reds were intermixed for a long time in Bâtard. The sale of the goods of the Perreney de Baleure family at the time of the Revolution specifies "white Bâtard Morachet". So there were reds here. In 1770 Béguillet noted that the "noirien blanc" was the only one grown here, as in all the great white vineyards of Burgundy. Noirien blanc or pinot blanc, this name was to last until the middle of the nineteenth century. But it was in fact a misnomer, for this stock was really the chardonnay, which can be identified from its leaf whose petiolar sinus (the indentation between the lobes) is in the shape of a lyre and has a smooth underside. It is the king of vines of the great white wines of Burgundy, from Chablis to Pouilly-Fuissé. A relatively vigorous plant with a high yield, it needs pruning so as to leave a solid structure of old wood in order to restrict the flow of sap when the vine buds in spring. It produces elegant golden bunches, more elongated than those of the pinot. The grapes, less compact, are small and have a deliciously sweet juice.

If Montrachet came late on the scene, this was the fate reserved for the whites. For in the Middle Ages Burgundy was a heavy red wine which quickly went to the head. It was a wine for the rich. There were doubtless white wines, *clarets* or *galants*, but these were less famous. In the sixteenth and seventeenth centuries the ruby wines gradually became *rosés*, lighter in colour, but they were still reds. The whites were just beginning to emerge. It was only from the beginning of the eighteenth century that the white wines became great Burgundies, while the reds began to develop those characteristics which were to make them famous: deep in colour, full-bodied, rich and complex. The whites meanwhile developed at a snail's pace, changing less in nature and style than the reds. The chardonnay is very successful in Montrachet because it suits this hot dry climate and the thin soil perfectly, whereas the pinot noir needs deeper land and is relatively less susceptible to the vagaries of the weather. A marriage of love between the soil, the *climat* and its stock, as Olivier de Serres wrote, for where Sauternes needs three grape varieties, Montrachet needs only the chardonnay. However, this homogeneity is comparatively recent: even today there are still several rows of aligoté in the heart of Bâtard. Between 1920 and 1930, black grapes and sometimes simple gamay lived side by side with the illustrious chardonnay in the *Grands Crus* of Chassagne and Puligny. The pinot gris or beurot (tokay in Alsace) was

A Burgundy proprietor visiting his cellars. Detail from an oil painting on canvas by Pierre-Victor Olagnon, 1829. Musée du Vin, Beaune. ▶

also fairly common, and in the nineteenth century some people suggested using it here to produce a dessert wine. It has practically disappeared.

"The great white wines of Burgundy are the result of one of the most astonishing successes in viticulture: variations on a single theme," wrote Pierre Poupon. "Indeed, whether a Chablis or a Pouilly-Fuissé, a Rully or a Mâcon-Villages, a Meursault or a Puligny-Montrachet, a Corton-Charlemagne or a Montrachet, all these white Burgundies with their infinite nuances and clearly discernible differences come from the same stock, the chardonnay. So one type of vine, whether planted to the north or the south, on this or on that hill-side, can create wines of the same type but with astonishingly different character. There is a difference of only some 250 kilometres between the wine of Chablis and that of Pouilly-Fuissé, but they are worlds apart, worlds of sensations. Here the chardonnay plays the oboe, there the flute. Here it engraves on copper, there it sketches in ink. But the chardonnay's chosen land, that where it is pleased to create its *chef-d'œuvre* in wine, is neither to the north nor to the south of the wine-producing lands of Burgundy, but in the centre, in the very middle, on the sacred hillside of the narrow Côte-d'Or."

"I once took someone (I forget whom) to this important site in the Côte. He was disappointed by its impoverished appearance and was unwilling to accept the reasons I put forward to explain this phenomenon of unique quality," Pierre Poupon tells. "No", said the visitor, "everything you have told me only half convinces me. There must be some other reason, less natural, more... psychological. And I think you have unwittingly helped me to put my finger on it. For you said, did you not, that Montrachet descends towards Chassagne as far as the road to Paris? Well, your Montrachet is merely an ambitious provincial. Like Rastignac, looking towards the capital and crying: 'Forward together now!', it has taken the shortest route to fame, the road to Paris. And it is a wine which has made it."

However, Pierre Poupon, author of *Vignes et jours* and many other excellent books on Burgundy, dismisses this theory: "Montrachet ambitious? A careerist? This wine always surprises me by its superiority, placing it clearly way above all the others. Whenever I come across it I am amazed by it, and I hope it will never cease to astonish me."

Grand Montrachet

The hierarchy of the *crus* has remained practically inviolate since the *appellations d'origine contrôlée* were established between 1920 and 1930. If ever a *Premier Cru* is raised to the rank of *Grand Cru* (as was the case with the Clos des Lambrays at Morey-Saint-Denis in 1981), a very firm consensus of opinion is essential. This sort of exceptional promotion can be the result only of a flagrant error or a regrettable oversight. Contrary to what the British and American press would have us believe, the "high society" of Burgundy *crus* is more exclusive even than English Court circles. It is hierarchy developed over a long period, for in Burgundy (though a few concentrated vineyards such as the Clos de Vougeot are exceptional), the appellation is based on the *climat*, an area of land distinguished by its microclimate, and not on the estate (as in Bordeaux), the grape variety (as in Alsace) or the name (as in Champagne). The essentials were already evident in the eighteenth century. In the nineteenth century serious writers tried to create classifications based on established and objective criteria: a reputation beyond question, suitability of the soil, and traditional methods. Their aim was to eliminate fraud and the many abuses of the time, and they wanted transactions to be conducted ethically and to inspire confidence in the consumer. In 1822 André Jullien wrote: "Meursault... produces many highly appreciated white wines which, as they leave the area, often take on the name of the wines of Mont-Rachet which they resemble to some degree, though they do not have all their fine quality." A century earlier, in 1728, the priest Arnoux warned his readers against "the vines which are neighbours to that vineyard, for they somewhat resemble it in quality and sometimes pass for Montrachet". "That is why you should be sure of having a trustworthy agent if you wish to procure some", he advises.

The viticultural associations, particularly the Beaune Agricultural Committee, were soon to join in this argument, in which they naturally had a considerable financial interest, for depending on their classification, a parcel of vines and its wines might command a higher or lower price. It should also be noted, incidentally, that this investigation was carried out with surprising rigour and was entirely independent of all political pressure.

A latecomer in Chassagne-Puligny (1840), the Land Register states the situation precisely. But nothing is simple, as you would imagine. Indeed, the Chassagne town council had outlined the plan for its Land Register on February 24, 1791. The first section, designated "Morachets", stretched from the road from Couches to Gamay, and from Puligny to the main road. The 1840 Land Register united under the name of Montrachet the *climats* of Criots, Blanchot, Vide Bourse, Remilly, Dents de Chien, making altogether over 13 hectares in the one commune of Chassagne. The Montrachet section of the Land Register also joined together several small localities, including Le Montrachet. Gradually other *crus* were to appear, some survivors from the past, others of more recent date. These too took the name of Montrachet, as though wishing to be associated with some illustrious family. But the one and only holder of the title was the *clos*, or enclosed vineyard, Montrachet itself, and had been clearly and unambiguously defined as such for more than two hundred years. The enclosed vineyard was most probably created between

The oldest plan of Montrachet: the Land Register of Jean-Baptiste Rigoley, lord of Puligny, carried out between 1741 and 1747. Two hundred and fifty years later, we find Domaine de Laguiche practically unchanged. Puligny town hall. ▶

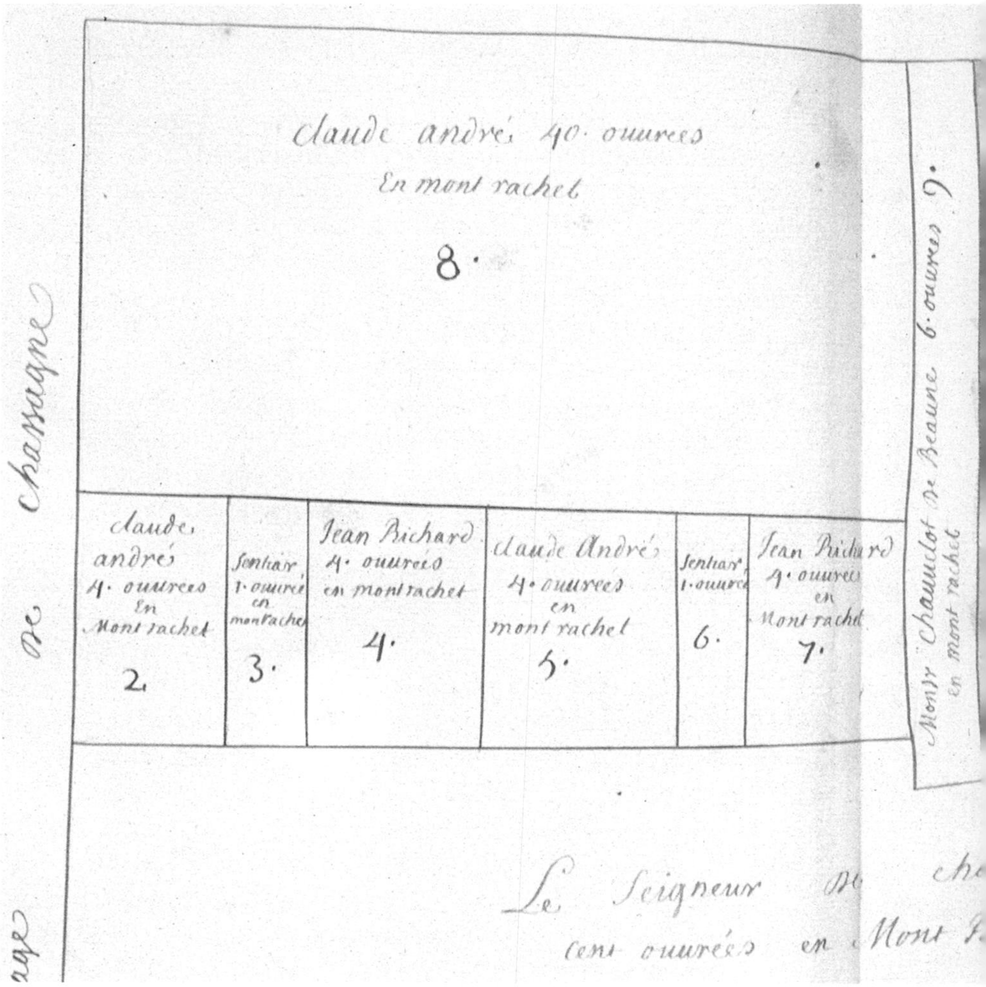

claude andré 40. ouurées

En mont rachel

8.

chamagne
de
nage

Montr Chamulot de Beaune en mont rachet
6. ouurées 9.

claude andré 4. ouurees En Mont rachet 2.	Sentiar 1. ouurei en montache 3.	Jean Richard 4. ouurees en montrachet 4.	claude André 4. ouurées en mont rachel 5.	Sentiar 1. ouurc 6.	Jean Richard 4. ouures en Mont rachet 7.

Le Seigneur de che
cent ouurées en Mont

the fifteenth and sixteenth centuries, its boundaries marked by a wall. But here is another conundrum. In most cases such walls formerly marked the extent of a single proprietor's attempt at consolidating his holdings. The wall of Montrachet therefore constitutes the only concrete historical evidence of the presence and extent of the *cru*. But as stone is mute and it is impossible to tell its age, we can only make deductions. Without being able to prove it, we can assume that this wall dates from the beginning of the eighteenth century, when the Clermont-Montoisons realized their ambition of becoming the largest proprietors in Montrachet and establishing a policy of seeking quality. But perhaps it already existed? Even if only in part?

Was Montrachet considered as a vineyard before the eighteenth century? There is no evidence of this. In 1770 Béguillet speaks of a vineyard, as does the priest Arnoux as early as 1728. André Jullien pinpoints matters in his *Topographie de tous les vignobles connus* (Topography of all known vineyards): "It is on the terrain of this commune that Mont-Rachet is situated, famous

les chartreux de Beaune, 10 ouurees en montrachet

Sieur Delarue 10 ouurees en montrachet

Mr Jecqaus de Beaune 24 ouurees en Mont rachet

Mr Dugon de La Rochelle, 24. ouurees en Mont rachet

Monsieur Villes de Dijon 6 ouurees en mont-rachet

Seigneur de Puligny 4 ouurees en mont rachet

11. 12. 13. 14. 15. 16.

Reposoir.

rue ou heritages ou Plan. S

for the excellent wines it produces. Although harvested on the same land and from the same strain of stock, they are of different quality, the result of the vines' exposure. They are distinguished by the different names of *Mont-Rachet aîné, Chevalier Mont-Rachet* and *Bâtard Mont-Rachet*. The first, superior to the other two, is harvested on that part of the mountain which is exposed to the east and the south; it combines all the qualities which go to make a perfect wine. It has body, a high alcohol content and great finesse, a very agreeable flavour of hazelnut, unique and distinctive, and in particular, a vitality and bouquet whose intensity and smoothness distinguish it from the other white wines of the Côte-d'Or. The *Chevalier Mont-Rachet* shares all the characteristics of its elder, though not to the same degree. The *Bâtard Mont-Rachet* follows *Chevalier* closely and sometimes shares with it the praises of the connoisseurs."

Christened Montrachet the elder (as if it were a family business), Montrachet is identified as an individual *cru*, superior in quality to its relations. Similarly, Doctor Denis Morelot, writing at more or less the same time (1831), never ceases to sing the praises of Montrachet, raising it alone to the rank of "tête de cuvée" among the whites. "In good years", he says, "its lightness, its perfume, its finesse, its extreme delicacy, its liveliness without being dry, its sweetness without being insipid, make it one of the best white wines you can drink. Chevalier-Montrachet, Bâtard-Montrachet, the Meursaults, the Blagnys are nearly all similar in flavour and characteristics. Less fine than the real Montrachet, they none the less have a very agreeable taste and are very spirituous; accordingly, it is also acknowledged that they very quickly go to the head."

In 1855 Doctor Jules Lavalle also speaks of the "real Montrachet" to distinguish it from the others. In his book on the Côte-d'Or, which appeared in 1925, the geographer Henri Drouhot mentions "Grand Montrachet" as an appellation and not simply as an existing wine. What is more, several nineteenth-century stone portals in Montrachet are engraved with the inscription "Grand Montrachet". In his book *Bourgogne tastevin en main*, written in 1949, Georges Rozet paints a reverent picture of "true Montrachet, le Montrachet simple". This has become an American custom. In the United States labels read "Le Montrachet" and not "Montrachet" as everywhere else in the world. What subtlety!

Whether it was the elder, the real, the great or just Montrachet, the *cru* then stretched over 7 hectares 49 ares 10 centiares (18.5 acres). Doctor Jules Lavalle seems to have counted differently in 1855. He calculated 3 hectares 95 ares 30 centiares (9.8 acres) of Montrachet in Puligny, and 13 hectares 53 ares 89 centiares (33.5 acres) in Chassagne without making it clear whether one is included in the other. So we arrive at a total of around 10 or 17 hectares, depending on whether we subtract or add. But looking more closely at the figures, we realize that an error has crept in. The original figure should read "3 hectares" in Chassagne and not "13 hectares". Now the calculation is correct – 7 hectares 49 ares 19 centiares (18.5 acres). Camille Rodier gives almost exactly the same areas in 1920.

At the end of the eighteenth century the priest Claude Courtépée spoke of Montrachet as a *cru* of 7 hectares 70 ares (19 acres), a figure which he had undoubtedly rounded up, and from which we can see that Montrachet has not changed over the years.

The royal family

At first, there was only Bâtard-Montrachet, an appellation in use from the eighteenth century. A document in the archives tells that in 1746 Pierre Gauthier, an equerry and tax official, sold vines in the little locality known as "Morachet-Bâtard". In 1786, a cabinet-maker from Dijon, Bertrand Desmoulin, announced in a newspaper that he was selling Bâtard-Montrachet by the *pièce* or in the bottle. It should be noted that the *terrier* preserved in

Puligny town hall dating from the middle of the eighteenth century does not mention the existence of Bâtard or of Chevalier, names which seem to have come into use at a later date. There are Chevaliers at Meursault but their etymology comes from the word *cheval* (horse). As for Bâtard, it is probably a colloquial appellation dating from before the name was admitted, recognized and officially declared a *climat*. The 1840 Land Register marks the Chemin des Chevaliers, obviously basing their information on traditional names. These intriguing place names, the only ones of their kind in Burgundy, have fired people's imagination, especially as there are Pucelles (Virgins) in the area. Jacques Prieur is often persuaded to tell this story, which I believe to be his own invention, at gatherings of the faithful, when wine enthusiasts come together in honour of the Tastevin and the Paulée.

"The lord of Montrachet often used to go riding along the road which ran in front of the Clos des Pucelles. One day, he thought he heard female voices calling to him. He tried to resist and continue his ride but his horse refused to go any further. He felt the blood surge in his veins, his temperature rise and his throat contract. He felt himself succumbing to that demon which tempts man in his middle years. It must be said that the lord of Montrachet did not resist for long. He went into the sacred enclosure and fell into the arms of one of the delightful creatures living there. The sequel is not hard to guess. Nine months later a new-born infant increased the population of the village of 'Puliné'.

"But later, after the disastrous return of the survivors of the Second Crusade, the lord of Montrachet learned that his dearly beloved son had died, a death which brought the family line to an end. He would have no heirs unless he were to adopt his bastard son. This is what he decided to do. So one day, amid great ceremony, this adoptive son was received into the château, flanked by a guard of honour of cheering peasants, who cried at the tops of their voices (doubtless to prompt the lord into bestowing largesse upon them): 'Welcome to the Bâtard of Montrachet!'

"Now the lord was over sixty and short-tempered. Unable to stand the young child's crying and screams, he would block his ears and mutter, '*A crio* (he is crying) *l'Bâtard!*' . The story came to the ears of the Duc de Bourgogne, a peace-loving and benevolent prince who liked things to be done correctly. Accordingly, he issued an edict stipulating that in the line of the Montrachets, the father would be called Montrachet l'Aîné, the deceased son le Chevalier-Montrachet and the youngest, le Bâtard-Montrachet. When the château was destroyed, these three names were given to the vines in order of the quality of the wines they produced, so respecting the family hierarchy."

The truth is probably entirely different. I think that, without being too precise about the area, people used to call the land just below Montrachet "Bâtard". Naturally, the higher part of the hill became Chevalier, in order to respect the hierarchy of things. Moreover Bâtard became a pejorative term only in the everyday language of the nineteenth century, and this son

of Montrachet had a right to the title of Grand Bâtard de Bourgogne, as the term used to be under the Ducs de Valois.

In 1822 André Jullien put Montrachet, Bâtard-Montrachet and Chevalier-Montrachet under the heading "première classe". In 1855 Doctor Jules Lavalle ranked Montrachet *hors ligne* (Chassagne) and *tête de cuvée* (Puligny). Then, as *première cuvée*, came the Chevalier-Montrachet and the Blagny white, les Combettes, la Platière, les Referts and les Charmes. The classification used in 1860 by the Beaune Committee is less generous. The only wines given the right to be called *première classe* were Montrachet, Chevalier-Montrachet and the highest part of Bâtard-Montrachet. The writer Bertall hid behind the opinion of the "most qualified experts" and classed Montrachet *hors ligne*, and Chevalier and Bâtard as *première cuvée*, along with les Gouttes d'Or, les Genevrières or Corton-Charlemagne. Similarly, in Paul Jamain's classifications of 1901, only Montrachet is *hors ligne*; *Premier Grand Cru*: Chevalier-Montrachet and Corton-Charlemagne; *Second Grand Cru*: Bâtard-Montrachet. As for Camille Rodier, in 1920 he placed Montrachet as *tête de cuvée*, Chevalier and Bâtard as *première cuvée*. The "lowest part of Bâtard" was placed as *deuxième cuvée*, after les Folatières, les Combettes, la Garenne, les Chalumaux, Champ Canet and the white Blagny, all classed as *première cuvée*.

The 1921 judgement

We come now to the judgement given by the tribunal at Beaune on May 12, 1921 regarding the *appellations d'origine* at Montrachet. The case was heard on February 17. Certain proprietors in Chassagne and Puligny had written the name Montrachet when they had registered their harvest return figures, among them Madame Martini-Rosé, the proprietor of the Clos de Vougeot, Joseph Leflaive, Luther Jouard, Paul Latour, Fernand and Gabriel Coffinet.

Other proprietors, considering that this claim was unjustified, took the matter to court. Among these were Julien and Joseph Bouchard, the Marquise Henriette de Rochechouart-Montmart, the widow of the Marquis Philibert de Laguiche, Anne d'Harcourt, née de Laguiche, the Marquis Pierre de Laguiche, the family of the Comtes Lafon, Baron and Baronne Thénard, Charlotte Serres-Renoult, the widow of Baron Jules de Montbrun.

The aristocracy of the *cru* was defending its rights and, it must be admitted, its legitimate privileges, which was entirely legal. In fact in 1919 the legislature entrusted the magistrates with the job of defining the *appellations d'origine contrôlée* in order to put an end to the frequent abuses. This was a legally binding ruling and lasted until the creation of the law covering the

◄ *The banner of Puligny-Montrachet's brass band.*

AU GRAND MONTRACHET (Clos de Vigne)

AUTRES VIGNES FINES EN ROUGE

telles que : le Clos Saint-Jean, le Clos Voillon, les Pucelles et autres climats

MAISONS D'HABITATION et D'EXPLOITATION VINICOLE

Caves, Cours, Dépendances

Sis sur les communes de CHASSAGNE-MONTRACHET et PULIGNY-MONTRACHET, canton de Nolay arrondissement de Beaune (Côte-d'Or)

A VENDRE en DÉTAIL et aux ENCHÈRES PUBLIQUES

SUR LICITATION

Le Dimanche 24 Novembre 1918, à 1 heure de l'après-midi

En la maison commune de Chassagne-Montrachet, par le ministère de Mes LEVERT et DÉNOYERS, notaires à Beaune

AOCs in the mid-1930s. This procedure, which was invoked several times in Burgundy, notably for Chambertin, required magistrates to acknowledge the reality of *usages locaux, loyaux et constants*, or local custom and practice.

The Beaune judges recognized the existence of "a justly celebrated *cru*, Montrachet", produced from the chardonnay grape, coming from vineyards known by the name of Grand Montrachet, Vrai Montrachet or quite simply Montrachet, delimited to the east side by the road from Chassagne to Meursault, to the west by a wall and rocks, and to the north and south by various local roads. In their view, the defendants' vineyards had had, from time immemorial, the name of Bâtard-Montrachet, Chevalier-Montrachet, Bienvenues, Pucelles or other names, but never that of Montrachet without any other qualification. They also observed that the wines produced by these vineyards had never been sold under the name of Montrachet, with, however, one exception relating to several parcels of Dents de Chiens, small indentations into the *cru*'s established boundary, situated in Chassagne. So Montrachet increased in size from 7 hectares 49 ares (18.50 acres) to 8 hectares 7 ares 87 centiares (20 acres). This is what today's Land Register shows. But the *Institut national des appellations d'origine* lists 7 hectares 99 ares 80 centiares (19.8 acres), though nobody knows how the difference of 8 ares (0.20 acres) came about. The majority of books or articles published at the time still spoke of 7 hectares 50 ares (18.5 acres), basing this figure on previous works and without taking the 1921 judgement into account. The figure is inaccurate, though it is given, for example, in the monumental *Larousse des vins et vignobles de France*, published in 1987.

The court annulled the offending harvest return figures and prohibited the proprietors of other parcels from using the name of Montrachet, under penalty of paying 1000 francs damages with interest to each claimant for ev-

▲ *Announcement in the local press of the Drapier sale in 1918. The term "Grand Montrachet" is still used to distinguish Montrachet from its neighbours.*

ery infringement that was proved. Was there to be an appeal? The owners of the vines in Chevalier and Bâtard bowed before the Beaune judgement. What would the proprietors of Montrachet do? Their lawyer advised prudence: "It is true we have to accept that Dents de Chien has now been assimilated into Montrachet. We have not received satisfaction on this point, but such a slight increase is of little consequence." What the lawyer added revealed that the affair was not already a foregone conclusion: "The Bâtards and the Chevaliers are refused the appellation of Montrachet without qualification, despite the 1860 classification which is clearly contrary to our request. This is a result which we should risk compromising were we to go to court, especially as our adversaries have no intention of taking the matter further." So the matter was closed.

Between this judgement and the official AOC law, a plan to protect the appellation emerged in 1931. The Comte de Moucheron, a proprietor of Montrachet and owner of a château in Meursault, proposed that the other proprietors should all join forces. The idea came from Jacques Prieur, a proprietor in Meursault. "You will not be unaware of the desirable tendency which is presently developing among consumers of authentic wines," wrote Comte de Moucheron. "In order to guarantee this authenticity, on-site bottling would seem to be the best procedure. We consider that in view of the small number of proprietors of our famous Montrachet and its restricted size, it would be in our interest for this wine not to leave our cellars except in the bottle, with a stamp proving its undisputed origin." So the proprietors of the *cru* would "control the marketing of this wine". The Comte went on: "Prices are bound to remain at a relatively high level. For Montrachet, the fact of being the first of the *Grands Crus* in Burgundy to take the initiative in practising on-site bottling exclusively will make us leaders in the field." The plan was readily adopted. All the harvest of Montrachet was to be bottled at the property of the respective owner (this was not to be a "cooperative"). Each proprietor would put his name on the labels and the corks. In off-years the proprietors would decide together whether to declassify the wine, which would then take the name of Chassagne or Puligny-Montrachet, and the obligation to bottle would be waived. After every harvest, the proprietors would meet in March to establish a minimum price per bottle. Beyond that, they would be free to fix their own price.

This plan was conceived in April 1931. The proprietors of Montrachet discussed it on June 15 and reached a general agreement on the broad issues. They even wanted to register the creation of the association officially. The next meeting was scheduled for the month of August. But just like at the Clos de Vougeot where similar ideas are frequently conceived, all this came to nothing. They did not even create a "federation" as in Chambertin or at the Clos de Vougeot. Why did it fail? Perhaps because of what was considered the overbearing influence of the Meursault "clan" (the Comte de Moucheron, Comte Lafon and Jacques Prieur being the most active in the association). Perhaps too the trade, in particular the firm of Bouchard Père et Fils, looked with no great favour on the prospect of an agreement between the proprietors laying claim to control of the *cru* and the market. Here today, perhaps elsewhere tomorrow.

A difficult birth

During the 1930s, when the *appellations d'origine contrôlée* were created, the laws of July 31, 1937 and June 13, 1939 simply ratified the judgement of 1921 as far as Montrachet was concerned. By contrast for the other appellations classed here as *Grand Crus* matters were more complicated. Chevalier-Montrachet and Bâtard-Montrachet did not even have a precise delimitation. In May 1938 the Ferré Commission, a working party of "wise men", was entrusted with the task of making proposals to the *Comité national des appellations d'origine*. Its members went to Chassagne and Puligny to hear what those concerned had to say and to study the situation on the spot. It was a difficult birth. Louis Ferré was the director of Burgundy's Oenological Centre in Beaune. He knew the vineyards, the wine and the people inside out. No one questioned his competence and impartiality. At his side was the Marquis d'Angerville, who was also highly respected.

First of all, Bâtard-Montrachet: in Chassagne, this *cru* is situated in one of the six subsections of the Montrachet section of the 1840 Land Register. It is a subsection called "Bâtard-Montrachet" but includes the following localities:
– Bâtard-Montrachet (5 hectares 81 ares 80 centiares or 14.4 acres)
– Les Criots (1 hectare 51 ares 75 centiares or 3.7 acres)
– Blanchot Dessous (2 hectares 3 ares 80 centiares or 5 acres)
– Vide Bourse (1 hectare 42 ares 50 centiares or 3.5 acres)
– Les Encégnières (1 hectare 96 ares 30 centiares or 4.9 acres)
This gives a total of 12 hectares 76 ares 15 centiares (31.6 acres).

In Puligny this *cru* lies in the section called Les Houillères on the Land Register, Bâtard-Montrachet forming one of its nineteen subsections with two localities:
– Bienvenues (6 hectares 1 are 60 centiares or 14.9 acres)
– Bâtard-Montrachet (3 hectares 71 ares 47 centiares or 9.2 acres)
Strictly according to the Land Register, the Bâtards of the two communes account for barely 9 hectares, and that is all. Topographically, these parcels have the same exposure as Montrachet, albeit at a lower altitude and with a different geology. In 1860, the Beaune Agricultural Committee had distinguished two classes within Bâtard. Although "justified by the geological nature of the terrain which gradually changes on leaving the hillside of Montrachet", the Ferré Commission considered that it was not proper to create distinctions between these parcels, since they were marked on the Land Register in Bâtard-Montrachet and their wines had always been produced and declared under this appellation.

But requests to extend were formulated:

– by the Federation of Growers of Puligny-Montrachet, with a view to obtaining the Bâtard-Montrachet appellation for Cailleret, Pucelles, Folatières, Clavaillon, Referts, Charmes, Combettes, Champ Canet, Chalumaux, Hameau de Blagny, Blagny-Sous le Puits, Garenne and Champ Gain;

– by a proprietor in the *climat* of Bienvenues (Puligny) and by eight proprietors of Bâtard-Montrachet.

The Ferré Commission dismissed the Federation's claims, which were admittedly surprising, out of hand, considering that they were excessive and unjustified.

The second request, more restrained than the first, gave rise to bitter controversy. Twenty-one proprietors of Bâtard-Montrachet in Puligny and Chassagne were opposed to it. Moreover, thirty-eight proprietors in Chassagne were against any extension of Bâtard, even going so far as to threaten that if any extension were made they would apply this appellation to all the white wines coming from chardonnay grapes harvested in Chassagne.

The Commission tried to study the situation calmly: its report shows how the INAO conducted its deliberations in such complicated cases. In the matter of Bienvenues claimed as Bâtard-Montrachet, the petitioners invoked the Land Register: it was not an extension of Bâtard, for the 1840 plan had Bâtard-Montrachet as a general denomination (subsection) with Bienvenues coming after as a separate small locality. The Land Registers prior to 1840, the Commission recalled, were not divided into subsections or localities. But from 1840, only the names of the subsections were mentioned in on the Land Register. Such was the case for Chassagne and Puligny. From then on, the name of Bâtard-Montrachet on the Land Register did not constitute a right to an appellation, since these parcels were marked in Bienvenues.

The petitioners also referred to the 1840 plan drawn up by the Beaune Agricultural Committee. These parcels were classed as Bâtard-Montrachet. Not a bit of it, replied the Ferré Commission: in respect of the communes whose Land Register was drawn up from 1840, this plan mentions only the subsections. Moreover this is why Chevalier-Montrachet does not feature on it. It was then included in Montrachet, and the judgement of 1921 took that into consideration. So it was clearly a case of a request for an extension rather than for the recognition of an existing situation. People could then, and rightly, speak of Vrai Bâtard-Montrachet... or of Grand Bâtard.

The petitioners explained that there was no natural boundary between the neighbouring *climats* of Bâtard-Montrachet and Bienvenues. No more than between Montrachet and Chevalier-Montrachet. Finally they declared that the 1921 judgement proved them right. The court in Beaune mentioned

---

Harvesting: everyone has his own ideas, methods and habits. ▶

Bienvenues, indicating that these wines were "generally and mainly" sold under the name of Bâtard-Montrachet. The Ferré Commission returned fire with "generally and mainly" does not mean "invariably".

However, after sweeping these arguments aside, the Ferré Commission did recognize that the proprietors in Bienvenues were defending legitimate claims. For their parcels were in every way identical to those classed as Bâtard-Montrachet, "probably superior in quality to the wines coming from Bâtard-Montrachet classed in the second class". The plan clearly shows the existence of a boundary for Bienvenues conforming with that of Bâtard, between the first and second class. None the less, it was surprising to see the Ferré Commission using these arguments based on the work of the Beaune Agricultural Committee (1860) when it had dismissed them in respect of Bâtard itself... The Ferré Commission also commented that the higher part of Bienvenues had always been planted with chardonnay whereas the rest

of the *climat* had formerly had pinot noir. It admitted then that an extension of Bâtard was conceivable in the first class part of Bienvenues. So it was proposed to classify as Bâtard-Montrachet not only the 5 hectares 81 ares 80 centiares (14.4 acres) in Chassagne and the 3 hectares 71 ares 47 centiares (9.2 acres) in Puligny, but also 2 hectares 30 ares (5.7 acres) in Bienvenues at Puligny, that is a total of 11 hectares 83 ares 27 centiares (29.2 acres). In addition, "as has been done for Chambertin" (Mazis-Chambertin, Charmes-Chambertin, etc.), the experts suggested agreeing to the following three appellations: Bienvenues-Bâtard-Montrachet in Puligny, Criots-Bâtard-Montrachet and Blanchots-Bâtard-Montrachet in Chassagne. But finally, on May 31, 1939, after protracted trench warfare in Chassagne, the Ferré Commission signed a report limiting the extension to Criots-Bâtard-Montrachet (with the disappearance of Blanchots-Bâtard-Montrachet, whose destiny had been hanging by a thread). The final decree was dated

June 13, 1939. This happened all over again in respect of Chevalier-Montrachet. The same procedure was adopted by the Ferré Commission in May 1938. This time matters appeared simpler, for there was only Puligny to be considered. But appearances can be deceptive. The section on the Land Register under the names Hameau de Blagny, Champ Gain and Montrachet was divided into ten subsections. The two localities included on the 1840 plan – Chevalier-Montrachet and Montrachet – were part of the subsection Le Montrachet. These two *crus* were classed in the first class by the Beaune Agricultural Committee in 1860, clearly differentiated by the judgement of 1921. The Ferré Commission considered that Chevalier-Montrachet was precisely defined by history and local custom. The appellation would be granted to all the parcels there "with the exception of certain parcels corresponding to *murgers* or roads connecting various localities".

But nothing is simple in vine-growing country. Louis Jadot and Louis Latour, highly respected merchant-proprietors in Beaune, claimed the Chevalier-Montrachet appellation for their vines in Puligny, situated in Cailleret (1 hectare 2 ares 70 centiares, about 2.5 acres), resembling in every respect those of Chevalier-Montrachet. All the proprietors of the traditional Chevalier rebelled, producing a petition drawn up by Joseph Leflaive and signed by everybody in Puligny: the claims of Louis Jadot and Louis La-

▲ *Comte Jules Lafon (left), Joseph Leflaive and François Virot (right): the history and legend of the* cru.

tour were considered excessive. What did they have to say for themselves? These vines, acquired on the death of Léonce Bocquet in 1913, had been sold to them, according to the title deeds, as "in Chevalier-Montrachet or Cailleret". The publicity concerning the sale had mentioned "in Chevalier-Montrachet". "So we have paid for the name", stated the two purchasers. All previously known sales of these wines already bore the mention "at Chevalier-Montrachet" and, attested by the lawyer's stamp, were duly registered as such in 1887 and before. Before that we find 86 ares (2.1 acres) in Montrachet and 33 ares 50 centiares (0.8 acres) in Cailleret (1857), and still 86 ares in Montrachet (1846) and 85 ares 70 centiares (2.1 acres) in Chevalier-Montrachet (1829). So Chevalier-Montrachet had existed since 1829. The two Beaune merchants, having a sense of the *climats*, called the lot Chevalier-Montrachet "Les Demoiselles". Which Demoiselles? Since the 1820s these 86 ares (2.1 acres) had belonged to General Voillot. His two daughters, Adèle and Julie, both spinsters, inherited them and sold them in February 1846 to another family from Beaune, the Moreau-Guillemots. Louis Jadot and Louis Latour claimed the right to call their wines both Chevalier-Montrachet and "Les Demoiselles" in posthumous honour of Julie and Adèle Voillot, "demoiselles" meaning "young ladies". "Have the Grèves Bouchards ever been taken to task or questioned as to their right to use the name Grèves de l'Enfant-Jésus?" they asked, referring to the ancient vineyard of the Beaune Carmelites.

Joseph Leflaive replied that this was simply a case of wine merchants pretentiousness, that this vineyard had been classed in the second class in 1860 and was marked as Cailleret on the Land Register, that a road separated Montrachet from Cailleret, that the petitioners' use of the term "Demoiselles du Chevalier-Montrachet" was an abuse of the name, and that all the parcels in Cailleret should be allowed to be Chevalier-Montrachet. Supported by good lawyers, Louis Jadot and Louis Latour refuted each of these arguments in turn. A road? The Romanée Saint-Vivant is split in two by a road, as are Les Teurons in Beaune and Les Boucherottes in Beaune and Pommard, and so on. And the second class of 1860? What about Dents de Chien assimilated into Montrachet by the judgement of 1921? "Les Demoiselles du Chevalier-Montrachet"? Wrong: the labels read "Chevalier-Montrachet – Les Demoiselles. The extension to Cailleret? In the Corton case, the court in Dijon reasoned in the same way as Joseph Leflaive. Yet this ruling had been overthrown in Paris. If the other proprietors of Cailleret had considered it pointless to call their wines differently, they could not claim another appellation today. As for improper use, why had the proprietors of Santenots called their wines Volnay-Santenots?

This debate shows the extent to which appellations which to us today seem clear and inviolable gave rise to bitter acrimony at the time when names and *crus* were being decided. The Ferré Commission was doubtless highly embarrassed and washed its hands of the matter: "As the arguments invoked by both parties are essentially of a legal nature, the experts consider that they are not qualified to give a ruling on this request and refer it back to the *Comité national des appellations d'origine* to have the matter decided by the law." In the expectation of their favourable opinion (which they must have presupposed to some extent), they made the addition of:

– 6 hectares 11 ares 80 centiares (15.1 acres) in Chevalier-Montrachet, and

– 1 hectare 2 ares 70 centiares (2.5 acres) in Cailleret,

representing a total of 7 hectares 14 ares 50 centiares (17.7 acres) in Chevalier-Montrachet.

The INAO's legal action decided in favour of Louis Jadot and Louis Latour. The decree, dated June 13, 1939, extended the Chevalier-Montrachet appellation in Cailleret by one hectare. It remained to be seen whether the subsidiary appellation of Les Demoiselles, used constantly since, was, if not legal, at least legitimate. This was an enormous problem. The proprietors of the Clos de Vougeot had been forbidden to refer to this ancient vineyard's *climats* from the past (Musigny, for example). Would it now be possible to do the same in the *Grands Crus* of Puligny and Chassagne? The designation Louis Latour's vineyard had used had not varied in form, but other people considered it an abuse.

As for others extensions, in 1955 the Chartron family requested that a parcel in Cailleret be classified as Chevalier-Montrachet. This parcel was made up of several old parcels included in an entirely haphazard way in Chevalier-Montrachet and Cailleret. When it had been replanted, it had had other "sterile" land which was not fit to be cultivated added to it. This land was also in Cailleret. The Viticultural Federation dragged the affair out for nearly ten years before in 1964 a favourable decision was given. The Delimitation Committee, an imposing body including the Inspector General of Rural Affairs, Rivers and Forests, an honorary member of the Faculty of Science in Dijon and others approved this new classification in Chevalier-Montrachet in 1970, dismissing at the same time any claim to an AOC for the neighbouring parcels deprived of their soil. The INAO sanctioned this in February 1974. So Chevalier-Montrachet gained 25 ares 23 centiares (0.6 acres).

So there were Chevalier, Bâtard, Criots-Bâtard and Bienvenues-Bâtard...-Montrachet. Les Criots (a diminutive of *crais* – stony land) is one of the oldest localities in the parish. As for Bienvenues, the word comes from land taken on *métayage*, said to be "welcome" (*bien venues*). This may seem fanciful, but the archives of the Abbey of Maizières mention purchases of "welcome" vines in 1397 and 1418. Danguy and Aubertin quote this *climat* in their book (1892) but Doctor Lavalle makes no mention of it in 1855.

Before the creation of the AOCs, the wines (here a 1928 Puligny red) had to request a "certificat de pureté" from the Oenological Centre in Beaune. ▶

Lying wholly in Puligny, Chevalier-Montrachet stretches laterally above the part of Montrachet which is situated in the commune, covering an area of 7 hectares 33 centiares (18.1 acres). This has varied considerably over the years, for Doctor Lavalle gave it 27 hectares 71 ares 80 centiares (68.5 acres), whereas Camille Rodier counted only 6 hectares 24 ares (15.4 acres).

Straddling Chassagne and Puligny, Bâtard-Montrachet now covers 11 hectares 86 ares (29.3 acres). Camille Rodier reckoned its area at 9 hectares 73 ares (24 acres) in Puligny and 12 hectares 79 ares 85 centiares (31.6 acres) in Chassagne, that is over 22 hectares (54.4 acres). Part of this difference lies in the area of Criots in Chassagne (1 hectare 57 ares or 3.9 acres) and

Bienvenues in Puligny (3 hectares 68 ares or 9 acres). Tradition has it that these parts of Criots and Bienvenues were promoted to "son of... Bâtard" to balance out the parcels of *Grand Cru* between Chassagne and Puligny. And there is no doubt that an endeavour was made to increase the surface of Bâtard to some extent: the growers of Chassagne have proved that the trade always used to buy Criots as Bâtard and have invoices to prove it. The Ferré Commission did its best, but it was caught between Chassagne and Puligny, each commune defending its own interests. At the height of the argument, the Chassagne town council decided to give rulings on the appellations. For the parcels named as Bâtard-Montrachet, the white wines were to have this appellation; for the others the appellation was to be *Grand vin blanc de Chassagne*. But each grower wanted his voice to be heard at the meeting. "If the appellation is extended to Criots", said Monsieur Deléger, "it will also have to be extended to Blanchot Dessus." "The geography of the place should be taken into account", reckoned Monsieur Villard. The mayor of Puligny pointed out that Cailleret had never been synonymous with Chevalier. But before the law of 1919, the wines of Cailleret were sold under the name of Montrachet. Doctor Jules Lavalle was here referring to red wines, however. As for Bienvenues, Julien Monnot assures us that they were planted with "good red sets and even gamay formerly". The growers present contested this. Criots was gained after an epic struggle by Edmond Delagrange, which proved (with documentary evidence) that since 1919 he had been declaring his Criots as Bâtard-Montrachet. The other proprietors were doubtless selling their wines as Chassagne-Montrachet or Criots. But his case was watertight and he managed to convince the Ferré Commission. The proprietors of Blanchot Dessous, Encégnières and Vide Bourse, on the other hand, were unable to furnish the same proof: from this it can be seen how much determination, astuteness and tact was needed at the end of the 1930s to obtain classification as *Grands Crus* in Chassagne and Puligny – classifications which have since become eternal and sacrosanct.

The founders of the AOC did their best, and it should be recognized that they had a difficult case to judge. These regions of appellation were established not only by local custom but also by business practice. Furthermore some *climats* disappeared or were assimilated into a more dignified appellation (Vide Bourse, for example, meaning "empty purse" would have an unfortunate effect on any label!) A great number of other communes in Burgundy have done the same thing.

On March 8, 1977, on the initiative of its former president, the Viticultural Federation in Puligny called for the abolition of the Bienvenues appellation, requesting that it be taken into Bâtard-Montrachet. The matter never went any further. The Burgundy AOCs are like a house of cards: it is difficult to move one piece without upsetting the balance of the rest.

Montrachet could hope for better things as a result of the 1937 ruling. For the first time in all its history, it was equal with its Chevalier and Bâtard as a

Grand Cru. Would its true greatness now be recognized? Would a separate category be created for it?

Even if other members of its family often have the same qualities and the same virtues, Montrachet is like no other. It owes its empire not only to its own qualities , however, but also to commercial astuteness. For anything that is rare is expensive, and anything that is expensive, is sought after. Raymond Dumay rightly remarks that the more expensive a wine is the greater are its chances of being good. Moreover if it is hard to find, if "you have to drink it on your knees", – as Alexandre Dumas is believed to have said – its fortune is made.

Since the eighteenth century everyone has stressed the absurd price of this wine and the difficulty of getting hold of it. "It is always sold at a very high price and despite this it is rare for the price to cover the proprietor's costs and overheads", wrote Doctor Denis Morelot in 1831. "Should the wine of Montrachet be considered as one of those rare marvels the chance of appreciating whose perfection is granted only to a chosen few?" asks Doctor Jules Lavalle in 1855. "Let the man who is able to buy a few bottles of the best vintages consider himself fortunate, whatever the price; he will never have paid too much." So that sums up everything: on the one hand, the wine does not cover the proprietor's costs, and on the other, you will never have paid enough for it.

The fame of this wine beyond price was already firmly established in the eighteenth century. Speaking of the small quantity available, the priest Arnoux writes: "Accordingly, it sells at a very high price, and to obtain some, you have to order it a year in advance, because it is always reserved before it is even made." This is confirmed by a *Recueil de Mémoires historiques* of 1766, which reproduces texts from the middle of the eighteenth century: "Montrachet and La Romanée are extremely limited *crus*. For this reason, these two wines are the foremost and most sought after in the whole of Burgundy. They are more expensive than the wines of the Clos de Vougeot and Chambertin. When these latter are selling for 800 livres, the others fetch 1200 livres. If you want any, you are obliged to order it before the harvest." "Limited" here means "of modest dimensions". Little-known and amazingly modern, this text explains everything. The rarity of Montrachet is responsible for its price, not to mention any snob value.

Two centuries later Alexis Lichine echoes these words: "Vines whose wine is sold practically before even being made and almost at any price." No one can doubt that Montrachet has played this trump card adroitly. It has the business world in its pocket, and no one can reproach it for that.

The secret is in the wine

From whatever point of view we consider this problem or in whatever light, all the explanations seem convincing but none seems adequate.The enigma of Montrachet lies neither in its history, nor in its soil, subsoil, microclimate or grape variety. No doubt all these factors and all these influences play their part. But their balance is so subtle and so changeable that it depends more on art than on science.

The wine of Montrachet is a miracle of nature, at one and the same time a gift from heaven and the work of man. When a survey organized by the review *Cuisine et Vins de France* was conducted in France in April 1982, people's replies revealed how little the French really know about wine. Is Montrachet...

– a white wine from Burgundy?	7%
– a red wine from Burgundy?	8%
– a white wine from Touraine?	8%
– don't know	77%

And the 77% had probably never drunk any! A similar survey conducted four years later by the same review showed that little progress had been made... 10% now identified Montrachet as a white wine from Burgundy.

But wine lovers, for their part, do not get it wrong. After stirring up a hornets' nest when it organized the Olympiades du Vin some ten years ago, Gault et Millau repeated this competition in 1986-1987. The two rounds of chardonnay hurdles were a highly cosmopolitan obstacle race: Italy, Brazil, Austria, Spain, Chile, the United States, Australia, Argentina and France. What came (just) in the lead on these two occasions? A Chevalier-Montrachet Domaine Leflaive 1983 and a Chevalier-Montrachet Louis Jadot of the same vintage. Honour had been preserved!

The word "Montrachet' has become a sort of symbol. The firm of Oxenham in Mauritius formerly produced a wine locally called "Monachet". It

---

◄ *The cork of practically every bottle of Montrachet is of Spanish or Sicilian origin and bears a proud "signature".*

is now called "Ange d'Or" (Golden Angel) after discreet "diplomatic rep-
resentations". Although the name Montrachet is no longer applied to wines
made in various parts of the world, we could still read recently in *The Wine
Spectator*: "When Montrachet is too much" (March 31, 1987); or another
headline, "The Montrachet of Australia" (May 1, 1986).

Bernard Portet, an oenologist of the Clos du Val in the Napa Valley, revealed one day that after a stay in Chassagne at Domaine Ramonet, he had
the feeling of "living in complete harmony" for the first time in his life.
"Everything was at one", he said. "The environment, the wine, the aromas,
the taste, even the men." Moreover, I had the same curious, exciting impression when, on entering the Ramonet family's kitchen, a sort of oenological
laboratory, I smelt the very essence of their wine, as if it had somehow become impregnated into the people and their surroundings over the years.

Delicate vines

"When I was appointed to Dijon at the beginning of the 1950s," recounts
Raymond Bernard, "I quickly perceived that in Burgundy viral diseases are
highly traumatic. Yellow spots appear on the leaves during the growing
season, particularly with the whites. Everybody has his own opinion: "It
has always been like that!", or again, "It comes from the veins in the land".
The same reactions as at the time of phylloxera. We marked plants and
identified the diseased ones. We took grafts from healthy plants and selected
them. It was the beginning of a programme which has occupied us now for
nearly forty years." Raymond Bernard is the delegate of Onivins (Office
national interprofessionnel des vins) for Burgundy, Alsace and Champagne.
He studied in Montpellier under Professor Jean Branas, who has done so
much to bring ampelography, or the science of grape varieties, up to date.
He has become one of the leading experts in the field of clones. But what is a
clone? The reproduction of a vine-plant by vegetal multiplication. Whether a
pinot noir or a chardonnay, clonal selection has two objectives: one for health
(the obtaining of a healthy strain with no viral diseases) and the other for variety (the selection of the best types of stock). From now on to speak merely
of chardonnay means nothing. For today there are hundreds of varieties of
chardonnay. Rather, we should speak of clone 76 or clone 95. The INAO is
beginning to take an interest in this and we can foresee that one day labels
will have to indicate the clone. In fact some are much better than others,
and an enlightened public will soon call for such details to be given.

It goes without saying that the vineyards of Montrachet are well organized
and planted. At the present time they are suffering from erosion by rainfall,
which is considerable in Chevalier. An explanation is being sought. Is it a
result of doing away with the walls and the *murgers*? Undoubtedly. And the
systematic use of chemical herbicides? Perhaps, but ploughed land is also
vulnerable to erosion. Vineyards which had been ploughed crumbled away

at Auxey-Duresses. In any event, it seems that an effort should be made to re-create the historic defences against erosion, and especially the walls which have been so casually abandoned.

As for the vineyards, everybody agrees that although the old ones give little juice, they make the best wine. Yet it is difficult to define what constitutes an old vineyard. There are some which are 50 to 80 years old but their plants have been replaced over the years, rather like those Gothic cathedrals which no longer have any of the original stonework. André Ramonet is opposed to these "replantings", which in the long run complicate the situation. At one time when a vineyard was uprooted, it was replaced for some years by oats, lucerne or sainfoin on the hillside. This practice has now disappeared and the land has scarcely over a year's rest.

Does Montrachet have its own version of AIDS? By this, I mean a viral disease provoking considerable damage. It does indeed, and it is called *court noué*. "Thirty years ago it was a real disaster", Raymond Bernard goes on. "The vines in the white vineyards of the Côte caught this disease and had to

---

▲ *From Chablis to Pouilly-Fuissé, the chardonnay has fallen in love with Burgundy's terrain.*

Brown or white under the snow, the vines always turn Cistercian in winter. ▶

be uprooted after fifteen years because they were exhausted. It is nothing like phylloxera. The rods appear to be screwed up tight. The nodes are separated by smaller ones which appear between them. These increase in number and then diminish up to the eighth or ninth eye. The plant's growth is stunted, it becomes dwarfed and at the end of ten or twelve years it dies, although the normal average age of a vine is from forty to fifty years. The leaves shrink, so restricting photosynthesis, and quality suffers. They look like ducks' feet and have more pointed serrations. Pollination is faulty. Another type of *court noué* exists called *fan leaf*, an infectious bright canary-yellow streaking. Yet another problem with the chardonnay is *enroulement*, which happens in autumn. The leaves become thicker and curl up on themselves, the veins becoming more contrasted. This produces the same sort of effect as the folds of a cigar. *Enroulement* particularly affects the sugar content. Unlike *court noué* it does not affect the whole plant, but it is still a risk to guard against."

Are there any unusual varieties found in Montrachet? As in Meursault, here we sometimes come across a rare chardonnay with pink berries, musky and aromatic. This is a spontaneous mutation, a genetic peculiarity, like the one discovered in 1899 in Vosne-Romanée by the grower Camuzet, a pinot noir which produced bunches in three colours, the same plant giving pinot noir, pinot gris and pinot blanc!

A tractor which straddles the vines replaced the horse in the 1950s, and today even helicopters sometimes help with spraying the vines. Should we disapprove of this intervention of modern technology? Whenever disease or parasites threatened a parcel, several days often used to be needed to treat it by hand. Nowadays the enemy is combatted in two hours. The results are on the whole positive, even if the helicopter is somewhat noisy and lacking in finesse. As for pruning, it is generally done conscientiously enough, though there are abuses here and there.

Like Santenay, Chassagne has a different system of pruning from that of the rest of the Côte. Many vines are pruned by the Cordon de Royat rather than the Guyot system. The latter annually renews the principal branch which will produce the fruit-bearing rods, whereas the Cordon de Royat system removes only the young shoots. This practice certainly has an effect on the quality of the wines. The vines are often cultivated by the proprietor and his family, if they are growers. Where it is a case of vines belonging to a proprietor living some distance away or to a proprietor who does not look after the vines himself, *métayage* or tenant-farming is the most common solution. Thus local growers can enlarge their own holding and add to the appellations they can offer. René Lamy told me: "You know, it is a great thing for a grower to be able to say that he has Montrachet or a *Grand Cru* in his cellar. That is why we make every effort to get hold of some whenever there is an inheritance in the offing!"

Vines belonging to non-residents are sometimes looked after by salaried workers or *tâcherons*. Although this has become pejorative in the language of today, it is a perfectly respectable term implying a worker who works as he thinks best, undertaking to do the job to the best of his ability. Up to harvest time the *tâcherons* do all the work on the vineyard. Such is the case with Henri Bonnefoy. This young man of 35 from Chassagne loves vines and all that goes with them. But he himself has only about 20 ares (half an acre). So he became a *tâcheron*. In 1981 he took on part of the Montrachet belonging to the Marquis de Laguiche, which he has looked after completely since 1985. Today he tends nearly four hectares. So it is he who works all the year round in the famous Montrachet of the Marquis de Laguiche.

Is he given guidelines? No, he is trusted completely. And pruning? "Every plant should be considered separately", he says. "I prune according to each plant." Does the Montrachet receive special attention? All the vines are treated with the same care. How much is he paid? Whether it is a simple Bourgogne appellation or the Montrachet, the official rate in Côte de Beaune is the same, something in the order of 7,300 francs per *ouvrée* (4 ares 28 centiares, that is to say about a tenth of an acre) in 1987. That is about 40,000 francs per year for cultivating these two hectares of Montrachet, a total income for the *tâcheron* of round about 80,000 francs per year, that is a monthly income of about 6,500 francs, which represents some fifteen bottles of Montrachet. Henri Bonnefoi does not complain. He considers it an honour, even a pleasure, to work here. His one regret is that he can only rarely drink the wine he helps to make. "At one time", he says, "they used to keep a few bottles at the 'domaine'. Every time we had a particularly back-breaking job to do, such as breaking up the land, we would drink wine produced by its vines. If it was in Montrachet, we drank Montrachet. It was a good tradition. Now vinification no longer takes place on site and they do not keep any bottles for special occasions. I hardly get a chance to drink the wine from the vines I work. But that's life..."

From grape to cask

Every year the yields are fixed in accordance with official rulings at an average of around 40 hectolitres per hectare, with a possible increase of some 20%. These yields, which are quite reasonable, are extremely variable and depend on the age of the vines. The "Commission of Five", whose president is Edmond Delagrange-Bachelet, pays a visit to the vineyards of the *Grands Crus* in August and September to determine the base yield.

"At Domaine Thénard, the Montrachet was always first to be harvested," Jacques Bordeaux Montrieux remembers. "It was a religiously respected tradition. We used to say that we had to *see to the Montrachet first*. In fact, this was ridiculous. Now we go about things in a different way. As harvesting here lasts for ten days or so, we choose a fine sunny day for the Montrachet – the best moment." An early harvest? A late harvest? If it is bad weather, they harvest without waiting. But if the weather is set fair, the custom is to wait for complete, even excessive, ripeness. This was the case in 1986. Over-ripeness presents risks, however. They sometimes say that the crop has "turned". The grapes take on a chocolate colour, are attacked by rot and are threatened by oxidization. "This often happens after a thunderstorm", Jean-Marc Blain-Gagnard remarks. With the 1987 harvest, the "noble rot" was so intense that we had to take a basket to each plant to collect the grapes which were dropping off the bunches. Bouchard Père et Fils respects to the letter the precept of "rest on the seventh day" and never harvests on Sunday. "I once saw them gathering grapes on a Sunday morning", continues Jacques Bordeaux Montrieux. "It had to be an emergency. I quickly did the same."

Harvesting generally takes place at the end of September or the beginning of October. I have in front of me a chart of dates showing when harvesting began in Chassagne from 1740 to 1843. They coincide with today's dates, the earliest falling around September 15 and the latest October 15. There is no mention of August, although some old jottings refer to such early harvests. This is certainly not true. Are we to see mechanical harvesters on this illustrious hillside? Fortunately the area lends itself less readily to them than the people. One grower whom I asked gave me this reply, which came in a series of hiccoughs: "I've bought one... But fortunately it doesn't work... And you know, I shall never use it in Montrachet... Anyway it's too big to get into the vineyard..."

Nothing could be more typical of Burgundy! This reply could well serve as an exercise in literary comprehension. For each statement is followed by a denial, revealing the astonishing richness of afterthoughts in Burgundy's mental subsoil. Even if mechanical harvesters were able to operate successfully here, let us hope that we never see them. This is less a question of technology than of ethos. The grapes for such a wine call for loving hands and gentle secateurs, strong shoulders and tender glances. Do we cut diamonds in the same way as we hew trees? When a bottle is sold for 700 to

1000 francs, the sale represents not only the wine but a name and an image, a tradition and a reputation – in a word, Burgundy.

Harvesting is one thing, vinification another. It is then that the real work of producing the *Grand Cru* begins. Once cut, the grapes arrive rapidly at the vat-house: the golden rule says within two hours. It is a race against time lasting a day and a night – no longer – in order to avoid any oxidation.

Everyone has his own principles, methods and style. In the main, the work follows a standard procedure: crushing in the vat-house (often carried out with such care that sometimes it is hardly done at all in order to keep the harvest intact), then a light pressing without removal of the stalks. These stalks (which at this stage in the vinification process will have been removed if harvesting has been carried out mechanically) will facilitate the pressing process, for they add solid elements to the bulk of the *marc* to be pressed. The musts produced by the crushing and those from the pressing are then carefully blended together. Sulphur dioxide (sulphite treatment) is now added to the juice which is collected in a vat. It is decanted so as to separate the clear part from the cloudiness which occurs as a result of flocculation. This juice is aerated and sometimes yeast may be added. It will then ferment for one or two weeks in oak casks. Everything depends on the activity of the yeasts, the temperature of the building, the nature of the vintage and the practices of the establishment. The secondary fermentation (malolactic) sometimes follows this initial alcoholic fermentation very quickly, or may well take place several months later (1969, 1972, 1978). All the world's specialists in the field of wine microbiology have tackled this problem, but no one can really explain it. One other unknown factor is the excessive effect of potassium in relation to the tartric acid, as was the case in 1977. Why? "As long as the malolactic fermentation has not taken place, I cannot sleep easily," a grower from Puligny told me. Does he give his Montrachet greater attention than any other wine in his cellar? "I am more anxious about it", he replied. They do not have the right to fail with such a *chef-d'œuvre*. The *Grands Crus* always enjoy the privilege of being treated like royalty.

It is dangerous to put large quantities of casks of white musts to ferment in a badly ventilated cellar. The carbonic gas builds up and the grower must wear an oxygen mask when he visits his cellars. Prudence recommends taking a lighted candle. If it goes out so should he, and on the double! In Chassagne, Constant Laberge lost his dog in this way, suffocated in the cellar. In 1969 Pierre Lacroix was overcome and the Chagny fire brigade had to be called out. It was a year of uncontrolled fermentation, like 1947, when casks which were only two-thirds full bubbled over. At one time they used to place a basin of whitewash in the cellar, but the best solution of all is to pump the gas out. In any event the workers need to carry matches, even if only for testing for gas in the cask. If the match goes out, there is no risk of oxidation. If it burns brightly, the cask should be filled completely and a bung placed in the top.

The technology of presses has developed considerably. "I can still see my father-in-law in front of the Vaslin press," recalls Edmond Delagrange. "Heavens above", he would say, "the *marc* comes out by itself. No need to cut it out."

There are several other operations in addition to those listed above. Chaptalization consists of adding sugar before fermentation (17 grammes per litre to obtain one degree more). This practice is legal in Burgundy, with a tolerance of two extra degrees. It is an old custom, for the monks of Cîteaux are said to have introduced it at the Clos de Vougeot at the end of the eighteenth century. In certain years, such as 1985, a natural 15° or so is reached. 13° or 14° are not uncommon. This is nothing new: 14.9° was achieved in 1825, for example. Sometimes sugar is not added at all by some producers, sometimes its addition is symbolic. "We add a pinch of sugar to be on the safe side," one of the most famous producers of the *cru* told me. Safe side? Indeed, the exact amount of sugar transformed into alcohol is an enigma. What the future degree of the wine is to be cannot be known as long as it has not been chaptalized. In 1976 they thought the white would have 15° to 16° of natural sugar. Yet in the end none had more than 14°. This varies from year to year, as the former director of Burgundy's Oenological Centre, Max

◄ *Harvesting in Chassagne-Montrachet.*

The grapes must not lose a single second between the vineyard and the vat-house. The juice will be put in cask a few hours later.
▶

Léglise, points out. What is more, there is a maximum and a minimum degree. In 1979 a new rule concerning enriching wine in France (as a general practice and not as sanctioned by courts of appeal, as previously), created several new obligations: a definite date for starting the harvest, monitoring ripeness and fixing a maximum degree for each appellation. In general, this was based on the appellation's minimum degree plus 3°, with an upper limit of 14.5°. The decrees have since been modified. For the three appellations Bâtard-Montrachet, Bienvenues-Bâtard and Criots-Bâtard, an error had crept in at administrative level. The minimum degree has now been corrected to 12°, as for Montrachet and Chevalier-Montrachet. A long text published in the *Journal officiel* on February 28, 1987, finally fixed the following figures. Montrachet and Chevalier-Montrachet: a minimum of 12 natural degrees; the other three *Grands Crus*: 11.5°; the maximum for all to be 14.5° when chaptalization has been carried out; if the alcohol meter gives a reading of more than 14.5° of natural sugar the appellation will be granted. Chaptalization calls for particular skill and absolute integrity. It can unbalance a wine, making it heavy, over-generous, alcoholic, with too strong a flavour of alcohol, a defect rare in the *Grands Crus* of Montrachet but one which is sometimes off-putting for the taster. It slightly increases the wine's volume and this temptation has to be conscientiously avoided. What happens when the natural degree exceeds the legal limit? It is ignored and matters are settled afterwards. A small quantity of water has even been tipped into the future wine, and it has to be admitted that this is a shame! In 1990 the EEC regulations will insist on chaptalization with grape sugar instead of cane or beet sugar. The Burgundians are very reluctant...

Casks of oak, naturally. New ones? Generally the proportion of new casks is one-third, with a skilful marriage of the cooper's deliveries and the casks of one to three years' use. Recent research in Burgundy, and in particular in the Côte des Blancs, has shown that in every case ageing in new oak casks gave the best results. This was well known, but now it is certain. Just as for the degree of alcohol, the pronouncement of the Delphic Oracle is heeded: *ne quid nimis*. But everything in moderation, for too many new casks produce an excessive flavour of wood and give the chardonnay a flavour of Californian wine. But one question haunts me. Why was Montrachet produced in small (114-litre) vats (*feuillettes*) up to the end of the nineteenth century? René Fleurot assures me that great white wine benefits from the effect of the wood and its tannins in such casks more than in the larger ones of 225 litres. This practice has disappeared (even from people's memories) but I wonder whether it was not a tradition which was simply convenient. As for the lees, they are responsible for the bitterest of religious wars in Montrachet. Racking separates the clear wine from the deposit it throws – lees – which gather at the bottom of the cask. Certain firms, and I am thinking in particular of Domaine Ramonet, age their wine on the lees, carefully preserving this deposit with its well-nigh magical virtues. Others do not take the risk. For a risk it is. Domaine Thénard considers that it is not worth the candle, or that at least there are limits. So it adopts a cautious approach. On the other hand, Domaine des Comtes Lafon racks off the "thick mud" after the first fermentation, then leaves the wine for two years on its fine lees. They say it is the best agent against oxidation and it reduces the amount of sulphite treatment necessary. Everybody makes wine in his own way.

Moreover, the problem is not straightforward and has not been clarified. Michel Feuillat, a Professor of oenology at the University of Burgundy, has been studying it for some years. "After the alcoholic fermentation in oak casks, great white chardonnay wines are traditionally left for seven to eight months on their lees," he explains. "This is when the malolactic fermentation takes place. Many cellars still practise 'stirring' which puts the lees back in suspension. Ageing with yeasts in order to improve the quality of a wine and in particular its aromas is a recognized phenomenon in the Champagne-making process. We wanted to know if during the ageing of great white Burgundies on their lees autolysis of the yeasts also occurred, and, if the practice of regularly stirring them up had an effect on this phenomenon, how such wines finally developed." From 1982 to 1985 experiments were carried out in Meursault, with one cask racked without lees, one cask with lees but with no regular stirring, one cask stirred up once a week (the lees being kept in suspension), and casks with no lees but with yeast autolysis. What conclusions were drawn? "The white wines aged with their lees are richer in nitrogen and amino acids from the yeasts", Michel Feuillat records. "This is how the malolactic fermentation is helped along. From what we know today, tasting does not allow us to give substantial preference to wines aged on their lees, whether stirred or not. Wines which have been racked seem more flattering as young wines. As for wines aged on their lees, they develop less quickly but have a longer life. They can be distinguished from the others after eighteen months."

"I can still hear my mother," Edmond Delagrange recalls. "During the vinification period, she used to shout to us: 'Have you stirred it?' And if we had not done so, she would haul us over the coals, yelling 'It must be stirred!' We used a broom handle. But there are mysteries. We had old vines in Cailleret in Chassagne. I had put a cache to one side to make what the old folk used to call the 'hypocras', the very best. Well, this wine never fermented. There was insufficient deposit, not enough lees, not enough yeast." Vincent Leflaive and many others too in Chassagne or Puligny repeat: "Let nature do its work." In particular, the malolactic fermentation should not be hurried. He adds, "Absolute cleanliness is indispensable to ensure the awakening of a wine. An enormous amount of water is required to ensure

However exhausted they may be, the harvesters are always ready for a "fête" in the evening. They are also the first to welcome the new vintage. ▶

that the wine-making equipment is impeccably clean. A vat-house should be cleaned three times a day, like a nursery."

Fining is done with bentonite or casein, a milk protein, or even with milk, but skimmed milk is unreliable. Fining is difficult in certain years (1973, 1977), but why this is so remains a mystery. At one time, people used to bottle their own white wine at the Easter half-moon, generally without fining it. And they often succeeded. Why? Another mystery. Filtration? Yes, just a light one after sixteen to twenty months' ageing in wood, or no filtration at all. Wines were generally bottled after eighteen months and sometimes after two years. It is only after bottling that their story really begins. It can last ten or fifteen years, or even more... But, you may ask, what about those infamous

pitfalls? A Chambertin from Trapet is not the same as a Chambertin from Camus or a Chambertin from Rebourseau. These differences in vinification are perhaps more perceptible in reds than in whites, particularly because of the length of the fermentation period. But there are certainly distinctive styles in Montrachet. The old families are still faithful to those long-lived wines which at first are rather closed up, but whose development is fantastic, fully repaying the patience of those who are willing to wait. Other vintners make wines which are for earlier drinking. We shall not even mention those who dare to put their bottles on sale after only twelve months and who have been heard to say, with some impudence, that early bottling "captures the wine's youth".

How do they go about producing these doctored wines? With rapid fermentation, freezing, rigorous racking, heartless blending; all this can soon put a wine on its feet. But what will its body be? And its bouquet? Yet everything is gone into. For example, the correct use of cold, which has its fervent partisans and fierce critics. Vincent Leflaive goes so far as to say that good wine will defend itself against any aggression. "If you frighten it, it will retreat into its shell like a snail!"

Obviously the cork plays an important part. Certain producers use "top-class" suppliers who supply cork from very old trees in Sicily. Others prefer Spanish cork. The majority use good corks. The practice of marking the name of the firm and the vintage has been preserved. Such is the case with Domaines de Laguiche, Bouchard Père et Fils, La Romanée-Conti, Louis Jadot, Leflaive, Fontaine-Gagnard and Comtes Lafon. And what about the bottle and its russet colour? Sadly its aesthetics are out of fashion.

Is the collective discipline what it ought to be? More often than not, but the region lacks a man such as François Virot, the overseer of Domaine Leflaive who died in 1967. He was a man of patriarchal authority who laid down the law in the community and even acted as watchdog. "He was fair," people say. They remember him with bitter-sweet respect. No one has inherited his power, based as it was on competence and impartiality. The existence of two villages and two viticultural federations did not help matters either.

A wine of the gods

Of so much care, of so much love is Montrachet born: "the most curious and delicious wine in France" (the priest Arnoux, early eighteenth century), "the most excellent white wine in Europe" (the priest Courtépée, late eighteenth century), "divine" (the Marquis de Cussy), "admirable" (Bertall), "precious" (Rodier), "unique" (Pierre-Léon-Gauthier), "divine" once again (Roupnel), "a star" (*Revue du Vin de France*). English-speaking wine writers and journalists also contribute to this chorus of eulogies: Hugh Johnson, Terry Robards, Jon Winroth, Serena Sutcliffe, H. W. Yoxall, Anthony Hanson, Alexis Lichine... "It is not a wine, it is an event!" exclaimed Frank Schoonmaker, who in 1938 was Domaine Ramonet's first American customer.

We constantly hear that "You should drink Montrachet on your knees, with cap in hand", a splendid homage attributed to Alexandre Dumas. When and where did he write it? He visited Montrachet during his voyage through France and Switzerland of which he published his impressions in 1833. But of Montrachet he breathes not a word, mentioning simply La Rochepot and Vauchignon, to which he consecrates several pages to record his admiration.

When the sun embraces moonbeams: the green-gold of Montrachet. ▶

His *Grand Dictionnaire de cuisine* confines itself to recognizing that "the wine of Montrachet, as such, is the best of all French wines". So where among the novelist's prolific output does this quotation lurk hidden? I consulted Raymond Dumay, who has taken a keen interest in the part played by wine in Dumas' romantic work. Although he is able to pinpoint the famous quotation of which Chambertin is so proud, he confesses he is unable to do the

same for the quotation concerning Montrachet. But perhaps Dumas merely said this one day, without committing it to writing? The Association of the Friends of Dumas cannot confirm the quotation either.

The virtues attributed to the wine of Montrachet by serious writers were already clearly summed up by André Jullien in the early nineteenth century: "all the qualities which make a complete wine". Body, a high alcohol content, power, a flavour of hazelnut, with vitality and an extremely intense, fine bouquet. But let us not go so quickly. Let the eye drink in its rapture. The colour of Montrachet has evolved with time. "They try to keep it colourless," said Doctor Morelot in 1831. "Which is why they make sure the cask is always full; this precaution prevents oxygen from being absorbed, for such absorption makes the wine yellow and causes it to lose some of its bouquet and lightness." It is probable that the strange greenish yellow colour of Montrachet deepened along with progress in the vinification and preservation of wines. In the eighteenth century it doubtless had the transparent pallor of a young priest at court. Greenish-gold? Chablis and Pouilly-Fuissé also claim this mysterious blend of colour and its reflections. Yellow? "No", they say in Chassagne, "Puligny is yellow." Yellow? "No", they say in Puligny, "Meursault is yellow." Gaston Roupnel speaks of the "magic greenish reflections of this liquid gold". It is not always easy to pin them down, but this green-gold is a colour which is certainly not yellow; it is clear and bright and often looks like a combination of moonbeams and sunlight.

To the nose, Montrachet has hints of hazelnut or honey, almond or ripe grapes, hawthorn blossom or vanilla, fern or green apples. Honey, hazelnut and hawthorn are its most common aromas.

As the wine makes its slow and stately progress across the palate, it performs a miracle. Its body and bouquet are now inseparable. Structure and harmony merge into one, a perfect unity. That is Montrachet's secret. Unctuous yet dry, firm yet tender, complex and intense, it unites all the graces in one inflexible character. And this hand of pure gold in its silken glove, is it masculine or feminine? I would rather say that it is neither – its sex is that of the angels.

Hubrecht Duijker admits himself beaten: "It is almost impossible to find the words to do justice to this wine." It is true that wine literature sometimes has a disconcerting lyricism. Doctor Paul Ramain compares Montrachet to the A-flat slow movement of Beethoven's Twelfth String Quartet. The Belgian poet Maurice des Ombiaux, writing in 1925, saw it as a magnificat resounding in the vaults of a Gothic cathedral. When Frederick Wildman Jr drinks it, he has the same impression as when he first heard the Eroica Symphony. The priest Colin used to speak of a Bach fugue in liquid form. Montrachet rhymes with the French for violin bow.

If we stick to a strictly scientific vocabulary, the taster will confine himself to noting that in this complex he finds a hint of eugenol mingled with the aromas of lactones of 3-methyl-4-hydroxyoctanoic, masking the delicate

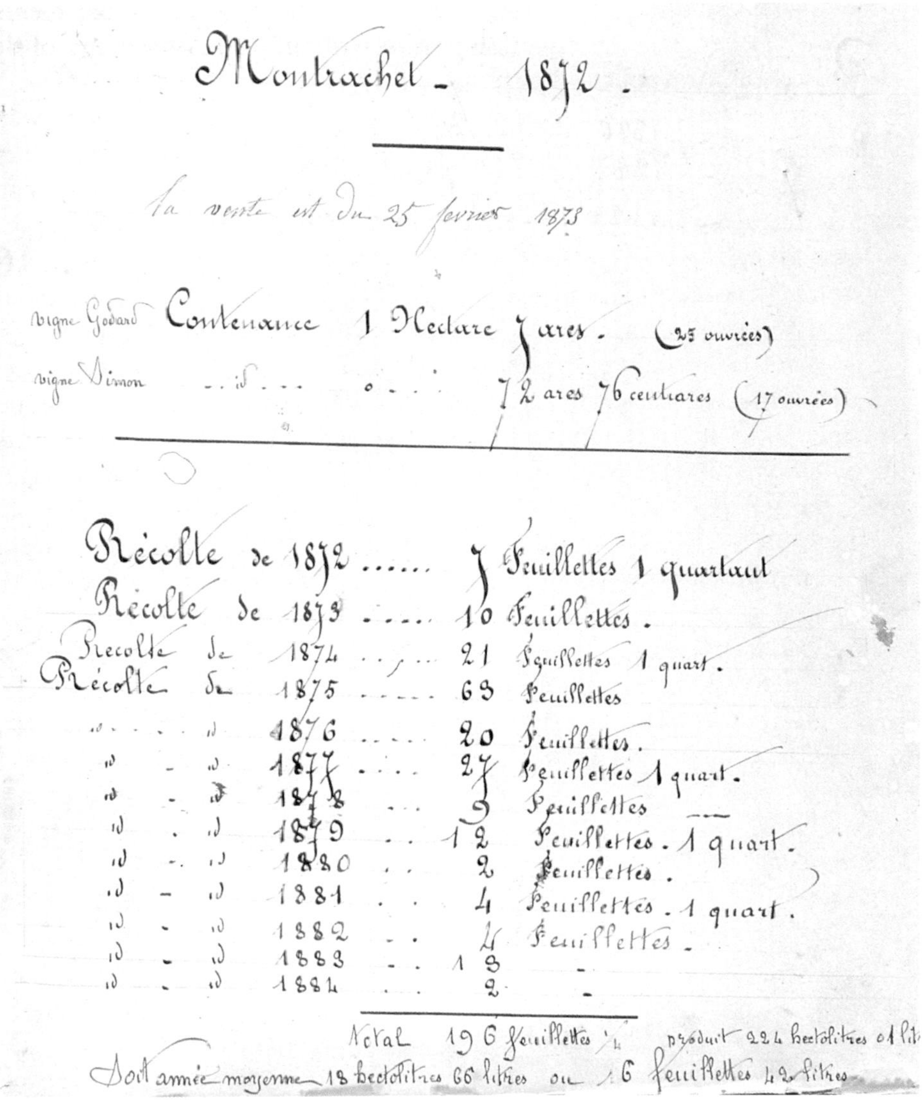

Montrachet — 1872.

La vente est du 25 février 1873

Vigne Godard — Contenance 1 Hectare 7 ares . (25 ouvrées)

Vigne Vimon — ...il... 0 ... 72 ares 76 centiares (17 ouvrées)

Récolte de 1872 ...... 7 Feuillettes 1 quartaut
Récolte de 1873 .... 10 Feuillettes .
Récolte de 1874 ../.. 21 Feuillettes 1 quart .
Récolte de 1875 ..... 63 Feuillettes
...........1876 .... 20 Feuillettes .
...........1877 .... 27 Feuillettes 1 quart.
...........1878 ... 3 Feuillettes
...........1879 .. 12 Feuillettes . 1 quart .
...........1880 .. 2 Feuillettes .
...........1881 .. 4 Feuillettes . 1 quart .
...........1882 .. 4 Feuillettes .
...........1883 .. 18
...........1884 ... 2 . —

Total 196 Feuillettes ¼ produit 224 hectolitres 04 lit.
Soit année moyenne 18 hectolitres 66 litres ou 16 feuillettes 42 litres

odours of 4-vinylguaiacol and 4-vinyl phenol arising from the bacterial decarboxylation of 4-hydroxy cinnamic phenylacrylic from the wood of the casks – difficult to slip into the conversation! In place of scents of wood, over-cooking, leather, carnation, coconut, or vanilla it is none the less true that the influence of oak on a great white Burgundy are summarized by this sort of rigorous terminology.

Everybody recognizes in Montrachet an exceptional fullness and a formidable intensity: "The mark of truly great wine," Hugh Johnson rightly con-

---

▲ *Baron Thénard's book of accounts, written in his own hand: the day-to-day life of Montrachet between 1873 and 1884.*

▶

1873

Janvier 22. Payé 116 journées de travail fait dans les réparations
de clos de Montrachet pr les murs a 2" 50 (l'une) . . . . 290 |

Payé 5 journées de maçons à 3" l'une — (pour les murs) . . . 15 "

27. Un voyage a Montrachet . . . . 3 " 50

Février 14. Un voyage a Montrachet . . . . 6 "

Février 25. Payé au vigneron pour journée . . . . . . 4 " 50

Payé 14 journées de manœuvre a Montrachet
a 3" et a 2" 50 l'une et timbre . . . . 41 " 60

Payé au maçon pour le raccommodage du mur
vieux et mur neuf et pierre qu'il a fourni . . 390 " 10

Février 25 Un voyage a Montrachet avec le maître maçon
pour toiser les travaux . . . . 6 " 50

.2. Versé au vigneron a compte . . . . 60 "

Mars 2. Payé au manœuvre de Montrachet pour
porter les terres . . . . 18 " 50

Achat de fumier . . . . 21 " 10

.2. Dépenses a Chassagne . . . . 3 "

Avril 15. Versé a compte a Bonnardot Pierre sur la culture de Montrachet 50 "

.2. aux vignerons du Montrachet venant de Mr Simon . . 100 "

Dépense a Chassagne . . . . . . 4 "

Port de panneaux pour Montrachet venant
de Calmay (voiture de Chagny a Chassagne) . . 3 " 25

A reporter . . . . . 1017 " 05

siders. "It earns its fame by an almost unbelievable concentration of the qualities of white Burgundy." Its concentrated flavour left the late Alexis Lichine aghast, a man who had drunk quite a few other wines. Chevalier and Bâtard have these qualities naturally in varying proportions, and depending on the personality and character of each. The Chevalier-Montrachet often seems more delicate, less powerful but with superb finesse. The Bâtard-Montrachet, having more body, is firmer, sometimes with a hint of the land and often a powerful perfume, "as big, even bigger than that of Montrachet", according to Lichine. They say here that the difference depends on whether the weather is wet or dry. If it is wet, there is greater finesse in the Chevalier. If it is hot and dry, the Bâtard is better. "When the plant suffers, the fruit feels the blow," says Edmond Delagrange. The nuances between Criots and Bienvenues, Bâtard's two comrades, are more subtle. They vary greatly depending on the bottle and whether they are from Chassagne (Criots) or Puligny (Bienvenues).

Expensive bottles

The total production of Montrachet in the 1980s was on average 250 hectolitres, against 190 hectolitres for the preceding decade, 147 for the 1960s and 112 for the 1950s. But replanting, improvements in cultivation methods resulting in healthier vines, and the nature of the vintage should all be taken into account. So production ranged from 107 (1984) to 442 (1982) hectolitres for the 1980s, 103 (1971) to 238 hectolitres (1970) for the 1970s, 97 (1961) to 186 hectolitres (1966) for the 1960s and 74 (1957) to 169 hectolitres (1950) for the 1950s. So the difference between a slender harvest and one when the grapes seem to come from Canaan has gradually increased in the space of forty years from 1 to 2, from 1 to 2.4 and then from 1 to 4.4 from decade to decade.

However unusual this might seem, these great differences are not at variance with the past. For example, the records of Domaine Thénard show that for the years 1872-1884 there were on average 16 *feuillettes* (half-casks) per year (nearly two hectares), the difference ranging from 2 *feuillettes* in 1880 to 63 in 1875. Domaine de Laguiche (two hectares) produced only one cask in 1923 and 1926, as against 12 casks in 1929.

These average yields rarely exceed 10 hectolitres per hectare up to the middle of this century, sometimes as much as 15, and as little as 3 or 4 hectolitres in certain years. Of course we cannot expect to find such a restricted production of Montrachet today. The average yield is around 25 to 30 hectolitres, proving a strict discipline. And it is no secret that 55 hectolitres per hectare was achieved in 1982 (a year of great abundance), a yield which can be sustained by the chardonnay but not by the pinot noir. So since the war annual production has increased from a maximum of 15,000 bottles to between 25,000 and 30,000 bottles.

And their price? Between 500 and 700 francs per bottle, rising to 1,000 to 1,100 francs – an absolute record in Burgundy with the exception of Domaine de la Romanée-Conti. If a bottle of Montrachet has always commanded a high price, it varied considerably depending on the vintage. Thus a barrel of Montrachet fetched 100 francs in 1889, 800 francs in 1890, 1,000 francs in 1891. In 1920, Camille Rodier reckoned that a bottle was worth between 25 and 40 francs depending on its quality. That works out at about 50 francs today. What a difference!

But this boom is recent. It probably illustrates the most important change in the Burgundy vineyards over recent years: the coronation of the whites. Whereas the American market used to absorb 5% of exports of Burgundy during the 1960s, it rose to 30% during the 1980s. This increase is essentially

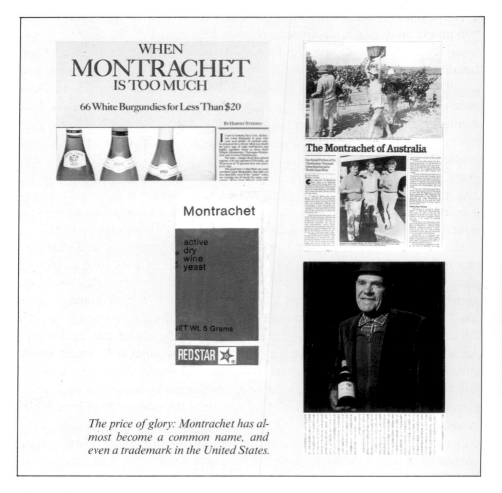

The price of glory: Montrachet has almost become a common name, and even a trademark in the United States.

due to the whites: 20% of Burgundy exported thirty years ago, more than 50% today. This evolution has come about as a result of the heavy international demand in this market, notably from the United States. Perhaps whites are easier to appreciate. Whatever the case, out of 5 bottles of Montrachet, 3 or 4 go for export of which 2 or 3 go to the United States. It is more advantageous to France's balance of payments than to her consumers.

Today Montrachet and Pouilly-Fuissé, Chablis and Corton-Charlemagne are drunk with veneration by enlightened wine lovers, or heedlessly as an aperitif by wealthy snobs. For this reason Burgundy, which is known and appreciated in France and Europe as a red with a warm colour, vigorous in temperament and well-structured, sometimes with subtle grace (a wine for the "hale and hearty"), suddenly in the New World becomes a dazzling, voluptuous charming white in its evening gown. This is a mutation imposed by business and even more by the preferences of customers.

Do tastes, and with them the wine, risk changing? In 1986 the British journalist Christopher Fielden wrote an article in *Decanter* entitled "California in Burgundy". He had just tasted the 1983 chardonnays and had detected a Californian flavour. We should doubtless modify this claim. And yet the two major faults of the Californian chardonnay (excessive alcohol and woodiness) lead to the creation in the United States of a flavour sometimes unfortunately also to be found in the Burgundy chardonnays. This phenomenon is partly due to the desire to please the American consumer, whose ideas dominate the market, and partly too to a sort of unthinking contagion. Fermentation at low temperatures (12°-14° C, 54°-57° F) as practised in California and Australia sometimes gives a chardonnay which is too aromatic and artificial. The Burgundy tradition is 16°-20° C (61°-68° F). In his remarkable essay entitled *La Mort du vin*, Raymond Dumay put forward an original and gripping proposition. Wine, he says, has always been the expression of a political and economical hegemony, creating the flavour in its wake – so American wine will end up dominating all the rest. We should be wary.

Historically and all over the world the Burgundy pinot noir and chardonnay have constituted the touchstone for the flavour of these two stocks. A wine was judged good if it had these Burgundy qualities. Although the pinot noir has no equivalent, this is no longer the case with the chardonnay, which has "exploded" all over the planet – California, Oregon, Australia, South Africa, New Zealand. And as the majority of wine critics are British and American, they give welcome support to the new vineyards which speak chardonnay with an English accent. These young vineyards know that the hurdle to be jumped is precisely the one represented by these two most complex stocks. If they are successful, they can sit at the table of the Great Vineyards, where Burgundy, Bordeaux and Champagne have long since had their crests engraved on their cutlery and etched on their glasses. These young vineyards concentrate particularly on the grape varieties because, having no known famous appellation, having no history, no past, this is all they can turn to advantage. Even if this Californian flavour is not a threat to the Burgundy vineyards, there is still a real risk. Are we to make wine which the international consumer calls for, bowing before the nefarious practices which have come about through contact with Californian bottles, whose wine is often excessively alcoholic and reeks of new wood, or rather to continue making wine in the way we have always done?

To give an idea of the boom which has taken place in the market, here is the evolution of average prices for one cask of Montrachet sold to the trade (per cask of 228 litres or 300 bottles):

1980: 30,000 francs (other *Grands Crus* of the area: around 15,000 francs).
1981: 20,000 francs (other *Grands Crus* of the area: around 12,000 francs).
1982: 25,000 francs (other *Grands Crus* of the area: around 20,000 francs).
1983: 46,000 francs (other *Grands Crus* of the area: around 23,000 francs).
1984: 60,000 francs (other *Grands Crus* of the area: around 23,000 francs).
1985: 80,000 francs (Chevalier: 50,000 francs; Bâtard: 47,500 francs; Criots: 41,000 francs; Bienvenues: 40,000 francs).

1986: 70,000 francs (Chevalier: 38,000 francs; Bâtard: 36,000 francs; Criots and Bienvenues: 35,000 francs).

In 1990, after a pause of some years, a cask of Montrachet regained the price of 80,000 francs reached in 1985. At the highest point, a bottle of Montrachet went above 300 francs direct from the property, 600 francs on the lists of the négociants, and reached 1,000 francs in restaurants. A great vintage can fetch $1,000 a bottle in the United States, $300 or $400 being the price of a young wine.

And the price of the land? This is a delicate subject. Rumours are rife. Is the official price always the one paid? Of course sales are always for small parcels, but they are rare. Many of the proprietors of the *cru* own considerable fortunes, so they may be ready to invest here if only for the prestige, an investment which would represent the price of an elegant flat in Cannes, just as other people might buy gold mines on the stock exchange. Even celebrities show an interest, like the popular singer Pierre Perret who considered for a while buying vines in Montrachet.

In 1990 an *ouvrée* (4 ares 28 centiares or 0.1 acres) of Montrachet was worth approximately 1 million francs, that is 24 million francs per hectare. This puts the entire vineyard at a value close to 200 million francs. Prices have nearly doubled between 1987 and 1990, reaching 600,000 francs per *ouvrée* in Bâtard-Montrachet. These are merely hypothetical estimations, for Montrachet is not a monopoly susceptible of tempting an American conglomerate, a Japanese investor or a French insurance company. In the mid-1970s an American group offered 7,200,000 francs for the two hectares of the Marquis de Laguiche. The proposition was brushed coldly aside.

As far as the other *Grands Crus* are concerned, an *ouvrée* is worth 400,000 to 600,000 francs, that is around 12 million francs per hectare. To clarify things, in 1990 an *ouvrée* in Chambertin was worth approximately 600,000 francs, and around 300,000 francs in the Clos de Vougeot. The prices of white burgundy are climbing and only the great red burgundies are following. In about 1965 a hectare of Chambertin and of Montrachet fetched the same price. For the record, the current price for a hectare of arable land or meadowland in the Côte-d'Or is between ten and fifteen thousand francs. Very good meadowland or fine woodland in the Auxois commands a price of around twenty-five to thirty thousand francs per hectare. Fifty years ago a good farm or well-kept woodland sold better than a vineyard. And what about prices before that? The equivalent of 100,000 francs for a hectare of Bâtard in 1892 and the same amount for a hectare of Montrachet in 1918. A sale of Montrachet took place in 1967 on the basis of 750,000 francs per hectare: three-quarters of the price of an *ouvrée* today!

Outlying properties (that is lying outside the area, or even the canton) are exceptional, and in the jungle of the world of real estate it would be difficult to imagine who could deprive Chassagne and Puligny of what is rightly theirs. There is an old law which still holds true: vines always end up belonging to the people who work them, because they are divided into such small plots that the only person likely to be interested is their nearest neighbour, especially if he is a friend of the seller. This explains the appearance in Montrachet of the firms of true growers Ramonet-Prudhon and Delagrange-Bachelet.

Is the land becoming more concentrated or increasingly divided up? As far as Montrachet is concerned, it is no more divided up than in the eighteenth century and perhaps less than in the preceding century. At the time when the 1840 Land Register was drawn up, the average size of a parcel was 107 ares (2.6 acres). Today it is about 50 ares (1.2 acres), as a result of division among families over the last fifteen years. Inheritances and family partition are gradually reducing this concentration of land to a certain extent. By contrast the long life of the *domaines* appears remarkable. With one break during the Revolution, that of the de Laguiche family goes back to time immemorial (this is undoubtedly the only such example in the Burgundy *Grands Crus*). Those of the Regnault de Beaucaron family, the Guillaumes and the Bouchards pre-date 1850; that of the Thénard goes back to 1873. If there are eighteen proprietors here, the four oldest represent an area of 5 hectares 66 ares (14 acres) out of a total of 8. Together with La Romanée-Conti, 75% of the total vineyard is accounted for by only five *domaines*.

Chevalier-Montrachet has seen a large number of parcels of land grouped together, so whittling down the share of the small estates in this *cru*. Rolande Gadille has shown that from the middle of the nineteenth century up to the present day, the area under the control of people owning land of less than 25 ares (three-fifths of an acre) went down from 32.5 to less than 10% of the total whereas those of over a hectare went up from 33 to 55%. Today five *domaines* own 85% of the appellation.

On the other hand, Bâtard-Montrachet remains the privileged area of the small and average-sized property. In the middle of the last century, the average parcel covered less than 12 ares (0.3 acres). Today it is even smaller, and we can see that the phenomenon so much criticized at the Clos de Vougeot is not an isolated case. The record for splitting up land is certainly held in Burgundy, by the *Grands Crus* of Bâtard-Montrachet, where no concentration of land exceeds 1 hectare and where the majority of the holdings cover about 15 ares (0.4 acres).

Foreign capital? No, unless we count Domaine Louis Jadot, whose shareholders are American, and the British Bâtard-Montrachet of Simon Oliver (Coombe Castle Fine Foods). Foreigners in Burgundy? Families are split up and proprietors live all over France. But this is the exception; most of the growers do live in the area. And the part played by the merchant grower in the property? This is not a negligible one, especially because it often increases as a result of privileged marketing agreements, and sometimes privileges of vinification, to the advantage of firms such as Louis Latour, Joseph Drouhin and Remoissenet. Indeed in Puligny several growers sell the whole of their production to the trade in must or wine. However, the estate re-

mains largely a growing entity, especially at Chassagne and Puligny and the surroundings (Saint-Aubin and Gamay, Saint-Romain, Santenay, Meursault, within a radius of 4 or 5 kilometres). But this is less so in the Côte de Nuits, except for the Domaine de La Romanée-Conti. Each of the two Côtes keeps its own space.

And profitability? Obviously everything depends on the origin of the land, and how it was taken on or bought. Cultivation and vinification costs scarcely differ, whether we are speaking of Montrachet at 600 francs per bottle or wine from an aligoté at 20 francs per bottle. Putting aside taxation, it is obvious that there is considerable variation between wines which are so different. Today in the *crus* they calculate their profits at about 2 to 3%, if account is taken of the cost of land. This profitability has dropped sharply over twenty years (in 1967 it was between 6% and 8%) as a result of the price increases in land. The major problem is that of inheritances, for with each generation, the state takes its share and is the principal beneficiary from price increases.

Formerly, Montrachet was a *cru bourgeois*. I have in front of me the account books of Baron Thénard, written in his own hand between 1873 and 1884. He disregards capital investments, but he notes everything else:
– a voyage to Chassagne (rail fare and other costs): 20 francs;

▲ *An eighteenth-century wine-seller's sign in carved wood. Musée du Vin, Beaune.*

– paid to the vigneron for 3 days' work including harvesting: 80.50 francs;
– paid to the mason for repointing the old wall and for new walls in stone provided by him: 390.10 francs;
– purchase of manure and *marc* for the enclosure: 26.50 francs;
– Montrachet tax-office: 118.15 francs, etc.

In 1875, the baron's expenses rose to 1,642.85 francs against an income of 1,891.50 francs. But in 1878, his expenses were 1,177.70 francs as against receipts of only 325 francs (only one *feuillette* sold at this price). The accounts more or less balance over a ten-year period but they do not repay capital expenditure. Yet it is still in the family a century later. This is how "investment yield" should always be considered in the vineyards of Burgundy.

How and with what to drink it

Paying for it is one thing, drinking it another. The prince of great meals and illustrious banquets, Montrachet has been drunk by all their imperial highnesses, royal or republican, on every continent. "I always used to send a case to the Elysée on Christmas Eve during the time of General de Gaulle", says Jacques Bordeaux Montrieux (Domaine Thénard); "The Vatican even ordered two casks of Montrachet at the beginning of the 1960s."

Napoleon is credited with a distinct liking for Montrachet. If there is positive historical proof of his love of Chambertin, the legend of Napoleon and Montrachet is founded on a letter reproduced by A. Patriarche in his

Famille royale des vins de France (*c.* 1910). A proprietor and merchant in Volnay, the author mentions a letter addressed on April 3, 1815, to his father by his cousin Bizouard, the postmaster at Rouvray: "I am writing in haste to tell you what happened here in Rouvray when the Emperor passed by on his way back from the island of Elba. He paid me the honour of stopping at my house at about half past one. He also paid me the honour of requesting a couple of bottles of wine, which he drank here at home. I gave him the wine you had been kind enough to offer me. He found it very good." It was a Montrachet, Marquis de Laguiche. The letter goes on to tell of the two decrees signed by the Emperor at the home of Rouvray's postmaster: the nomination of two mayors to replace the preceding ones, whose souls had doubtless been too royalist. We can only regret that these decrees did not confer the *Légion d'honneur* on Montrachet and Chambertin...

If Napoleon was fortunate enough to have been able to have "one for the road" in the form of a bottle of Montrachet (which is not everybody's good luck), such an event is not enough to justify the claim that it was the Emperor's favourite wine. In fact, Montrachet has no need of the prestige of its famous worshippers. It is rather they who are honoured by it...

"This wine should never be drunk cold," warns Doctor Paul Ramain. "To serve it on ice is a crime." It should be served cool, between 8° and 12° C (46° to 54° F). This reminds me of what is now an ancient argument between myself and Robert-J. Courtine concerning great Burgundy whites, which he always consigned to the ice bucket. Everything is a question of degree, for cool is not cold.

That great friend of the wine of Burgundy and nephew of Henry Bordeaux, Doctor Paul Ramain, gave the Brotherhood of the Chevaliers du Tastevin the motto of his *ex libris* : *Jamais en vain, Toujours en vin* (Never in vain, Ever in wine). His second piece of advice admits no argument: "It is improper to drink it other than in worthy company. This great lord should be tasted by fine connoisseurs." His third tenet concerns food: "And, like all very great wines, it can be drunk with any dish, except vegetables and stews, for it is never out of place."

Speaking of Montrachet, Georges Rozet considers that "the best homage it can be paid is for two to four friends to open a bottle, with glass and fork in hand, and drink it with a freshwater fish or a dish of mushrooms in cream, looking deep into one another's eyes. At this level of ecstasy, words become meaningless. A former student of Normale Sup, one of the prestigious French *Grandes Ecoles*, founder of the Brotherhood of the Chevaliers du Tastevin and a fine gourmet, Georges Rozet is an expert in the field. "In my view it is a wine which should not be prepared and served at any partic-

Soldiers demobilized after the First World War can finally enjoy a Montrachet which has been waiting for them. ▶

La Cigale
et la
Fourmi
③

Elle alla crier famine
Chez la Fourmi sa voisine
La priant de lui prêter
Quelque grain pour subsister
Jusqu'à la saison nouvelle.
Je vous paierai, lui dit-elle,
Avant l'oût, foi d'animal,
Intérêt et principal.

Septembre 1919

Menu

Banquet
de
Démobilisation

—

Hors d'œuvre variés
Petits pâtés
Poulet aux champignons
Perdrix aux choux
Salade de saison
Desserts
Tartes aux fruits
Bombe glacée
Fruits
Vins
Montrachet 1909
Vosne-Romanée 1915
Santenay 1906
Mousseux
Ecole de Viticulture
Café
Liqueurs

ular point in a meal. It is better drunk spontaneously, without any preliminary fuss intended to exalt it. Without any help, it alone will be the discreet prelude and rich development of an unforgettable symphony of flavours and aromas. So then, no advance-guard or lackeys before this king." Do not serve a Pouilly-sur-Loire before a Montrachet or you will see the latter take offence, shrink back into its shell like a snail and remain icily resentful.

In 1867 Antony Réal advised serving Montrachet at the start of dinner, with the soup. And during the last century Gaston du Coudray, another of gastronomy's apostles, suggested more exciting combinations: pyramids of freshwater crayfish, vol-au-vents, bouchées à la reine, stewed duck. Today, the journalist Jon Winroth advises poultry in cream, buttered sole, or a deceptively simple grilled lobster.

At the Troisgros restaurant, Bâtard is the accompaniment to eggs and caviar or escalopes of salmon with sorrel. At Robuchon's restaurant, a simple Puligny-Montrachet goes with seafoods, fresh spiced cod, bass with caviar. Pucelles is perfect with salmon. Dry white for the flat Brittany oysters, Puligny for hot oysters and all these *crus* for crayfish. And the dessert? You might try slightly warm pear flan or pears in a caramelized puff-pastry case with Chevalier, according to Nicolas de Rabaudy and Jean-Luc Pouteau, who since 1983 has born the title of the World's Best Sommelier. Lobster claws for the Bienvenues-Bâtard-Montrachet, declares Jacques Puisais – "a strong, harmonious combination". On recent menus I have seen Montrachet with fresh turbot, braised Schleswig trout with tarragon, and rolled braised turbot in cream. More often than not, then, with fish: "It is the most wonderful wine for trout," is the advice of Pierre Bréjoux, "especially if you have caught it yourself." Or again, with a foie gras served at the start of a meal.

In Burgundy? Robert Euvrard and Joseph Fonquernie suggested to me: "Creamed fish from the Saône: pike, perch, etc. A soup of freshwater fish from Seurre or Verdun, provided the croûtons are not too garlicky. Frogs' legs in cream. Breadcrumbed pike quenelles in Fagon style, freshwater crayfish with cream and a Nantua sauce. But old vintages of Chassagne and Puligny *Premiers Crus* are a splendid accompaniment to Morvan ham cooked with cream or a fricassée of Bresse chicken, or a chicken poached in a sauce..." There are some obvious heresies. For example that foie gras with Sauternes served with a Puligny-Montrachet at the Ritz in Paris for the Ernest Hemingway award in 1985.

There is an excellent restaurant in Puligny, called *Montrachet* of course. "Wine is my life", Jean-Claude Wallerand confesses. "To it I owe everything – my joys, my griefs, my pleasure at work and at leisure, and if over the years I have acquired a little knowledge and philosophy, it is thanks to wine. Wine teaches you benevolence and, as time slows you down, a deeper relaxation and a more serene judgement..." Nicely put, and indeed, these words describe the man himself. He comes from Valenciennes in northern France, where he was born in 1947. At the age of 14 he was already an

apprentice chef at the station buffet, arranging bottles of wine and collecting the labels. He devours all books on wines and vines. He has trained in Bordeaux, Beaune, Suze-la-Rousse, and was a pupil of Jacques Puisais. In 1979, he was finalist in the Ruinart trophy for France's Best Young Sommelier. The following year, he won the title of Best Head Waiter and Sommelier in the *département* of the Nord and for Champagne. In 1985, he was the Best Sommelier in Burgundy and the Franche-Comté; in 1986, he was finalist in the competition for France's Best Sommelier. Meanwhile, in 1984, he came to Puligny, where Doctor Collet and his wife Christine handed him the reins of this restaurant, which today has been resold to a hotel chain. "What do I prefer?" replies Jean-Claude Wallerand. "Marc Colin's Montrachet with the white meat of a Bresse chicken served with foie gras. Domaine Leflaive's Chevalier-Montrachet. Gagnard-Delagrange's Chassagne-Montrachet with crustacea, crayfish, lobster, freshwater crayfish, and Puligny-Montrachet from Domaine Etienne Sauzet or from Michel Colin..."

It would be difficult to find a family more typical of Burgundy than the Lameloises from Chagny. Pierre the grandfather, then Jean, and now today Jacques have succeeded one another in the kitchens of this restaurant, consid-

▲ *Jean-Claude Wallerand (left) and Jacques Lameloise (right): two of the staunchest apostles of Montrachet.*

ered since 1921 as one of the best on the R.N.6. When the road was diverted in 1954, and then some years later when the motorway was constructed, there were a few uneasy moments. But people already had the habit of making a detour to go to "Chez Lameloise". Jacques, who recently celebrated his fortieth birthday, received a good classical education at the school in Rue Férandy in Paris. While others were preparing their *baccalauréat*, he was already preparing exquisite dishes. The Savoy in London, Ledoyen, Lasserre – these are the schools through which he has passed. From 17 to 25, he learned the ABCs of his profession on the job. After marrying Nicole he returned to the nest, where his father entrusted him with the responsibility of the restaurant, though he still stayed on to help and advise. Broccoli flan with crayfish tails, puff-pastry cases stuffed with oysters and mushrooms, fillet steak cooked in Santenay and fricassée of Bresse chicken are some of the specialities of the house. With sixteen chefs at work and meticulous care taken with everything, Lameloise won its second Michelin star in 1974 and its third in 1979, not to mention the three *toques* in the Gault-Millau guide. In a word then, a panorama, nicely balancing the classic gastronomy of Burgundy with the better aspects of *nouvelle cuisine*. The "little restaurant" in Chagny has not had its head turned by dining at the table of the Greats. If Jacques Lameloise readily confesses his weakness for the Côte Chalonnaise, he has not lost sight of the golden line on the Côte des Blancs, for, as he says, "Burgundy is the wine of my birth." Succeeding Georges Pertuiset, Jean-Pierre Després has taken over as head *sommelier*.

Immortal?

Montrachet has a slightly greenish colour. Does that make it immortal? Indeed so perfect a wine ought to be. "Its life is almost indefinite," proclaimed Adrien Berger at the beginning of this century. At the time of the Exhibition of wines from the Côte-d'Or organized in Dijon on May 15, 1856, an impressive collection of old vintages was submitted to the jury. Among the whites, "the best of all was the Montrachet 1818, a wine beyond compare," reported one of the tasters. Its great age (38 years) had not caused it to lose any of its qualities.

Today as yesterday, everything depends on the vintage, the vinification and the care taken with the wine during ageing. Montrachet is not immortal like the yellow wine from the Jura. On the other hand, it can still retain its original brilliance after thirty to forty years in the bottle. A good vintage generally reaches its peak after fifteen or twenty years. Then the gold turns to old gold and the nose takes on a hint of madeira. In 1985, eight bottles of Montrachet (Domaine Fleurot) were tasted at a working session of the series of tasting glasses called *Impitoyables*: wines from 1918 to 1983, including 1928 and 1923. "With the exception of the oldest, which was highly oxidized, all the others were remarkable," the journalist Jean Clerc noted.

Good and great years in Montrachet

- 1720, 1728;
- 1731;
- 1743, 1745, 1746, 1748;
- 1750, 1753, 1759;
- 1760, 1762, 1764, 1767;
- 1770;
- 1795, 1798;
- 1802, 1806;
- 1811 (wine of the comet), 1815, 1818, 1819;

- 1822, 1825;
- 1834;
- 1842, 1846;
- 1854;
- 1865;
- 1870, 1875;
- 1881, 1883, 1886, 1889;
- 1891, 1894, 1898, 1899;
- 1904, 1906, 1907;
- 1911, 1915, 1917;

- 1921, 1923, 1926, 1928, 1929;
- 1933, 1934, 1937, 1938;
- 1947, 1949;
- 1950, 1953, 1959;
- 1961, 1966, 1969;
- 1976, 1978, 1979;
- 1983, 1985, 1989;
and all the great years
the Good Lord may yet send

"Brilliance, limpidity, finesse, aromas of aniseed, cinnamon, honey or almond; a powerful, subtle bouquet. All these great wines proved perfectly that a white wine can be one for long keeping." And it should be mentioned that when the *sommelier* was opening the bottle of 1918, he let the cork drop in and decanted the wine. Which killed it stone dead.

Too frequently, alas, this wine is drunk, when it has not had the time to open up. Happy they who are wise enough to offer it a long and serene rest, for their future happiness and that of their children. Buying a bottle of Montrachet is similar to planting an oak tree: one must first think of others.

If we study a vintage chart, we see that every decade has one to four memorable vintages. Years ending in the figure 9 have been great over a period of fifty years. But such judgements are partly subjective. Vintages such as 1970 or 1973 are remarkable for some wines, in particular Domaine de la Romanée-Conti. With Domaine Ramonet, the 1982s are preferred to the 1983s, the first seeming finer than the second. Such discussions could go on until we run out of breath... Whatever the case, as Albert Thibaudet used to say, "there are no good wines, only good bottles."

Siamese twins

Inextricably linked by the Montrachet they share, Chassagne and Puligny are Siamese twins. Nothing could be easier than to compare or contrast them. But although there is a justifiable rivalry between them, they both acknowledge their superiority over the whole world.

Do not ask the Delagrange-Bachelet family if Bienvenues is as good as Criots; do not question the Carillons in Puligny about the delights of Cailleret in Chassagne compared with the Cailleret opposite, even if the firm's son and heir feels himself halfway between the two by virtue of his marriage. The two villages seem so different: Chassagne more a village of growers, Puligny more stylish; one closer to the soil, the other closer to the sky; Chassagne modestly twinned with Saint-Martin in the Rhineland-Palatinate, and Puligny proudly twinned with Johannisberg, under the protection of Prince Metternich. The fashionable houses, the parks, the yew trees and cedars are more numerous in Puligny. But the two villages (454 inhabitants in Chassagne and 528 in Puligny, more than double last century's figures) resemble a casbah transported into Burgundy, consisting of houses tucked away in back yards and a maze of back streets with blackish stones, whose secrets are well shielded from the sun and well and truly hidden from the neighbours. Wine is not made on the village square.

In this eminently republican canton (Nolay belonged to the Carnot family for half a century under the Third Republic) which has as its *conseiller général* the former Minister for the Arts, Jean-Philippe Lecat, Chassagne votes to the right and Puligny ultra-right. The wine of Burgundy is like politics: red is to the left and white to the right. These villages appear smaller and more discreet than they really are. You will look in vain for a name-plate or some distinctive sign on the walls of Domaine Leflaive in Puligny. As for finding where Domaine Ramonet is hidden in Chassagne, there is simply no question of a name-plate or sign: people will ask you: "Which Ramonet?" then explain, "It is further up..."

◄ *Hot-air balloons are now to be seen drifting over the Burgundy vineyards.*

What is more, Montrachet as such is not signed at all. No road sign, no blaring publicity on the N6 road. Nothing except its vines and its old walls. During the harvesting period, tourists swarm round the *cru* like wasps round a honey-pot. Rich and poor alike, arriving in gleaming BMWs or old bangers, they stop to have their photographs taken in front of its illustrious walls. Pretty American students come by bicycle from Dijon to set eyes on this Acropolis. Their parents can afford the luxury of a trip in a hot-air balloon, with admiration inspired by Aragon, they all think that the most elegant alexandrine in the French language is

Montrachet, Montrachet, Montrachet, Montrachet...

I should also add in parenthesis that you can see how revealing the names of the *crus* are in Burgundy, and how well they go with their *climats*. Chambertin, noble, powerful, elegant, perfectly describes its wine. Romanée, as a red wine, has all it needs to be feminine. Corton is content with two syllables. The name Montrachet evokes all the elegance and fullness of a white. Chassagne and Puligny have fallen in love with this name and have taken it in marriage.

▲ *A pretty view of the village of Chassagne today, just as traditional as in an eighteenth-century engraving.*

On February 10, 1878, the Puligny town council passed the following resolution: "The Mayor points out to the town council that the commune of Puligny includes in its boundaries a good part of the famous *cru* known by the name of Montrachet; that the addition of the name of this *cru* to that of Puligny would give considerable advantage to the marketing of the wines produced in the areas of the land bordering the Clos du Montrachet, wines which are of considerable merit; that moreover, there are other communes in France with the name of Puligny, often creating confusion in mail or freight deliveries." In short, Puligny wanted to be called Puligny-Montrachet. On May 5 in the same year, Puligny town council renewed its request: "For the third time", we find written in the margin of the minutes. Chassagne-le-Haut, for such was its name, lost no time in making the same move. On August 4, 1878, its town council debated this historic motion: "The ouncil requests that the name of the commune of Chassagne-le-Haut be replaced by that of Chassagne-Montrachet (pronounced Morachet). The name 'Haut' used in conjunction with Chassagne is not logical, for the village is more on the plain than on the hill, whereas the name of Montrachet recalls that famous *climat* of vineyards producing the best white wine in the world. So the name of Chassagne-Montrachet would serve to propagate the name of this great wine and consequently would further the expansion of business."

This idea – brilliant idea, we might almost say – of combining the name of the commune with that of its most famous *climat* was first conceived in Gevrey. A decree by King Louis-Philippe gave this commune (Gevrey-en-

Montagne) the right to be called Gevrey-Chambertin. From October 17, 1847, this wildfire raged from village to village in the Côte: Aloxe became Aloxe-Corton (1862), Vosne became Vosne-Romanée (1866), Chambolle became Chambolle-Musigny (1878). Chassagne and Puligny were to be called Montrachet (November 27, 1879). Then followed Flagey-Echézeaux (1886), Nuits-Saint-Georges (1892), and Morey-Saint-Denis (1927). Each make up to the opportunity in turn. Today such claims would provoke violent local storms. Indeed, to quote only the first example, if it would seem legitimate to link the names Gevrey and Chambertin, the appellation Gevrey-Chambertin (310 hectares or 766 acres) was to benefit enormously from the fame of the *climats* Chambertin (13 hectares or 32 acres) and Chambertin-Clos de Bèze (15 hectares or 37 acres). Many carriages have attached themselves to this distinguished locomotive. Town councils and their debates make no secret of their desire to associate their land with the fame of the neighbouring *Grands Crus*. Of course we should realize that at this time business practice was not so strict and names were more readily granted. So for all these communes, a simple change of name was an exceptional promotional device. It cannot be said that the men of Burgundy had no sense of publicity. But who could blame them? The late and greatly missed Pierre-Marie Doutrelant perhaps, who in 1986 wrote five pages about Montrachet in *L'Express*. Saying what? "Montrachet, mount rapia." *Rapiâ*, tight-fisted. It is impossible to get a free bottle of good wine here. The only way is to claim in Puligny that one has been refused in Chassagne and vice versa. What journalism! Or again Anthony Hanson, in his provocative book on Burgundy, considered Montrachet as a "parvenu". Although this was probably a translator's error (*tard-venu* – a latecomer), the damage remains.

The Montrachet Viaduct

By contrast they would have gladly done without the "publicity" attracted by the plans to build a viaduct over the vineyards of Montrachet. However preposterous this idea might seem, it was a serious proposition, the brainchild of the Ministry of Transport. Although it did not ultimately become a reality, it came very near to it. The preliminary survey concerning the section of the Paris-Lyons motorway between Avallon and Chalon-sur-Saône started in 1955 but turned into a protracted affair. Among the many proposed routes, three were passed to the relevant government department. The route accepted in 1957 by the Minister of Transport, Edouard Bonnefous, crossed the Auxois and joined Chagny by Ivry-en-Montagne and La Rochepot. On September 11, 1961, Robert Buron finally adopted this route,

The tractor has replaced the horse in the vineyards.　　　　　　　　　　▶

which was to become the subject of a public enquiry the following year. The Route Nationale 6 was to have a big sister.

Suddenly people woke up... From the hill to the plain, the Ministry of Transport was proposing a viaduct over Montrachet! The environment's future defender, Edouard Bonnefous, had doubtless not noticed this a few years before. René Lafon remembers: "I saw the plans. I was shown where the base of a pylon was to be dug into the Montrachet vineyard. As to sunshine under this viaduct, the engineers had not given it a thought..." In the face of the outcries this project provoked, the authorities behaved in the traditional way and resisted tooth and nail. Then, by pure chance, someone saw that a trunk-road linking Beaune and Chagny could be used to construct the motorway on a line Chagny-Beaune-Dijon-Langres, thus reducing costs. And so the "Beaune alternative" was born. It took two years to make headway. In 1964, weary of battle, Marc Jacquet, the former minister, officially rejected the first route in order to give Beaune a better crack of the tourist whip, so freeing Montrachet from its motorway nightmare...

Since then it has constantly been asserted that the government was ready to spend six million francs more (in 1965 francs) to spare Montrachet the troubles of the motorway. But in reality, as this plan was rightly considered absurd, the state simply opted for the least damaging solution at the same price.

The people of the cru

Essentially, Montrachet has belonged to the same families over many years – from the aristocracy and the upper middle-class on the one hand, and on the other from a social group which has come to be known in Beaune as the "Lords of the Cork". The marketing of their wine was generally based in Beaune and carried out by the Burgundy merchant-vintners. More recent than in the other *Grands Crus*, the democratization of the vineyards has created a new social group and a new wine: the grower and his wine.

At one time the grower was, strictly speaking, the proprietor's salaried worker, his tenant-farmer or sometimes his *métayer* and, whatever the case, a worker on the land. "Poor vigneron", people used to say, so many were the afflictions and deprivations that rained on his head. And when these were increased by marital problems, he became the very personification of Nono, the character who gave his name to Gaston Roupnel's popular novel (1910). But just as the chef has emerged from his kitchen to vie for fame with stars and cabinet ministers, the vigneron has completely changed his social status. In selling a part of his wine himself, or sometimes the whole of his production, and having his own name on the bottle, he has acquired an identity and a personality. Journalists visit all the cellars, awarding them points, putting them under the microscope, lauding them to the skies or condemning them to hell fire. For there now exists the wine "critic", just as for the theatre or food, filling column inches in every newspaper and review in France, Switzerland, Belgium, Great Britain and the United States. This has affected Montrachet to some extent and Chevalier a little, since the arrival in these *crus* of growers representing the local property and their family holdings. By contrast it is particularly marked in Bâtard, Criots and Bienvenues.

The grower no longer walks behind his horse. As proud as any Roman emperor returning to Rome in his chariot, he perches aloft on his tractor. But machines cannot do everything. The contribution of man – and particularly of woman – so necessary for the vine, still rests in an agile hand and an aching back. It is an extraordinary way of life: firstly that of a grower attached to a perennial plant whose whims are always unpredictable, and secondly that of a vintner transforming the grapes into wine – a work of art. The profession of businessman, advertising specialist, public relations person, actor and playwright rolled into one; in short, the man who transforms art into great art, wine into great wine.

All this came about with "the bottle", that is, with direct sales by the proprietor. When did this phenomenon start? Late in Puligny, for the lack of cellars due to the high level of the water-table forced early sales, and in the cask. During the 1930s Domaine Leflaive, operating on a large scale, led the way. But even today, out of more than eighty people registering harvest return figures and forty growers, only five or six bottle their own wines. Perhaps the road had something to do with this. They say that in Chassagne people bought cars sooner than elsewhere. In any event, we were soon to see cars passing along the Route Nationale 6 and being enticed to stop. "The bottle came about as a result of the car", says one grower.

Indeed, Chassagne started direct sales just before the war, in 1937-1938. An American, Frank M. Schoonmaker, came to France to write a book about wine. He met Raymond Baudoin, the founder of *Revue du Vin de France*, a man who knew Burgundy inside out. Baudoin took his guest round some of the famous cellars and made a suggestion to him. Why, instead of writing a book, should this American not select excellent Burgundy wines on site to resell in the United States? These were difficult years and the wine used to remain in the cellars for a long time, often over three or four winters. The growers were delighted with this godsend and Frank Schoonmaker became an importer and merchant, though he continued writing. It was mainly he who was responsible in the United States for establishing the practice of using the name of the grape variety to designate American wines (pinot noir, chardonnay, sémillon, niagara, etc.), so moving from the arbitrary use of generics (burgundy, claret, chablis, champagne, chianti, sauternes, etc.) to the use of "varietals", which is rather more precise (the stocks). Although

A "dragon's tail", as it is known in Burgundy: when the sun is hidden as it starts to set behind the Côte. ▶

Frank M. Schoonmaker played a real and important role in getting "proprietors' wines" known in the United States, it is only fair to mention that he acquired his first experience with Ridgway B. Knight, collaborator of the firm of Frederick Wildman in New York, and future ambassador for the United States and president of the American Club in Paris. It was he who was in at the birth of the American infatuation with Montrachet.

In the section devoted to Domaine Ramonet the reader will find the colourful story of Frank M. Schoonmaker's first contact with Montrachet. Thanks to Raymond Baudoin and the firm of Frederick Wildman which opened up the way for him, this American was handed the keys to the best in Burgundy: Pierre Ramonet in Chassagne, Jacques d'Angerville in Volnay, Leflaive in Puligny, Rebourseau in Gevrey-Chambertin. "In Chassagne", says Edmond Delagrange, "from the 1930s everybody was already doing some bottling for French customers."

But this revolution of man and wine has come about only since the beginning of the 1960s. It has sometimes unsettled people and turned their heads, troubled consciences and turned the wine. Can it be easy to remain indifferent before a river of gold, in the face of so many pleas ("Please, please sell me just three bottles...") and such obvious temptations? We must however acknowledge that the large majority of families have remained entirely honourable. The Côte-d'Or is not the Côte d'Azur, and if land is very ex-

pensive here, it is for planting... Direct sales at the property, and the appearance of innumerable guides to domaines have created a new phenomenon. Whether a personality featured in *Who's Who* or an anonymous tourist, everyone wants to meet the grower noted on his list. And everyone wants to visit a cellar at all costs. In her book *Croque-en-Bouche*, Fanny Deschamps (who is from Burgundy) relates what used to happen nearly every day at Ramonet-Prudhon. In the shed, a minister is waiting for the bottles he has been promised. "We have sold him a few because he had a letter of introduction from a doctor we know and admire. Otherwise...," Madame Ramonet explains. "My husband is not too keen on selling to any old stranger. And after all, this minister is not on the telly very often, so I didn't recognize him. Yesterday we had a visit from a pair of lovebirds. Real darlings, they were. Afterwards, I saw from their visiting card that they were princes. We get more and more visitors: doctors, lawyers, teachers, politicians. I don't know why. They can find our wine at the merchants. But no, they simply must come and see the vines for themselves and sniff the casks, as if we had time to pander to them. They are all nice people, mind you..."

◄ *Simpler than those of the Clos de Vougeot, the portals of Montrachet are of a more human dimensions.*

"We have our work to do", says one of the growers. "They should realize. We cannot be opening the doors ten times a day for people who are nice enough but who turn up without warning..." This is undoubtedly the result of selling "by the bottle." "You discover that business is a profession and that it has its constraints", the merchants say ironically. Following the growers of Puligny, who back in 1898 created a tasting cellar (which later disappeared), those of Chassagne, including the Ramonets, decided in 1986 to open a collective cellar for tasting and sales, where all the wines could be found: a good idea which has been successful. In the first year the turnover figure was 1.3 million francs for the 25,000 bottles sold. Even if it is rather frustrating for the visitor, it is the only possible solution for the future, and Chassagne is one of the first communes to have understood this. Puligny, taking the cue from its past, opened a new tasting cellar in 1990.

You have only to read the telephone directory to realize how viticultural dynasties seem to be flourishing. You will not find any Prosper Duvieux-ceps or Léontine Tâtevins, names which in certain communes all seem to lead back to the same merchant's switchboard. But there are Chavys, Colins, Moreys, and then it starts to get confusing: there is Gagnard-Dupont and Gagnard-Delagrange, Ramonet-Prudhon and Bachelet-Ramonet, Colin-Deléger and Deléger-Niellon... When, as is often the case, the spouse brings along vines in her dowry, the *domaine* takes a double name, that of husband and wife. That is how Delagrange-Bachelet became Gagnard-Delagrange in the following generation, and then Blain-Gagnard and Fontaine-Gagnard a generation later. But although Pierre Ramonet is called Ramonet-Prudhon, his son André is simply Ramonet.

Their character

On May 19, 1987, Jean-Baptiste Colin was buried in Chassagne. Colin, with his round face and round, 1930s-style spectacles, was a priest of the Roman Catholic church, former mayor of the village and estate manager of Domaine de Laguiche – all at the same time, and one of the very best of men too.

He was born in Chassagne in 1907, the son of Jean-Baptiste Colin, already estate manager for the Marquis de Laguiche. He studied at the seminary of Flavigny in the Côte-d'Or then at Louvain. Ordained in 1935, he became a teacher in a school at Troyes. Released from his functions in the ministry by agreement with his bishop, he came back to Chassagne in 1948. There, without removing his cassock, he took in hand the day-to-day administration of the *domaine* of which his father had been in charge all his life. From 1964 to 1971 the inhabitants of the village elected him mayor, just as the people of Dijon did Canon Kir. He had a rare sense of smell. The locals called him the "truffle-sniffing priest", for he had no equal when it came to finding black truffles. He gathered 50 kilos (110 pounds) in 1931 and kept a specimen of just over 320 grammes (11 ounces) preserved in alcohol on his mantlepiece

as a souvenir. "May God, the Divine Vintner, welcome His servant and give him a place in His vineyard", were the words pronounced on the day of his funeral. Preaching during the festival of Saint Vincent in 1970, Colin addressed the vines as "a wife, sometimes unfaithful, but always loved, as one always ends by loving whatever has made one suffer". Montrachet was something special: "You will understand, my children, why the wines which Christ has bidden us drink with Him in the Kingdom of His Father, should decline certain unions, certain misalliances, without race, character and nobility. It is the wine of France and this wine alone which our ancestors have bequeathed to us. Let us be proud of it!" In this sceptical and tolerant region, wine enters the church only for marriages and funerals, but it is not blasphemous, and has no intention of replacing the Almighty. The *Manuel des vignerons associés de Chassagne* of 1844 begins with the Ordinary of the Mass and finishes with different recommendations concerning the harvest, the way to look after the grapes, and a table of wine prices since 1740.

Another child of the area, adoptive this time, is Jean Lenoir, the *nez du vin*, the Cyrano of today. Another astonishing life: born on September 23, 1937 at the height of the harvest, he was the grandson and son of farmers from Labergement-Foigney. He worked for the Post Office in Dijon, fought in Algeria and became a teacher in special education. After found ing the Youth Centre in Dole, he became deputy director of the Maison de la Culture in Chalon-sur-Saône. In his view, wine is part of culture – wine which he

▲ *Jean Lenoir, the "nez du vin" (left) and the priest Jean-Baptiste Colin, mayor and vigneron (right).*

discovered during his childhood with the Pillot family in Chassagne. He improved his knowledge in this field, took courses at Dijon University, and coached Georges Pertuiset to run for the title of France's Best Sommelier. During this time he conceived a new idea. "I wanted to create something which would be a source of emotion. I discovered that the most apparently simple perfumes, acacia, violet, honey, provoke an intense emotion when you detect them in wine. This idea was to turn into the *Nez du vin*, a collection of phials of aromas to which the taster can habitually refer. For Burgundy reds for example, blackcurrant, banana, hawthorn blossom, cinnamon, liquorice, vanilla, truffle or violet."

Jean Lenoir works for himself now. When I first became his friend, I marvelled to hear him remain so faithful to his Burgundy accent, which rolls its "r's" in a way no longer permitted by the genteel, and to see him happily sniffing at everything, fruits, flowers, grasses, spices and, of course, wines. He "translates" his perfumes abroad, as far away as Japan. With this unusual creation, he divides his time between Yerres in the Ile-de-France and Carnoux-en-Provence where his team works. He has not been unfaithful to his Burgundy olfactory roots. What does he think of the great whites? "The Chablis often astound me with their aromas of menthol tending towards the button mushrooms of the fields. The Meursaults have hints of hazelnut, then honey and beeswax. Corton-Charlemagne? More spicy, crystallized fruit. The wines of Puligny evoke fern, because of the proximity of the water-table. As for those of Chassagne, in my opinion they are the most harmonious, with nuances of milk and butter. Rather like what you smell when you pass by a bakery... Hot croissants!"

Their wines

The *Grands Crus* in Chassagne and Puligny cover barely 30 hectares. Only five in number, they yield considerably less wine than Corton-Charlemagne alone, another to wear a crown of gold in the Côte. On the other hand, their contribution to the great white *crus* of Burgundy is essential. Montrachet and its "satellites", as the term used to be, represent a modest proportion of the wines of these two communes.

Puligny excels in whites, which represent practically its entire production – some 9,000 hectolitres (1,200,000 bottles) as against 350 of red (46,000 bottles). The vines cover a total of 215 hectares, of which some 100 are classed as *Premiers Crus*. In the middle of the last century, most of the land was planted with gamay. Chardonnay and pinot were found on the hillside of Blagny.

Old labels. The oldest (Labaume l'Aîné) dates from the beginning of the nineteenth century – a simple sheet of printed paper from which the purchaser of wine by the cask cut out small labels to stick on the bottles. ▶

"Fruity and distinguished", according to Camille Rodier, the chardonnay has a wealth of charm. The *Premiers Crus* are spread out over twenty-four named localities, themselves grouped into fourteen *climats*. All, or nearly all, are on the hillside, on the extension of the vineyard of Montrachet in the direction of Meursault. Exposure, soil, subsoil and nuances in vinification distinguish them clearly.

Les Demoiselles (or La Demoiselle): adjacent to Chevalier-Montrachet, this terrain belongs to Cailleret. On two occasions it was partly included in Chevalier-Montrachet (L. Jadot and L. Latour in 1938-1939, then more recently, J. Chartron), but by contrast, certain of its parcels were declared unfit for cultivation.

The terrain of Cailleret is described by its name: the soil is mixed with *cailloux*, small pebbles. The 3 hectares 93 ares 23 centiares (9.7 acres) belong wholly to Domaine Chartron. They are not entirely planted with chardonnay. A small plot of pinot noir (8 ares or 0.2 acres) divides it in two. This is reminiscent of Aloxe-Corton, where the white Corton are only a few metres away from the reds. The quality comes close to that of the neighbouring *Grands Crus*, whether it is a question of volume, aromas, or persistence.

Les Combettes (6 hectares 76 ares 14 centiares or 16.7 acres) is one of Puligny's war horses and one of the glories of Domaine Sauzet. On outcrops of rock among deep trenches of good land, the soil is clayey and then, further up the slope, chalky. It produces a chardonnay of admirable finesse and constancy. It is one of the best of the area, rather resembling the wine of Meursault.

Les Pucelles (of blessed memory, for, says the story, they lost their virginity as a result of the ardent attentions of the Bâtard-Montrachet): their 6 hectares 76 ares 34 centiares (16.7 acres) give an irresistible perfume of honey, and a roundness which is enchanting. Perhaps less complex than certain other *Premiers Crus* in Puligny, Pucelles – very close to Bienvenues-Bâtard-Montrachet – have an instant appeal. They are more popular with restaurateurs than with wine lovers wanting to add to their cellars. "This wine is a young dancer going to the Opera," says one grower.

Clavaillon (or Clavoillon) is almost wholly owned by Domaine Leflaive (5 hectares out of the *climat*'s total of 5 hectares 58 ares 55 centiares or 13.8 acres). Between Pucelles and Perrières, it has rich deep soil which at one time produced great reds. Today the whites have a nose typical of Montrachet, with bouquet and body. They are substantial wines of solid structure.

Perrières (4 hectares 48 ares 84 centiares or 11.1 acres) is intermingled in a rather complicated way with Clos de la Mouchère (3 hectares 91 ares 98 centiares or 9.7 acres) and Referts (5 hectares 52 ares 47 centiares or 13.7 acres). Formerly this was the *climat* called Les Referts, split up between several named localities. The Clos de la Mouchère recalls the former presence of "sugar flies". Perrières recalls subterranean quarries. Its land contains limestone reddened by iron oxide and beds of marl. Pinot noir was grown here at one time. Today, the chardonnay gives a well-structured white, rich and round, with seductive aromas of fern and honey, which ages well.

Folatières (17 hectares 63 ares 76 centiares or 43.6 acres) is situated above Clavaillon, beside Cailleret. It is unstable land and easily washed away by heavy rains. Very chalky and pebbly, sometimes mastered by dynamite, the banks of soil are greatly revered. Benefiting from the same amount of sunshine as Chevalier-Montrachet, over the years Folatières has absorbed several named localities which are less "commercial": Peux Bois, Au Chaniot, En la Richarde. A precocious wine, though less exuberant than a Pucelle or a Combette, a Folatière surprises by its breeding and its suitability for laying down. The experts sometimes find a hint of hazelnut and truffle. If you know the Eve in the Rolin Museum in Autun, the wines of Folatières share her sensuality.

Like Champ Gain (5 hectares 67 ares 71 centiares or 14 acres), Truffières (2 hectares 48 ares 22 centiares or 6.1 acres) lies on very chalky land which has been developed for some years now. Although their aromas resemble those of Folatières, their structure does not have the same harmony.

Opposite Folatières on the road to Blagny are Champ Canet (3 hectares 25 ares 66 centiares or 8 acres), Jaquelotte (80 ares 11 centiares or 2 acres), Chalumaux or Chaumeaux (5 hectares 79 ares 30 centiares or 14.3 acres) and Clos de la Garenne (1 hectare 53 ares 23 centiares or 3.8 acres). On this land close to the quarries, the marl and scree form a scanty reddish earth in which the roots probe deep into the fissures in the rock. These are light, fruity wines which can be appreciated when they are fairly young, except for Chalumaux, whose tender finesse and aromatic power equal Genevrières in Meursault. Clos de la Garenne has an absolute purity of flavour.

The Matrot and Montlivault families live in the hamlet of Blagny. On this hillside are Hameau de Blagny, Sous le Puits and Garenne, whereas other named localities lie more towards Meursault (Jeunelotte, la Pièce sous le Bois, Sous le Dos d'âne). These have white and red vines along the slope (20 hectares 94 ares 39 centiares or 51.8 acres) on marls covered with scree. At the top, brown chalky land then land of clayey limestone. Although it suits the pinot well, it has been rather submerged by the wave of chardonnay. The reds have plenty of character and they often evoke the *crus* of the Côte de Nuits. They used to be known as "medicinal wines". Those of La Garenne are fuller-bodied.

The Puligny-Montrachet (Village) appellation is for reds and whites. Of modest extent, it gives very different types of wines: well-structured, with a fine bouquet and for long keeping on the Chassagne side, rich and substantial on the Meursault side. Burgundy red and white is also produced here as well as aligoté over some 50 hectares.

Although Puligny's trump card is white, Chassagne cannily takes care not to put all its bottles in one basket. The village has always produced whites and reds and these latter have known their moment of glory. Now somewhat eclipsed by Montrachet, they are no less abundant and have a good reputation. Camille Rodier recognized in these reds "an indisputable analogy with certain good reds of the Côte de Nuits". Coming from the pen of a man from Nuits-Saint-Georges, this is evidently a compliment! In about 1850 there were still pinot noir, gamay and even pinot gris or beurot, peculiar to the region.

Out of a total area of vines of some 350 hectares of which 159 are in *Premiers Crus*, the average harvest is 7,500 hectolitres (100,000 bottles) of reds and 58,000 (770,000 bottles) of whites.

In the *Premiers Crus*, in which parcels of white and red are often to be found, a distinction should be drawn between law and habit. But this is not easy. Indeed, a good forty named localities have been classed in *Premiers Crus*. So these names can legally feature on a label.

But for obvious reasons of simplicity, there has been a certain amount of grouping together. This is legal and honest, though not always consistent. One example will illustrate the situation. Clos Saint-Jean has 5 hectares 7 ares 80 centiares (12.5 acres). All well and good. But added to it are Rebichets,

Scale 1:20,000

SAINT-AUBIN

Chassagne-Montrachet

SANTENAY

400

En Pimont

La Grande Montagne

Pot Bois

Le Parterre

300

Les Combards

Clos Saint-Jean

Les Baudines

Bois de Chassagne

Les Embazées

En Virondot

Chassagne du Clos Saint-Jean

La Romanée

La Grande Montagne

En Cailleret

Vigne Derrière

Les Murées

Les Rebichets

Les Grandes Ruchottes

Clos Pitois

Frencherront

Tête du Clos

Les Grands Clos

Les Petits Clos

Les Petites Fairendes

Les Fairendes

Les Champs Gain

La Maltroie

Chassagne

Ez Crets

Les Places

La Grande Borne

Les Brussonnes

La Cardeuse

Morgeot

Morgeot

Vigne Blanche

Morgeot

Les Masures

La Canière

Les Chênes

Les Voillenots Dessus

Clos Devant

Clos Chareau

Les Boirettes

La Chapelle

Ez Crottes

Guerchère

Les Chaumes

La Boudriotte

Champs Jendreau

Les Chaumes

Le Clos Reland

Les Essarts

Clos Bernot

Puits Merdreaux

Meuchottes

Voillenot Dessous

SANTENAY

REMIGNY

Les Battaudes

Les Benoîtes

Champs de Morjot

En L'Ormeau

La Platière

La Goujonne

Les Morichots

Le Concis du Champs

Les Chambres

Champ

SAÔNE-ET-LOIRE

Les Benoîtes

Champs de Morjot

La Platière

Les Lombardes

Le Poirier du Clos

La Corvée

Sur Matrange

Bouchon de Corvée

Dessous les Mues

Les Pierres

CHAGNY

R.N. 6

CORPEAU

LYON

Montrachet
Chevalier-Montrachet
Bâtard-Montrachet
Bienvenues-Bâtard-Montrachet
Criots-Bâtard-Montrachet

Chassagne-Montrachet

Puligny-Montrachet premier cru
Chassagne-Montrachet premier cru

Puligny-Montrachet

Puligny-Montrachet premier cru (white)
Blagny premier cru (red)

Puligny-Montrachet (white)
Blagny (red)

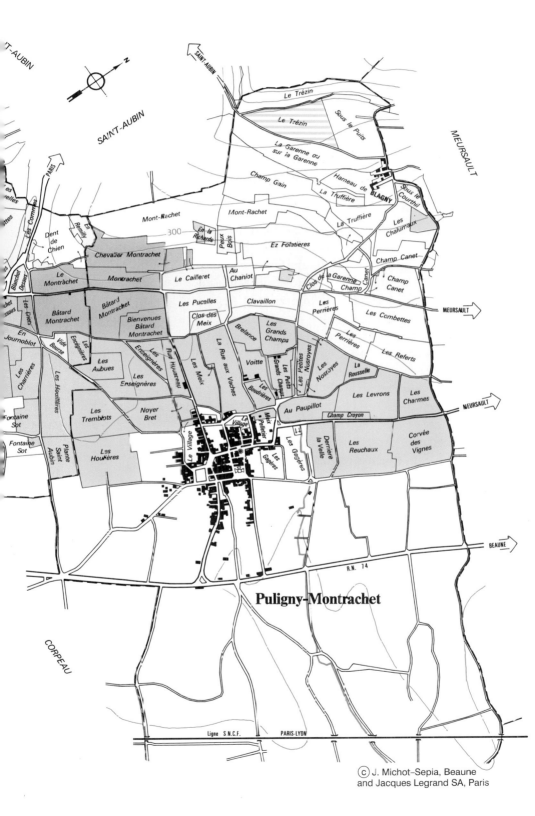

Puligny-Montrachet

© J. Michot–Sepia, Beaune
and Jacques Legrand SA, Paris

known as Clos Saint-Jean (5 hectares 45 ares 7 centiares or 13.5 acres), Murées, known as Clos Saint-Jean (1 hectare 60 ares 93 centiares or 4 acres) and the Chassagne du Clos Saint-Jean (2 hectares 2 ares 21 centiares or 5 acres), also known as Clos Saint-Jean. So the growers have the choice between the many and varied appellations of Rebichets, Murées, Chassagne du Clos Saint-Jean... or Clos Saint-Jean. Now comes the Chinese puzzle: what is the exact area of Clos Saint-Jean? In round terms, 5 hectares *stricto sensu*, or the 15 or so hectares which have the right to this appellation?

Having thus assuaged my conscience, I can now attempt to finish my task with the help of René Lamy, the president of the Viticultural Federation, whose affable assistance is invaluable. The list of Chassagne's *Premiers Crus* is reproduced on the page opposite.

These are the true figures! And just for one single little commune in Burgundy, already amply provided with *Grands Crus*! If I have been anxious to give an exhaustive list, it is to highlight the real situation in Burgundy. It is impossible to establish or publish a clear and complete list of the *climats* of any one commune in Burgundy, indicating their exact areas. Admittedly, Chassagne is a particularly complicated case, but the majority of reliable authors fail to distinguish the *climats* from the named localities. We have just glimpsed here what this is all about.

But mysteries occur. I have been told that the appellation Bois de Chassagne is not in use, yet it unambiguously covers 5 hectares. So under what names are these wines sold? It is normal to resort to such regroupings, while still respecting the unity of the *climat*. Often dating from time immemorial, the named localities were not destined to give birth to *crus*. They simply distinguished the parcels in accordance with local practice and needs. Those which invented their own names did not have growing uppermost in mind. To some, these nuances will appear trifling. But they are not. Burgundy is a carpet in *petit point*, not an industrial product. Boudriotte is not Morgeot; the Cailleret of Chassagne is not the Cailleret of Puligny. The local growers make no mistake when they taste these wines. This diversity is in the very nature of the region. When he was the Minister for Agriculture, Edgard Pisani asked French viticulturalists if it would not be simpler and more business-like to do away once and for all with these AOCs and call the wines "Bordeaux", "Burgundy" or "Alsace". It is not difficult to imagine the reply.

Formerly, the most famous appellations of Chassagne were Clos Saint-Jean and Clos Pitois. An old estate of the convent of Saint-Jean-le-Grand d'Autun, abolished under the Revolution after a thousand years of history, Clos Saint-Jean is the oldest *cru* in Chassagne. 90% of its wines are red and it perhaps owes to the late-lamented nuns a more feminine, less robust temperament than Morgeot. Situated on the hillside, the vineyard lies on thin red earth. Its wine has great delicacy of bouquet after a sometimes hard initial attack. There are aromas of plum and peach. They are wines which are rather "earthy" when young. There are still many walls in Clos Saint-Jean,

Premiers crus of Chassagne-Montrachet

- Clos Saint-Jean (5 ha 7 a 80 ca)
- Les Rebichets or Clos Saint-Jean
  (5 ha 45 a 7 ca)
- Les Murées or Clos Saint-Jean
  (1 ha 60 a 93 ca)
- Cailleret or Chassagne
  (1 ha 14 a 47 ca)
- Chassagne du Clos Saint-Jean or Clos
  Saint-Jean (2 ha 2 a 21 ca)
- Cailleret or Les Combards
  (65 a 33 ca)
- Les Chaumées (7 ha 43 a 36 ca)
- Les Vergers or Petingeret
  (1 ha 75 a 37 ca)
- Les Vergers or Les Pasquelles
  (2 ha 44 a 83 ca)
- Les Chenevottes or Les Commes
  (1 ha 5 a 94 ca)
- Les Chenevottes or Les Bondues
  (1 ha 73 a 10 ca)
- Les Chenevottes (8 ha 15 a 97 ca)
- Les Macherelles (5 ha 18 a 96 ca)
- Les Vergers (5 ha 21 a 2 ca)
- En Remilly (1 ha 56 a 42 ca)
- Dents de Chien (63 a 76 ca)
- Vide Bourse (1 ha 32 a 43 ca)
- Blanchot (1 ha 17 a 15 ca)
- La Maltroie or Chassagne
  (2 ha 89 a 74 ca)
- La Maltroie or Les Places
  (2 ha 40 a 87 ca)
- La Maltroie (4 ha 18 ca)
- Ez Crets or La Maltroie
  (2 ha 30 a 22 ca)
- Les Brussonnes or Morgeot or
  La Grande Borne (1 ha 73 a 22 ca)
- La Cardeuse or Morgeot or
  Les Brussonnes (96 a 20 ca)
- Les Brussonnes or Morgeot
  (2 ha 87 a 81 ca)
- Abbaye de Morgeot or Morgeot
  (3 ha 98 a 22 ca)
- Vigne Blanche or Morgeot
  (2 ha 23 a 72 ca)
- Morgeot or Ez Crottes
  (2 ha 35 a 72 ca)
- Morgeot or Guerchère
  (2 ha 17 a 78 ca)

- Abbaye de Morgeot or La Chapelle
  or Morgeot (4 ha 57 a 35 ca)
- Morgeot or Les Brussonnes or
  Les Boirettes (2 ha 83 a 74 ca)
- Morgeot or Les Brussonnes or Clos
  Chareau (1 ha 98 a 58 ca)
- Les Embazées or Bois de Chassagne
  (5 ha 19 a 30 ca)
- Morgeot or Tête du Clos
  (2 ha 11 a 64 ca)
- Bois de Chassagne
  (4 ha 78 a 28 ca)
- La Romanée or La Grande
  Montagne (3 ha 35 a 50 ca)
- Morgeot or Les Petits Clos
  (5 ha 9 a 49 ca)
- Morgeot or Les Grands Clos
  (3 ha 92 a 82 ca)
- Morgeot or Les Brussonnes or
  Francemont (2 ha 38 a 86 ca)
- Clos Pitois or Les Brussonnes
  or Morgeot (2 ha 97 a 48 ca)
- La Roquemaure or La Baudriotte
  or Morgeot (61 a 48 ca)
- Morgeot (31 a 15 ca)
- La Baudriotte or Les Chaumes
  or Morgeot (2 ha 69 a 19 ca)
- La Boudriotte or Morgeot or Champ
  Jendreau (2 ha 10 a 54 ca)
- La Boudriotte or Morgeot
  (2 ha 23 a 20 ca)
- En Virondot or La Grande Montagne
  (2 ha 27 a 99 ca)
- En Cailleret (6 ha 11 a 31 ca)
- Cailleret or Vigne Derrière
  (3 ha 76 a 45 ca)
- Les Champs Gain
  (4 ha 62 a 6 ca)
- Les Fairendes or La Boudriotte
  or Morgeot (7 ha 16 a 34 ca)
- La Boudriotte or Morgeot or
  Les Petites Fairendes (81 a 55 ca)
- Les Grandes Ruchottes or La Grande
  Montagne (2 ha 13 a 26 ca)
- Tonton Marcel or La Grande
  Montagne (49 a 50 ca)
- Les Baudines or Bois de Chassagne
  (3 ha 60 a 43 ca)

for they hold back the mountain side. Highly appreciated in the nineteenth century, Clos Pitois no longer enjoys the same reputation. Without any good reason, moreover. Like Clos de la Chapelle and Cardeuse, it is a monopoly.

Morgeot exists in both red and white with plenty of variety. Rich in body and well-structured, the reds are wines for long keeping and age well. The whites are fruity and very stylized, agreeable and complete. But it is difficult to pass a single judgement on whites coming from vineyards which are so different: piles of pebbles in Vigne Blanche, sand in Grands Clos, white earth in Tête du Clos, soil of loam and clay in other places.

Once red, Cailleret has turned over to white. "An image of quality", say the growers of the village. "It is always good if you take care of it." Another up-and-coming *climat* is La Boudriotte, particularly well served by Domaine Ramonet. Half red, half white, Boudriotte is like an island in the heart of Morgeot, being right in the middle, between Morgeot and Clos Saint-Jean: less hard, lighter, very well balanced, with aromas of kirsch.

Flagrant and floral, Chenevottes and Vergers are gradually going over to whites. We can see here that exceptional land gives equal chances of success to the pinot noir and the chardonnay. On the southern tip of the Côte, Chassagne succeeds in producing the very synthesis of these two great Burgundy varieties, and can afford to plant them side by side without the risk of any cruel disappointment.

Faced with so many names, we sometimes wonder if our growers do not sometimes extend the list somewhat, as with the famous Tonton ("Uncle")

▲ *Between Chassagne and Santenay, the former Abbey of Morgeot.*

Marcel, for example' In fact, the name of this named locality really indicates a menhir or a dolmen, long since disappeared but still remembered. Chenevottes, Vergers and Macherelles are neighbouring *climats*. They have good land which was once devoted to the cultivation of hemp or vegetables. Morgeot comes from Morgeot, a dependency of the Abbey of Maizières. Cailleret, a common name in Côte de Beaune, means land full of pebbles. Clos Pitois comes from the name of its first owner. Similarly, Boudriotte honours the name of a certain Boudriot. The majority of these names are *hors d'âge*, as we might say of an old brandy. They are in no way opportunist creations.

Wine: the work of men

Are we perhaps getting somewhere near the secret we have been searching for in vain since the beginning of this book? If we have not found the explanation in nature, history, the soil or the climate, clones or oenology, could it not be in man? Or woman, of course. No one can contest that this wine is more often than not admirable and sometimes sublime. It has its off-days. But do we reproach Stendhal or Mozart with a page scored out, a lack of inspiration owing to ill-health or domestic problems? For Montrachet is not a work of art but the complete work of an immortal artist.

Furthermore, I believe that wine can hardly be criticized objectively. At the risk of irritating the specialists ("those who, through knowing everything about everything end up by knowing everything about nothing", as René Engel said in the *Tastevin*), I think that wine cannot replace happiness. The joy of the moment plays an enormous part in the appreciation of wine and in remembering it. If you drink the most sumptuous Montrachet sad and alone, will it give you back the joy of living, love, confidence? On the other hand, you will find the most ordinary aligoté wonderful if you share it with the person of your dreams. Of course, a Montrachet will heighten your pleasure. But everything is in the mind, the heart, the soul, and not just in the body. Montrachet must be earned, and I would readily offer it to those most deprived, so that at least for once in their life they should have and share not this luxury (such a common word), but this beauty. There are wines born to give happiness, wines which would be out of place at a business lunch. Montrachet is one of them. Let us respect it.

But if man is in this wine, it is essentially because it is born of man. I have in front of me a sort of journal, a moving work written night after night by the priest Colin. It begins in this way: "Under the sign of light, life and love: the vine, wine, for they are light, life, love." Here are some ten years' work, chronicled with tenderness. The priest speaks of everything, from grafts to the mystic harvest, from mildew to the suffering of the Almighty, from malolactic fermentation to the Eternal Vine. "I am like a crow sitting alone upon my tree." he wrote in the evening of his life. "I flap my wings in vain;

I can no longer fly away, fly away to the stars..." Turning the pages of this simple private diary written in Chassagne, filled with wine and its joys, the vine and its torments, I said to myself: yes, this wine is first and foremost a work of man which lights up the heavens. Forget technique, competence, knowledge. Accept wine as a work of man. Think of those nights of frost, those squalls of hail, of the trouble taken and all the anxieties. Think of the love you are being offered when the wine is sold to you. During the most recent harvest, I passed through Montrachet one wet Sunday afternoon. Edmond Delagrange was going round his vines. He had come to look at his grapes which were beginning to rot. Blinded by his tears, he gazed tenderly upon them. Alone in his vineyards, he was talking to his grapes.

Catalogue of proprietors
of the Grands Crus

Thanks to the proprietors of the *Grands Crus* of Chassagne-Montrachet and Puligny-Montrachet, we were able to taste some fifty wines bearing the name of Montrachet. We thank them for their co-operation.

We would also like to thank our tasters, all superbly well qualified, who could only marvel at this historic "portrait gallery". Never before has this experiment been tried and proved successful.

Each proprietor or grower was free to present whichever vintage he or she wished. The panel tasted each bottle, presented anonymously (only the *cru* and the vintage were given), and judged it accordingly.

These judgements do not of course cover all the wines of the property or every vintage. They represent an average, for the tasting points were sometimes very different for the same bottle.

The overall impression was one of amazement. Rarely has a detailed survey of this kind in Burgundy revealed such riches, for no wine appeared unworthy of the name it bore. This at least bears witness to the high quality of the wines and proves that they can hold their own.

This catalogue requires several preliminary explanatory notes. As we needed a constant criterion, we chose ownership. But we found ourselves faced with a number of different situations:

• the proprietor runs the vineyard himself, making and marketing his own wine;

• the proprietor has relinquished ownership of the property but retains the usufruct;

• the proprietor entrusts the running of his land to a farmer or *métayer* who markets all or part of the fruit;

• the proprietor sells his harvest as grapes or juice after pressing but before fermentation;

• the proprietor has handed his vines over to a merchant-vintner who owns a viticultural estate elsewhere.

Details of such arrangements are given in the catalogue. Details are not given, however, of sales in the cask to merchants-vintners, generally from Burgundy, as such purchases vary from year to year.

In a vineyard such as Montrachet every inch of soil counts: we have thus kept the original French measurements in full. The following conversions may help:

1 *ouvrée* = 4 ares 28 centiares = 511.88 square yards.
1 hectare = 100 ares = 10,000 centiares = 2.471 acres.

AMIOT
Domaine Guy Amiot et Fils

◊ *Montrachet* (M)

Two parcels (6 ares 35 centiares and 2 ares 75 centiares) of Montrachet in Chassagne. bought after the First World War by Guy Amiot's grandfather, Arsène Amiot. They are part of the vines in Dents de Chien included in Montrachet by the 1921 judgement at Beaune. Amiot-Bonfils also has vines in Chassagne in Cailleret, Vergers and Champs Gain, and in Puligny in Les Demoiselles. In reds, it has Vergers, Champs Gain, Maltroie and Clos Saint-Jean in Chassagne. The Montrachet plants here are over 70 years old, and were planted in 1920. Work is carried out by hand, access being impossible for a tractor. The harvest was sold to the Savour Club until 1985 and is now aged at the property and sold retail to restaurateurs and collectors of rare bottles. Domaine Amiot has private clients who have been faithful for several decades. From 1925 to 1945 it owned a shop for retail sales in Paris.

Guy Amiot.

Proprietor:
Domaine Amiot-Bonfils
Manager: Guy Amiot
Rue du Grand-Puits
Chassagne-Montrachet
21190 Meursault
Tel: 80 21 38 62

Production (in hectolitres):

1981: 3.40	1986: 5.50
1982: 5.10	1987: 4.25
1983: 4.55	1988: 4.50
1984: 3.60	1989: 4.30
1985: 4.90	

Best vintages:
1964, 1971, 1978, 1983, 1985

Tasting:

M 1985. *Although still closed up, this bottle, tasted in 1987, already has a charming colour. Bright pale gold. Its aromas of citronella with overtones of vanilla give hints of great promise. A very round wine which fills the mouth. A great lord, undoubtedly. A Montrachet in classic style which will blossom as it ages.*

ANDRE
Veuve Maurice André

◊ *Bâtard-Montrachet* (BM)

Madame Maurice André, who lives in Beaune, owns this parcel of 39 ares 68 centiares in Bâtard-Montrachet which is run on *métayage* (three-fifths for the *métayer*) by Jean-Claude Bachelet (see Domaine Bachelet-Ramonet Père et Fils).

Proprietor:
Madame Maurice André
in Beaune

Metayer:
Bachelet-Ramonet Père et Fils
Chassagne-Montrachet
21190 Meursault
Tel: 80 21 32 49

BACHELET
Domaine Jean-Claude Bachelet

◊ *Bienvenues-Bâtard-Montrachet* (BBM)
This parcel of 9 ares and 42 centiares was bought in 1960 from the Dupaquier family by
J.-C. Bachelet's parents. He replanted it in 1971 and runs it with his wife together with
vines he inherited from his father in Bienvenues, and those of his mother in Chassagne
Premier Cru (Macherelles and Boudriotte), Puligny-Montrachet *Premier Cru* (Sous le
Puits, white), Saint-Aubin *Premier Cru* (Champlots and Derrière la Tour). For a few
years now, Bachelet has bottled practically the whole of his production and is looking
for opportunities to enlarge his *domaine,* which presently covers 7.5 hectares.

Proprietor: Domaine Jean-Claude Bachelet Saint-Aubin, 21190 Meursault Tel: 80 21 31 01	**Best vintages:** 1964, 1976, 1979, 1982, 1983, 1985.	*in the mouth. A fine wine which* *would benefit from losing a bit of* *weight.*
Production (in hectolitres): 1984: 3.74 1987: 4.37 1985: 4.70 1988: 4.65 1986: 4.69 1989: 4.27	**Tasting:** **BBM 1982.** *Rather too rich in* *alcohol for the vintage, discreet* *acidity, rich and mellow. Long*	

BACHELET-RAMONET
Bachelet-Ramonet Père et Fils

◊ *Bâtard-Montrachet* (BM), *Bienvenues-Bâtard-Montrachet* (BBM)
This Jean-Claude Bachelet shares his name with the preceding one. The Bachelets are
so numerous that they can no longer be counted in Chassagne. To try to make things
easier, as Christian names are not enough, each has a nickname: Pommier, Jules Perrin,
Guinguette... But this does not entirely avoid confusion, particularly on invoices! Today,
it is mainly Claude Ramonet who runs the business. His grandfather instituted a sort of
forerunner of direct sales at the property. It was risky at that period, for the limpidity
of the wines had not been fully mastered as it is today. The 1945 bottles, magnificent
wines, looked like aquaria! Fortunately, all that has changed.

The Bachelet-Ramonet business runs two parcels in Bâtard-Montrachet: one of 16 ares
75 centiares and the other of 39 ares 68 centiares, belonging to Madame Maurice André
in Beaune (see above). It also owns a parcel of 13 ares 20 centiares in Bienvenues-Bâtard-
Montrachet. The vines were planted in 1965 (Bâtard André), in 1980 (the other Bâtard)
and in 1971 (Bienvenues). Half the produce is marketed in the bottle.

There are also white vines (Cailleret, Ruchottes, Morgeot, Romanée, Grande Montagne) and red (Clos Saint-Jean, Boudriotte, Morgeot). Claude Ramonet's daughter and
son-in-law, Marie-Paule and Alain Bonnefoy, help to run the business.

Proprietor: Bachelet-Ramonet Père et Fils Chassagne-Montrachet 21190 Meursault Tel: 80 21 32 49	**Production (in hectolitres):** • **BM (include André's parcel)** 1983: 20.50 1987: 18.30 1984: 12.74 1988: 20.52 1985: 20.75 1989: 27.08 1986: 22.50	• **BBM** 1984: 6.27 1987: 6.33 1985: 9.92 1988: 6.84 1986: 7.92 1989: 6.33

Tasting:

BM 1985. *It is a pity its colour is so pale. Its nose is still lacking in eloquence. But it has youth on its side: sufficient acidity, mellow, warm and long in the mouth.*

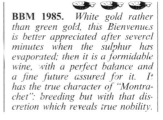

BBM 1985. *White gold rather than green gold, this Bienvenues is better appreciated after several minutes when the sulphur has evaporated; then it is a formidable wine, with a perfect balance and a fine future assured for it. It has the true character of "Montrachet": breeding but with that discretion which reveals true nobility.*

BAROLET-PERNOT
Domaine Barolet-Pernot Père et Fils

◊ *Bâtard-Montrachet* and *Bienvenues-Bâtard-Montrachet*

On December 18, 1986, André Barolet-Pernot and his wife, growers in Saint-Romain, inherited two lots of vines formerly belonging to Solange Latour, the wife of Lucien Pernot: 22 ares 57 centiares in Bâtard-Montrachet, half of which was acquired by the Pernot-Latours in 1952 and half by the Latour family from the previous generation; 9 ares 29 centiares in Bienvenues-Bâtard-Montrachet, also acquired by the Latour family. The parcels in Bâtard were planted in 1938 and that in Bienvenues in 1965. The new proprietors had their first harvest in 1987. Their land stretches over Saint-Romain, Puligny-Montrachet and Beaune: Saint-Romain red and white, Pucelles, Champ Gain, Hameau de Blagny, Enseignières in Puligny, Beaune les Teurons. The wine is sold to merchants, but some is also kept for direct sales to the firm's private clients.

Proprietor:
Domaine Barolet-Pernot
Père et Fils
Saint-Romain, 21190 Meursault
Tel: 80 21 20 88

BAVARD
Charles and Paul Bavard

◊ *Bâtard-Montrachet* (BM)

When they inherited the vines of their father Joseph, Charles received 33 ares 85 centiares in Bâtard and Paul, 33 ares 86 centiares, or one centiare more. But the family has not fallen out over it. Jean-Paul (Paul's son) and his wife have been tenant-farmers of Uncle Charles's vines since 1983. They also have Paul Bavard's vines on *métayage*, though not his Bâtard. All this at Puligny, of course. For several years now the wine has been sold in must direct from the press to the firm of Antonin Rodet in Mercurey.

Proprietors:	**Manager**	**Production (in hectolitres):**
Charles and Paul Bavard	**(Charles Bavard's parcel)**	**(Charles Bavard's parcel):**
Puligny-Montrachet	Jean-Paul Bavard	1986: 16.92 1988: 13.68
21190 Meursault	Puligny-Montrachet	1987: 13.11 1989: 13.11
Tel: 80 21 31 48	21190 Meursault	
	Tel: 80 21 38 17	

BELLAND
Domaine Joseph Belland

◊ *Criots-Bâtard-Montrachet* (CBM)

A native of Santenay, Joseph Belland succeeded his father and grandfather, and together with his son Roger runs the *domaine* from the family home which looks down over the valley of Santenay. Joseph Belland will warn you to be careful about Christian names if you pay him a visit in Santenay, for his three brothers also have vines there. Since 1982 he has owned half of the parcel of Criots, which he bought from the Marcillys and paid for within a week (this is why the parcel was not split up at the time of the sale). As it lies in a corner, all work on the vines has to be carried out by hand. The wines are aged in oak casks for at least eighteen months. During the first winter the cellar is heated to finish fermentation in the best conditions, and the following year the cold is allowed to penetrate to activate tartaric deposits before bottling. Half the sales are in casks and half in the bottle.

The Land Register marks "GFA Saint-Joseph": "That is the firm we have formed with the children", says the proprietor. "And why Saint-Joseph? Easy! Because my name is Joseph..."

His vines stretch out over Puligny and Chassagne in whites (Champ Gain, Clos Pitois); over Chassagne (Clos Pitois), Santenay (Gravières, Comme, Beauregard, Passetemps, Clos Rousseau); and Pommard (Cras) in reds. A splendid sample of *Premiers Crus* and the monopoly of Clos Pitois.

Proprietor:	Production (in hectolitres):	Tasting:
Domaine Joseph Belland	1982: 44 1985: 37	
Rue de la Chapelle	1983: 35 1986: 37	**CBM 1982.** *More yellow than*
21590 Santenay	1984: 29	*gold, this Criots has an agreeable*
Tel: 80 20 61 13		*woody nose with hints of vanilla*
	Best vintages:	*and linden. Acidity is giving way*
	1982, 1983, 1985	*to mellowness. It is fairly long in*
		the mouth. The overall impression
		is pleasing.

BLAIN-GAGNARD
Domaine Blain-Gagnard

◊ *Bâtard-Montrachet* (BM), *Criots-Bâtard-Montrachet* (CBM)

Claudine Blain-Gagnard is the daughter of Jacques Gagnard-Delagrange, granddaughter of Edmond Delagrange-Bachelet and sister of Laurence Fontaine-Gagnard: a solid and affectionate dynasty apparently under matriarchal sway, for with each generation, the women bring vines in their dowry and add their maiden name to that of their husband, so creating a new *domaine*. That is how many of the names of Montrachet *Grands Crus* has been created. Claudine married Jean-Marc Blain, the son of a veterinary surgeon from the region of Sancerre, who has adapted himself perfectly to this change of *climats*. The vineyard dates from 1980. Their eldest offspring, Lucie, will maintain the family tradition, but they also have a son to uphold the honour of the men. Like her sister Laurence, Claudine adores her grandfather, Edmond Delagrange-Bachelet (see below). Who would not? He has firmly inculcated into his heirs – son-in-law and daughter, and after them the grandchildren – a love of the land, sound practices, and a respect for long-lived wines which do not like to be disturbed and which will open up for those who are patient enough to wait. He heads a true family of growers with true Chassagne vines who always extend an unpretentious welcome. In this little courtyard with its pretty flowers no delusions of grandeur will be allowed to turn their heads. And the wine? In a word, divine. I know one grandfather who can be proud of his grandchildren, and a father (not to be forgotten) who need not be ashamed of his daughters or his sons-in-law.

Claudine and Jean-Marc Blain-Gagnard have the ownership without usufruct of 7 ares 83 centiares in Montrachet (usufructuary: Jacques Gagnard-Delagrange, their father and father-in-law), as well as vines given to them by their grandparents, the Delagrange-Bachelets, in 1978-1979: 34 ares 45 centiares in Bâtard-Montrachet and 20 ares 55 centiares in Criots-Bâtard-Montrachet. The other vines they own stretch over Chassagne (red *Premiers Crus* Clos Saint-Jean and Morgeot, white *Premiers Crus* Morgeot, Boudriotte and Cailleret), Volnay (*Premier Cru* Chanlin) and Pommard (la Croix Planet, les Combes). The wine is sold "by the bottle" and to merchants.

Proprietors:
Domaine Blain-Gagnard
Chassagne-Montrachet
21190 Meursault
Tel: 80 21 34 07

Production (in hectolitres):
- **BM**

1981: 10.12	1982: 23.94
1983: 15.96	1984: 11.94
1985: 11.50 (one vineyard uprooted)	
1987: 9.12	1989: 16.53
1988: 10.30	

- **CBM**

1981: 5	1985: 12.25
1982: 14.82	1987: 9.69
1983: 7.98	1988: 10.30
1984: 7.18	1989: 9.69

Tasting:

BM 1983. *If you come across this wine you will recognize it at once. At this tasting it was one of the best of the appellation. It has everything in excess – colour, aromas, body. But it manages to re-* tain a balance. A very rich wine, full and powerful. You might even say an enterprising wine. Typical 83 and a true Bâtard.

CBM 1982. *A "hit" for the Blain-Gagnard family, for this dazzling Criots really does honour both to the appellation and to the region. The panel lavished praise on it and with one voice finished with the words: "Bravo. Make us wine like that for ever."*

BLONDEAU-DANNE
Domaine Blondeau-Danne

◊ *Criots-Bâtard-Montrachet* (CBM)

Originally, Denis Blondeau-Danne, like his father, was not destined to be a grower. After studying to be a clockmaker, his father returned to the Château de Saint-Aubin on the death of his adoptive father, Charles Danne. Danne latter, an architect from Dijon who designed part of the town's Post Office building, had bought the château as a country residence and bequeathed it along with the vines to his only son. After studying electronics, Denis Blondeau returned to the calm of the château where he runs the family business.

The firm of Blondeau-Danne (the parents and their seven children) has vines in Meursault (Pièce sous le Bois), Volnay, Puligny-Montrachet (Garenne), Chassagne-Montrachet (Blanchot Dessous and Chenevottes) as well as in Saint-Aubin (Village and Combes). The 5 ares 4 centiares in Criots-Bâtard-Montrachet were replanted in 1979; they were bought on October 1, 1957 from Monsieur and Madame Perrot-Morey. The wine is sold exclusively to private customers. The excellent 1964 vintage has never been equalled.

The label, illustrating the Château de Saint-Aubin and mentioning a "fine wine" of guaranteed authenticity, is delightfully old-fashioned. It was designed by the Dijon firm of printers, Berthier, then copied by the firm of Filiber in Nuits-Saint-Georges. Denis, a confirmed nature lover, grows orange trees in the conservatory which serves as an entrance hall to the château.

Proprietor:
Domaine Blondeau-Danne
Château de Saint-Aubin
21190 Meursault
Tel: 80 21 31 46

Production (in hectolitres):
1982: 1.71	1986: 2.28
1983: 1.14	1987: 1.71
1984: 1.14	1988: 1.71
1985: 2.28	1989: 1.71

Best vintage:
1964

The Château de Saint-Aubin
(Domaine Blondeau-Danne).

BONNEFOY
Charles Bonnefoy

◊ *Criots-Bâtard-Montrachet* (CBM)
This parcel of 26 ares 27 centiares was bought as a life interest in 1976 from Joseph Deléger who wanted to hand it over to his vigneron. The gesture did him credit. Half the vines were planted in 1967 and the other half in 1972. The wine is sold exclusively to merchants (under contract to the firm of Louis Latour in Beaune). Moreover, Charles Bonnefoy is *métayer* of two twin parcels of 9 ares 66 centiares in Chevalier-Montrachet (Dancer and Courlet de Vrégille – see below). This harvest is sold in grapes to the firm of Louis Jadot in Beaune.

Proprietor:
Charles Bonnefoy
21190 Chassagne-Montrachet
Tel: 80 21 30 89

Production (in hectolitres):
1981: 6.63	1984: 11.40
1982: 18.47	1985: 15.70
1983: 15.71	1986: 14.63

BOUCHARD PERE ET FILS
Domaine et Maison Bouchard Père et Fils

◊ *Montrachet* (M), *Bâtard-Montrachet* (BM), *Chevalier-Montrachet* (CM)
Founded in 1731 and now owner of 92 hectares of vines (of which 71 are in *Grands* and *Premiers Crus*), the firm of Bouchard Père et Fils is a veritable institution in Beaune. How can we resist kneeling in adoration before the Vigne de l'Enfant-Jésus (Beaune-Grèves), which formerly belonged to the Beaune Carmelites? But these vineyards also stretch over Chambertin, Le Corton, Le Corton-Charlemagne, the *Premiers Crus* of Meursault, Beaune, Savigny-lès-Beaune, Pommard, Volnay... The principal cellars are situated beneath the bastions and against the ramparts of the fifteenth-century Château de Beaune: 4 million bottles, the oldest of which date from 1830, and nine generations from father to son. Like the firm of Louis Jadot, Bouchard Père et Fils were originally linen merchants. They originated in Dauphiné and worked in the north of France and Belgium. The idea of selling wine came quite naturally. Antoine-Philibert Bouchard, who

The topiarized yews of the Château de Beaune, planted in 1945.

died in 1860 at the age of 101, acquired the firm's first vines (7 hectares in Volnay). His descendants carried on after him, developing their activites as merchant-vintners. The firm benefits from having the exclusive distribution of La Romanée in Vosne-Romanée, a property of Canon Just Liger Belair, and several other *crus* of the Château de Vosne. It buys grapes, musts and young wines and vinifies and ages them. The *Premier Cru* Clos Saint-Marc in Nuits-Saint-Georges, for example, is vinified exclusively by this firm. The new vat-house, largely automated, bears witness to the importance attached in Burgundy to ultra-modern vinification equipment.

Claude and André Bouchard are assisted by the younger generation: Jean-François, who has qualifications from the Ecole supérieure de commerce de Paris (commerce and development), and Christophe, a qualified oenologist from Montpellier (vinification and ageing). Michel Bettane, the French wine journalist, carried out an interesting and detailed study of Domaine Bouchard (*Revue du vin de France*, Sept.-Oct. 1981). It is the third largest property in Montrachet with 1 hectare 9 ares 98 centiares. The vines were bought in 1838 by Bernard and Adolphe Bouchard from André-Adolphe-François, the Comte de Bataille de Mandelot, for the sum of 45,000 francs, payable over six years with interest at five per cent. Conversion is always difficult but we can say that the equivalent today would be about 400,000 francs per hectare, not even a tenth of the current price. This acquisition covered nearly half the former property of the Clermont-Montoisons. Through marriages, half of this went to the Cellard (Volnay) and Boillerault families, who today are to be found among the proprietors of the *cru*. Bouchard Père et Fils still retains the other half. These vines were replanted, in their different parcels, in 1950,

1960, 1964, 1970 and 1983. In Chevalier-Montrachet there are 2 hectares 2 ares 11 centiares, the largest of this great *cru*. Again in their different parcels, the vines here were planted in 1950, 1960, 1967, 1972, 1980, 1984 and 1985. Finally there are 7 ares 85 centiares in Bâtard-Montrachet in Chassagne. André Bouchard is the owner without usufruct, Madame Corne-Ozanon being the usufructuary, and the vineyards were once owned by Doctor Ozanon, famous in Burgundy for his passion for wine. The vines were planted in 1979. The harvest is sold in grapes to Bouchard Père et Fils. Among the most famous clients of these *crus* today is the cellist Mstislav Rostropovitch. The oldest "old bottle" of Burgundy sold at auction at Christie's in London on May 5, 1988, was a Montrachet 1864 from the cellars of Bouchard Père et Fils in Beaune, which was knocked down for £1,600.

Claude and Jean-François Bouchard: "père et fils".

Proprietor:
Domaine et Maison Bouchard
Père et Fils
Au château
BP 70, 21202 Beaune Cedex
Tel: 80 22 14 41

Production (in hectolitres):
• **M**

1984: 28.50	1987: 35.97
1985: 45.60	1988: 45.78
1986: 64.98	1989: 38.15

• **CM**

1984: 45.60	1987: 55.62
1985: 82.08	1988: 86.52
1986: 91.20	1989: 67.98

Changes in vineyards under production should be taken into account.

Tasting:

M 1983. *The very synthesis of the vintage, especially by its nose: more honey than in a beehive. A sturdy Montrachet. An intense deep yellow, it evokes dried fruit according to some, to others, crystallized fruits. More rich than elegant.*

CM 1983. *By contrast this is more powerful than rich. A charmer? Certainly, with a warmth that increases as it envelops you. A question of individual tastes. We might prefer rather more finesse and personality. Montrachet and Chevalier-Montrachet have the same style and character here.*

BRENOT
Domaine Brenot

◊ *Bâtard-Montrachet* (BM).
Three parcels forming 37 ares 44 centiares and belonging to Domaine Brenot in Santenay for several generations. After the death of Max Brenot in 1977, his son Philippe took over the family business (SCE Domaine Brenot). Apart from these vines in Bâtard-Montrachet, there are others in Santenay (notably in *Premier Cru*), Chassagne and Puligny-Montrachet, and Côte de Beaune-Villages. The vines were planted in Bâtard in 1960, 1971 and 1973. Two-thirds of the wine is sold to merchants and a third to private customers. Domaine Brenot had the parcel of Montrachet belonging to Jean Petitjean (see below) on *métayage* until 1988.

Proprietor:
Domaine Brenot
21590 Santenay
Tel: 80 20 61 27

Production (in hectolitres):
• **BM**

1984: 9.12	1987: 11.40
1985: 11.40	1988: 18.81
1986: 13.68	1989: 17.67

• **M (Petitjean)**
1987: 1.14   1988: 2.28

Best vintage:
1964.

CARILLON
Domaine Carillon Louis et Fils

◊ *Bienvenues-Bâtard-Montrachet* (BBM)

What a splendid dynasty of growers! Prosper Carillon succeeded Louis, Robert Carillon succeeded Prosper, Louis Carillon succeeded Robert. and today Jacques and François Carillon support their father and grandfather. A "small, proud, little family business", wrote Hugh Johnson about the Carillons. Passionately in love with the past, Louis adores the old stones and traditions of his village. His simple and original label reproduces the motif on the lintel of a door preserved in Puligny. As for the lintel of his cellar doors. they have a strange round shape, for they had to be hollowed out a little in order to allow the portly old casks across the threshold.

This is a rake, by contrast, grandfather Carillon relates the history of the area as no one else can. His philosophical approach encompasses both the hardships of former times and the comparative ease of today. Good wine interests him more than money. Discreet and modest, he is a wonderful old grower who has known more hours of toil during his life than hours of leisure, and who has happy memories of them.

More talkative than his father, although trained in the same rigorous school, Louis Carillon "inherited" this parcel of 11 ares 44 centiares in Bienvenues-Bâtard-Montrachet, bought by the family in about 1955 from the Dupaquiers and the Jolys (though they are not quite sure) and replanted in 1971. It completes a fine holding which includes among the *Premiers Crus* of Puligny Combettes, Perrières, Referts, Champ Canet and Champ Gain, the Puligny-Montrachet and Chassagne-Montrachet appellations in both red and white, and the Saint-Aubin and Mercurey appellations in red. The wine is sold to the firm's private clients and to distributors. Louis Carillon is a traditionalist, as you will have gathered.

Three generations and one love of wine: Louis Carillon (centre), son and grandson.

Proprietor:
Domaine Carillon Louis et Fils
Puligny-Montrachet
21190 Meursault
Tel: 80 21 30 34

Production (in hectolitres):

1981: 5.20	1986: 6.30
1982: 8	1987: 5.20
1983: 5.70	1988: 5.70
1984: 5 40	1989: 5.40
1985: 6.30	

Best vintage:
1959.

Tasting:

BBM 1985. *Although somewhat lacking in vigour, this wine with its very fine "Montrachet" colour has lively, floral aromas. It may not have a long life but at the present time it is wonderful. Very supple, it has a dazzling elegance and finesse. One fault: insufficiently marked acidity. However, the panel placed it among the most excellent bottles in this climat.*

CHARTRON
Domaine Jean Chartron

◊ *Chevalier-Montrachet* (CM)

Bought by Edmond Chartron from Domaine Billerey in 1917, this parcel of 96 ares 34 centiares in Chevalier-Montrachet was planted in 1946 and 1947. Jean Chartron, a dynamic personality, was mayor of Puligny-Montrachet, following three generations of mayor-growers in Puligny. The first, Monsieur Dupard, mayor in 1880, added the name of Montrachet to the name of Puligny. He was a cooper and wine-seller. Jean Chartron's father was called Jean-Georges and the present Chartron is Jean-René. Mischievous tongues have it that growers always give their own Christian name to their first male child "in order not to have to change the labels! " Jean-René Chartron runs Domaine Jean Chartron, the family firm of merchants, Dupard Aîné (created in 1860) and the firm of Chartron et Trébuchet (also merchants), not to mention two wine import firms in Germany (where he worked for twenty-five years before coming back to France). All of this is organized and administered perfectly. He married Jeanine from Alsace and they have three children.

Today his ambition would be to have the whole of the Clos de Cailleret (the monopoly of Domaine Chartron) classed as *Grand Cru*: a long-term project! Following the request made in 1955 by the Chartron family, who are the owners of several parcels in Chevalier-Montrachet and Cailleret (incorporated in one or the other of these *climats* in a rather unconvincing way, according to successive Land Register documents) the INAO decided in 1974 after long deliberation to recognize the Chevalier-Montrachet appellation for a parcel in Cailleret. Because the neighbouring parcels belonging to the same proprietor also situated in Cailleret had no soil, they were excluded from any right to an AOC. Very careful about the appearance of the vineyard, Jean Chartron has repaired the walls and doorways round his *cru*. His *domaine's* principal market is abroad (only ten per cent of his production remains in France, but he is hoping to increase this figure by making a special effort with the French market).

He used to spend at least an hour a day in the town hall, then would go back to his office (which has been the family home since the Revolution) to take up his duties as head of the firm and oenologist. The house is constructed over the cellars (there are no underground cellars in Puligny because of the water-table, which is only a few centimetres beneath the surface). He has a very sophisticated laboratory in which he carries out his own analyses and sometimes helps out his colleagues. His young oenologist is an ideal partner: he has great experience with red wines. Jean Chartron looks after the whites. The vineyard of Domaine Chartron is quite independent of these selling activities: 3 hectares in the Clos du Cailleret, one in Pucelles and 2 hectares in Folatières, the only red *Premier Cru* in Puligny.

Jean-René Chartron.

Proprietor:
Domaine Jean Chartron
Puligny-Montrachet
21190 Meursault
Tel: 80 21 32 85

Production (in hectolitres):
1981: 22.26	1986: 36.48
1982: 42.09	1987: 29.07
1983: 28.10	1988: 30.78
1984: 39.30	1989: 43.32
1985: 43.16	

Best vintages:
1947, 1949, 1959, 1967, 1969, 1973, 1974, 1976, 1979, 1983, 1985.

Tasting:

CM 1973. *This Chevalier has brought back from the Crusades pepper and spices. It has lost some of its brilliance, which is to be expected in view of its age. Its persistance in the mouth, stamina and power are proof of an out-standing development. The great richness of the 73 whites! It can never be said often enough: always wait for the Grands Crus of Chassagne and Puligny...*

CHAVY
Anne-Marie Chavy

◇ *Bâtard-Montrachet*
The parcel of 14 ares 11 centiares of Bâtard-Montrachet was inherited by Christian Chavy from his grandfather Albert Chavy. The Chavys are an old Puligny family which is no relation to the Chavys from Chassagne, and only very distantly related to the other Chavys from Puligny. On the death of Christian Chavy in 1982, his wife Anne-Marie and their children took over the business and they have approximately 6 hectares of vines in the following appellations: Puligny *Premier Cru* Referts, Puligny-Montrachet, Bourgogne red, Bourgogne white, Bourgogne Passe Tout Grains and Bourgogne Aligoté. Uprooted in 1985, the vineyard Bâtard was replanted and since 1988 is now producing again.

Madame Chavy's three daughters help in the work. Nathalie, the eldest (21), has studied viticulture and will eventually take over. The other two have other jobs: Valérie in photography and Isabelle in accountancy.

The red grapes and those of Bâtard are sold to the trade. The white grapes are vinified and then sold in wine. The bulk of the marketing is handled by the firm of Bouchard Père et Fils.

Proprietor:
Anne-Marie Chavy
Puligny-Montrachet
21190 Meursault
Tel: 80 21 33 99

CLERC
Domaine Henri Clerc et Fils

◇ *Bâtard-Montrachet* (BM),*Chevalier-Montrachet* (CM), *Bienvenues-Bâtard-Montrachet* (BBM) – The Domaine Henri Clerc, which recently gained a foothold in the Clos de Vougeot, has 18 ares 35 centiares in Bâtard-Montrachet. This parcel which would appear to be quite simple but in fact it is the result of a complicated reorganization of land: one parcel of 14 ares 80 centiares bought in 1903 by Joseph Patriarche on the sale of the estate of Charles Billerey, a proprietor and merchant in Beaune, who in turn had acquired it in 1882 from Henriette Brugniot, a proprietor in Meursault; one parcel of 1 are bought in 1893 from Julien Hondriot, a merchant from Nolay, and exchanged in 1959 for another parcel with the Lancier family from Meursault; and one parcel completing the whole was bought in 1918 from one of the Fontaine daughters of Volnay who had it through her maternal grandfather, Sebastien Gouverney. For the rest, for anyone interested, the 5 ares 10 centiares in Chevalier-Montrachet were the result of a purchase by Joseph Patriarche in 1923, auctioned as a result of distraint in 1908 on land belonging to Madame Gaudet-Desgouilles in Saint-Brice (Seine-et-Oise). As for the 64 ares 46 centiares in Bâtard-Montrachet, it is also the result of a purchase by Joseph Patriarche in 1923, from J.-B. Passerotte-Garnier in Saint-Romain. His father had bought these vines for his son in 1881 on the bankruptcy of Jean-Baptiste Philibert, a wine wholesaler in Saint-Romain. The present vines were planted in 1945 (Bâtard), 1970 and 1985 (Chevalier), 1978 (Bienvenues). Bernard Clerc set up on his own in 1965. Since his father's death, he has worked his parents' vines in return for half the profits, but he has largely increased the size of the family holding, from his father's 6 hectares to 26. His eldest son, Laurent, who is in his twenties, works with him. Bernard Clerc sells half of his harvest in bottle and the other half to the trade. He has a very large cellar which he has had constructed behind the family's home in the heart of Puligny village. This new cellar houses bottles, while the casks are in the cellar under the house. He also has another hectare of cellars in a sand quarry outside the town. Bernard Clerc planted all of the vines of the Domaine by himself. His son is now to take over the running of them. The vines in Bâtard are about 30 years old, those in Bienvenues 11 or 12, those in Chevalier 15 and 3. He also has Puligny *Premier Cru*: Pucelles, Folatières, Combettes and Champ Gain. Ninety per cent of his production goes for export, both *Grands Crus* and wines with regional appellations.

Proprietor:
Domaine Henri Clerc et Fils
Place des Marronniers
Puligny-Montrachet
21190 Meursault
Tel: 80 21 32 74

Production (in hectolitres):
• **BM**

1985: 10.98	1987:	6.8	
1983: 11.10	1988:	9.25	
1986: 10.83	1989:	8.81	

• **CM**

1985:	3.33	1987:	6.47
1983:	9.60	1988:	7.61
1986:	3.35	1989:	7.25

• **BBM**

1985: 38.68	1987:	30.93
1983: 38.68	1988:	32.48
1986: 38.68	1989:	30.94

Best vintages:
1959, 1969, 1973, 1978, 1983.

Tasting:

BM 1985. *It confirms the old precept: see with the nose and drink with the eyes. Nearly yellow, this Bâtard has very intense aromas, rich and varied: honey, linden, ripe fruit. The 85 vintage produced supple wines which will develop rapidly. But their balance will also ensure a long life.*

CM 1985. *Infinitely more delicate than the Bâtard, the Chevalier is superior. It has an average colour but its breeding is unmistakable. Floral and woody, clean and harmonious, a very elegant wine which should wait in the cellar. Although, value should not be calculated by the number of years, improvement will come with ageing.*

Bernard Clerc.

BBM 1985. *Less convincing than the other two: generally rather flaccid. Acidity too discreet and lacking in vigour. Still closed up or over the hill? Its fruitiness is in its favour and preserves its honour.*

COFFINET
Fernand Coffinet

◇ *Bâtard-Montrachet* (BM)
Two parcels in Bâtard with a total surface area of 26 ares 7 centiares. They belonged to Henri Coffinet who died in 1987, when his son Fernand inherited them. Today he runs them and his two daughters have married growers from Chassagne (Coffinet and Michel Morey). The wine is sold both to merchants and to private clients. Apart from Bâtard, this firm has vines in Romanée with the AOC Village white and red, and others.

Proprietor:
Fernand Coffinet
Chassagne-Montrachet
21190 Meursault
Tel: 80 21 31 22

Tasting:

BM 1981. *An 81, often said to be "a year to remember". Clearly young, this one has an agreeable nose of hazel-nut and almond, but already developed. It has what is known in the valley of the Loire* as a "cooked" bouquet. Its aromas are interesting. Its vivacity is just right but its finish is rather too short. We would prefer more body and substance. The impression would doubtless be more favourable with a more recent vintage.

COLIN
Domaine Marc Colin

VINS DE BOURGOGNE

Montrachet

Mis en bouteille à la propriété par
Marc COLIN

◊ *Montrachet* (M)

"A grower who is the very model of modesty and honesty," wrote the *Revue du Vin de France*. Nothing could be more true. Marc Colin and his wife Michèle (from a family of growers in Saint-Aubin) have four children of whom the eldest is soon to take up viticultural studies in Beaune. Marc Colin represents the fourth generation of growers in the family. He has a total of 10 ares 68 cantiares in Montrachet in four parcels, two of 3 ares 56 centiares and two of 1 are 78 centiares in Chassagne. They make up part of the area of Dents de Chien assimilated into Montrachet by the Beaune judgement of 1921. These vines were planted in 1940. Marc Colin does all the work by hand, for his parcel is in the middle of other vines, in the shape of an elongated pear. He sells his harvest in the bottle and is hoping to expand by developing land as soon as his children join him in the business. The other vines stretch out over Saint-Aubin (white *Premier Cru* la Chatenière, red in Village), Chassagne (white *Premiers Crus* Cailleret and Champ Gain, red and white in Village) and Santenay (red in Village).

Proprietor:
Domaine Marc Colin
Gamay, Saint Aubin
21190 Meursault
Tel: 80 21 30 43

Production (in hectolitres):
1981: 2.50	1985: 4.80
1984: 4.60	1983: 4.56
1982: 2.50	1986: 4.80

Best vintages:
1959, 1973, 1983.

Tasting:

M 1983. *A well-made vintage with excellent prospects for the future. We look forward to drinking it in the year 2000. Its aromas combine honey and vanilla against a subtle background of bitter almond. Its very power-ful structure overshadows the bouquet, but ageing will rectify this.*

Marc Colin.

DANCER ET COURLET DE VREGILLE

◊ *Chevalier-Montrachet*

These two parcels of 9 ares 66 centiares (19 ares 32 centiares all told) are the result of the Lochardet inheritance in Chassagne-Montrachet. They are worked together by Charles Bonnefoy on *métayage* (see above). The harvest is sold in grapes to the firm of Louis Jadot in Beaune. These vines were planted in 1958. Armand Dancer is a veterinary surgeon practising in the region of Mulhouse. Hervé Courlet de Vrégille lives in Dijon. They are respectively the godson and son-in-law of Armand Lochardet who, after making his career in public service, retired to Chassagne-Montrachet.

Proprietors:	Manager:
• Armand Dancer in Meursault • Hervé Courlet de Vrégille in Dijon	Charles Bonnefoy Chassagne-Montrachet 21190 Meursault Tel: 80 21 30 89

DELAGRANGE-BACHELET
Domaine Delagrange-Bachelet

◊ *Montrachet* (M), *Bâtard-Montrachet* (BM)

Edmond Delagrange-Bachelet is sometimes known as Prosper. "That is what they called me during my National Service and it stuck with me," he explains. "It was also my father's Christian name. But I prefer Edmond." He is the father-in-law of Jacques Gagnard-Delagrange and grandfather of Laurence Fontaine-Gagnard and Claudine Blain-Gagnard, all growers in Chassagne (see separate entries) – and I think, with his eighty years, grandfather of the whole village. Pierre Ramonet, who is almost the same age, is of a more retiring nature, while Edmond Delagrange is more gregarious. But it takes all sorts to make a world, and to make Montrachet too. Well-respected in both villages, Edmond Delagrange is president of the "Commission of Five", in charge of setting the yields of the *Grands Crus*. He retains the usufruct of 7 ares 80 centiares of Montrachet in Chassagne bought in 1978 from the Fleurot family, today the property of Laurence Fontaine-Gagnard. He also owns 15 ares in Bâtard-Montrachet bought from the Paquelin-Billard family in 1952.

With a wealth of stories to tell, Edmond Delagrange has lived for fifty years alongside the vines in Chassagne. His photograph has appeared in *L'Express*, in a Japanese newspaper, and a number of others. He regards this philosophically: "Life has not always been easy. In 1935, for example, I remember old Rossigneux who used to come and buy our wine. It was in new casks and a *tonneau* cost 100 francs. I wanted 315 francs. He stuck at 310. I said no deal. Why not 312.50? He refused. I sent him about his business and sat down at table. Suddenly, there was old Rossigneux again in the courtyard. He had come back to see if I had changed my mind. We argued interminably about the 2 francs 50 centimes. To give you an idea of what that represented, I bought a Citroën light 11 on December 31, 1938. It cost me 24,900 francs. That tells you what wine cost and how much we sold it for... It was my father-in-law who taught me about wine," he told me. "He knew it inside out... I was in Volnay and knew nothing about whites." He who does not find food for thought in all this will never understand Burgundy.

Proprietor:
Domaine Delagrange-Bachelet
Chassagne-Montrachet
21190 Meursault
Tel: 80 21 32 67

Production (in hectolitres):

• **M**

1985: 4.56	1987: 3.12
1983: 3.70	1988: 4.03
1986: 4.56	1989: 3.12

• **BM**

1984: 6.56	1987: 5.65
1985: 8.32	1988: 8.26
1986: 8.28	1989: 5.65

These vineyards increased from 11 ares 10 centiares to 14 ares 13 centiares from 1982.

Edmond Delagrange, one of Montrachet's patriarchs.

tractive nose of almond and fresh
lemon. This typical 82 Montrachet
has fruit and just what is needed
to give finesse. Its acidity does

not disturb the mellowness in the
mouth and it is sufficiently long.
In a word, it approaches the very
best.

DELEGER
Domaine Georges Deléger

◇ *Chevalier-Montrachet* (CM)

A parcel of 15 ares 95 centiares bought in 1936 by Edmond Deléger, grandfather of the present proprietor. Half Georges Deléger's vines in Chevalier were replanted in 1961 and the other half in 1977. In the winter of 1960-1961 he remembers having to make 22 holes in the rock with a miner's pick in order to be able to replant. In 1977 he was relieved to find that the work could be done by machine. Here the land changes without any transition from Chevalier to Montrachet, for there is no longer any wall.

From his large terrace, Georges Deléger can look at the houses of his two daughters, Bernadette Colin-Deléger (37) and Martine Anglada (35); Bernadette runs her own vineyards in Chassagne with her husband. In 1987 Georges gave all his red vines to his son-in-law on *métayage*. The vines extend over 4 hectares 30 ares (5 hectares if fully planted). Management and marketing are done by himself and his wife. He sells 90% of his wine to the United States; the Chevalier now passes through the door which Edouard Deléger opened in 1945 with Pierre Ramonet. The firms of Seagram and Robert Haas are faithful clients.

Proprietor:
Domaine Georges Deléger
Chassagne-Montrachet
21190 Meursault
Tel: 80 21 32 56

Production (in hectolitres):
1982: 9.69	1986: 9.56
1983: 7.95	1987: 7.65
1984: 7.66	1988: 7.58
1985: 10.26	1989: 7.65

In 1980 and 1981: 7 ares 15 centiares. From 1982: 15 ares 95 centiares.

Best vintage:
1978.

Tasting: 🥄 🥄 🥄

CM 1970. *With a colour still very young for a wine which was eighteen years old in 1987, this Chevalier has all the freshness of young wines while having the strength of character of good old ones. Its pure, clear aromas are lingering and powerful: an explosion in the mouth. To be able to*

taste a 70 is rare nowadays. We hope you may enjoy this pleasure.

DELEGER
Robert Deléger

◇ *Chevalier-Montrachet* (CM)

This parcel of 15 ares 95 centiares in Chevalier Montrachet comes from the property which Robert Deléger inherited from his father. The latter had bought these vines from the Villan family, who in turn had acquired them from the firm of Beuvrand de Poligny. The vines were replanted in 1980. Robert Deléger, a grower in Merceuil near Beaune which is by the way (the native village of Paul Masson, one of the founders of the Californian vineyards), is the brother of Georges Deléger (see above). His vines stretch over Chassagne-Montrachet and Saint-Aubin. He sells all his harvest in grapes to the firm of Louis Jadot (see below).

Proprietor:	Best vintages:
Robert Deléger	1961, 1969, 1970, 1971, 1973,
Merceuil	1976, 1979, 1982, 1985.
21190 Meursault	
Tel: 80 21 47 24	

DROUHIN
Maison et Domaine Joseph Drouhin

◊ *Bâtard-Montrachet* (BM)

A parcel of 9 ares 35 centiares bought from the Fleurot family in Santenay in December 1981 (see below). The vines were planted in 1946. For the firm Maison et Domaine Joseph Drouhin, see the section on Marquis Philibert de Laguiche.

Proprietor:
Maison Joseph Drouhin
7 rue d'Enfer
BP 29, 21202 Beaune Cedex
Tel: 80 24 68 88

Production (in hectolitres):

1982: 5	1986: 5
1983: 3	1987: 3
1984: 3	1988: 3.5
1985: 4	1989: 4

Best vintages:
1983, 1985.

Tasting:

BM 1984. *On certain fine summer evenings on the hill of Vézelay the light has this colour, and almost the same perfume of honey lingers in the air. An inspired wine, more Chevalier than Bâ-*

tard. But Robert Drouhin, whom we wish the same success in his new vineyard in Oregon (he is planting pinot there), invariably repeats: "A great Burgundy must above all be elegant."

FLEUROT
Domaine René Fleurot

◊ *Montrachet* (M), *Bâtard-Montrachet* (BM)

René Fleurot has a parcel of 8 ares 33 centiares in Montrachet. At the same time he looks after the parcel of his sister, Jacqueline Gaye (8 ares 21 centiares) of which he is tenant-farmer, as he is also for two parcels in Bâtard-Montrachet belonging to Jacqueline and his other sister, Marie-Claude Graindorge (4 ares 30 centiares and 4 ares 35 centiares respectively). Splitting up among the family has whittled down the size of the holding, which used to be larger in Montrachet: 15 ares 64 centiares sold to the Delagrange-Bachelet family (see above); and in Bâtard-Montrachet: 9 ares 45 centiares, sold to the firm of Joseph Drouhin (see above).

When he took on the family firm in 1966, René Fleurot gave it his name. Before that it was Domaine Fleurot-Larose, created in the nineteenth century in Santenay by Claude Fleurot, the husband of one of the Larose daughters. Hence the rose which features on the firm's crest. Claude's son Auguste succeeded him on his death in 1923, and himself died in 1935 at the age of 59. He left a large family behind him. His wife courageously took on both the vines and the merchant business. The latter no longer exists.

It was Claude Fleurot who, having first moved into the Château de Santenay-le-Haut, in 1921 bought the Château du Passe Temps, an attractive name which would make a good title for a novel. The name which is almost Bordeaux-sounding – is there not a Château Chasse-Spleen? Passe Temps is a little locality mentioned by Doctor Jules Lavalle in 1855, a (red) vineyard on which René Fleurot has the monopoly. Constructed in 1855, the house was for many years the property of the Duvault-Blochet family, and its cellars at one time housed the wine of La Romanée-Conti. It had belonged to Jules

The cellars of Château du Passe Temps in Santenay built on two levels.

Ouvrard, then to Paul Guillemot from Dijon, who resold it to the Duvault-Blochets from Santenay. And the cellars? They are really more of an enormous underground palace. "There are two levels underground, very spacious indeed, which form four cellars," René Fleurot told me as he led me down. "We can house all we need here." And indeed, these colossal cellars, which are absolutely dry, could be classed as a historic monument. Moss has woven its patterns over the old stones. As keen as his father on old vintages, René Fleurot religiously preserves, under their soft cover of dust, cobwebs and moss, standard size bottles, magnums, jeroboams, mathuselems and salmanazars which bear witness to the whole of Montrachet's history since the beginning of the century. The oldest go back to 1918. There are 1919s, 1928s and 1929s... "The 18s are still remarkable," says René Fleurot. "At a tasting of the Impitoyables in 1985 we opened one. It still had its original cork. Unfortunately it fell into the bottle and the waiter, acting for the best, served it in a carafe. You could not hold it against him, but it was a mistake. The wine oxidized at once. It lost everything. The impression would have been very different if the wine had been served from the bottle. However, the 28 was perfect and Vincent Leflaive, who is an expert, gave it ten out of ten." There were 8 vintages at this tasting of Domaine Fleurot (1983, 1976, 1974, 1971, 1967, 1928, 1926 and 1918): "unanimous and entirely justified compliments", wrote Jean Clerc in *Le Bien public* (December 14, 1985).

The Montrachet was bought on November 24, 1918 from Charles Drapier, a proprietor and merchant in Puligny. The Drapier family had bought it in 1870 from the family of the Marquis de Courtivron. There were 97 ares 70 centiares of vines divided into two by the 1918 purchasers, each paying 16,250 francs – Auguste Fleurot in Santenay and Comte Jules Lafon in Meursault for his sons Pierre and Henri, both in the army. The asking price was 30,000 francs, but the vines finally sold for 32,500 francs, that is rather more than 100,000 of today's francs. But another proprietor from Santenay, Léon Roizot, decided to make a higher bid for the Montrachet, as he was perfectly entitled to do. The notary explained that there would have to be a second séance for the sale and that it would perhaps be a better move to divide the vines into three, the Fleuron and Lafon families each handing over a third of their parcels. This is what happened on October 23, 1919. Discounting the walls, the vines now cover only 95 ares 28 centiares of which 30 ares 92 centiares belong to the Fleurot family. Assisted by his son Auguste, Claude Fleurot had expanded this business considerably. "My father did advanced business studies in 1906," tells René Fleurot. "He was a student in Paris with Paul Reynaud. He had travelled a lot. He was a very energetic man, president of the Old Students Association of the Hautes Etudes Commerciales, in charge of the Burgundy and Franche-Comté Football League, and so on. He died in 1935, just when the AOCs were being established. Moreover he was against them. He used to say "Wine is tasted in the cup." The English thought likewise until they entered the Common Market. He had grasped the inconveniences of the AOCs: "The right to an appellation is not a guarantee of quality. People sometimes rely on a right. And that is not to mention 'paper smuggling'*(trafic du papier):* just buying or selling the appellation without considering the wine..."

With the assistance of his son Nicolas, René Fleurot runs 11 hectares of vines of which he is owner or tenant-farmer: apart from the Montrachet and Bâtard-Montrachet, Roquemaure is an excellent Chassagne *Premier Cru* (monopoly), Abbaye de Morgeot, still in Chassagne (red and white), and Clos du Passetemps in Santenay (red). Contrary to what Hugh Johnson mistakenly wrote in his latest book, Domaine René Fleurot has no financial ties with the merchant firm of Prosper Maufoux in Santenay and has no vines in Pouilly-sur-Loire.

Proprietor:
Domaine René Fleurot
Château du Passe Temps
21590 Santenay
Tel: 80 20 61 15
Also in charge of the properties of Jacqueline Gaye of Brussels and Marie-Claude Graindorge of Saint-Mandé.

Production (in hectolitres):
• **M**

1981: 4.56	1984: 6.60
1982: 9.17	1985: 8.13
1983: 7.98	1986: 8.26

• **BM**

1981: 4.56	1984: 3.62
1982: 4.86	1985: 4.48
1983: 4.52	1986: 4.28

Best vintages (Montrachet):
1962, 1969, 1971, 1974, 1976, 1978, 1979, 1982, 1983, 1985.

Tasting:

M 1983. *A fine appearance, a wine which, said one member of our panel, speaks to an adult as a child would. It is probably a wine to leave for a long time in the cellar. Rather disappointing today, it will perhaps develop. Acidity is pronounced, insufficiently mellow, structure more square than round. A thrilling nose: white flowers and fresh foliage, then a hint of mineral and spices, almost grassy on the second inhalation. In short, this wine has its own character.*

BM 1983. *If I am to believe a wonderful connoisseur of this climat, there should always be a hint of the aggressive in Bâtard. This one has not yet sown its wild oats but what virility! It is with such children, the fruits of love, that a race is preserved. A restrained nose with hints of vanilla and honey. It will open up. Long in the mouth, mellow, rich, with a general harmony making an admirable bottle. For long keeping of course.*

FONTAINE-GAGNARD
Domaine Fontaine-Gagnard

◊ *Bâtard-Montrachet* (BM), *Criots-Bâtard-Montrachet* (CBM)
The daughter of Jacques Gagnard-Delagrange and granddaughter of Edmond Delagrange-Bachelet, Laurence Fontaine-Gagnard is the sister of Claudine Blain-Gagnard. With each generation of this family the wife always brings along the vines and her name. Laurence and Claudine are extraordinarily devoted to their grandfather who, it must be said, deserves such veneration. This dynasty makes excellent wine! Laurence Gagnard began by selling wine under her maiden name. Then she married a member of the air

force whom fate had landed in Beaune. This is how Domaine Fontaine-Gagnard was born in 1985. Laurence Fontaine-Gagnard has the ownership without usufruct of 7 ares 80 centiares in Montrachet in Chassagne, bought in 1978 from Madame Graindorge-Fleurot (the former Fleurot-Larose property). Her grandfather retains the usufruct. She has 30 ares 27 centiares in Bâtard-Montrachet and 33 ares 13 centiares in Criots-Bâtard-Montrachet, a gift from her Delagrange-Bachelet grandparents in 1978-1979. The wine is sold "by the bottle" and to merchants. The vines stretch out over Chassagne (red *Premier Cru* Morgeot, white *Premiers Crus* Morgeot, Maltroie, Vergers and Cailleret), Volnay (*Premier Cru* Clos des Chênes) and Pommard (*Premier Cru* Rugiens).

Proprietor:
Domaine Fontaine-Gagnard
Chassagne-Montrachet
21190 Meursault
Tel: 80 21 35 01 and 80 21 35 50

Production (in hectolitres):
• **BM**

1982: 20.89	1986: 13.11
1983: 15.43	1987: 10.54
1984: 12.82	1988: 15.83
1985: 13.10	1989: 14.82

Vineyards under production have fallen from 30 ares (up to 1984) to 22 ares since 1985.
• **CBM**

1982: 22.80	1986: 18.81
1983: 14.82	1987: 15.10
1984: 12.54	1988: 17.26
1985: 19.65	1989: 16.24

Vineyards under production have increased from 20 ares (up to 1981) to 33 ares from 1982.

Tasting:

BM 1985. *Attractive and clear, its aromas seem to combine the floral and the fruity. Behind the oak of the new casks, very pronounced, we believe we detect honey and vanilla, fern and green apples. But there is a lack of substance in the mouth despite its mellowness and an honourable finish. A true 85.*

CBM 1985. *Here is a young marquis in a suit of gold silk who will break every heart. Long life is ensured, at least for some years to come. Perfectly perfumed, it would seem born for a Grand Siècle dance floor. Density is not its strong suit, but what grace! There is not much acidity. But in Versailles, Saint-Simon and Bossuet were not judges of elegance.*

Laurence and Claudine, Jacques Gagnard-Delagrange's two daughters with Claudine's husband.

GAGNARD
Domaine Jean-Noël Gagnard

◊ *Bâtard-Montrachet* (BM)

The *domaine* of Jean-Noël Gagnard, grower in Chassagne, perfectly illustrates the many charms of the wines of the area. For we find the *climats* Morgeot *Premier Cru* (red and white), Cailleret *Premier Cru* (white), other white *Premiers Crus*, La Maltroie *Premier Cru* (red), Clos Saint-Jean *Premier Cru* (red), appellation Village (white and red) as well as a *Premier Cru* from Santenay, Clos de Tavannes.

At the head of this list is Bâtard-Montrachet. Jean-Noël Gagnard has 36 ares 40 centiares (of which a small area is taken by a little house used as a shelter among the vines). He received this parcel as a result of the division, registered by deed of gift, by the

Gagnard-Coffinet parents to their three children on May 24, 1960. Née Renée Coffinet, Madame Gagnard has a parcel of 52 ares 15 centiares inherited from her father Gabriel Coffinet-Lelarge who died in 1937. He had received it in 1914 following the death of his mother Marie Paquelin, the widow of Fernand Coffinet-Paquelin. The latter had acquired a parcel of 96 ares 50 centiares in Bâtard on November 13, 1892 for the sum of 10,000 francs. The acquisition was made at a public auction organized in the town hall at Chassagne. The notary conducting the auction was acting on the orders of Madame Moyne and Pierre Neuzillet her brother, the heirs of their paternal uncle Pierre Neuzillet-Gathey living in Virey (Saône-et-Loire). This catalogue of land ownership shows how over one century a parcel of nearly one hectare has been gradually divided up, although remaining in the same family of growers in Chassagne. The vines here were planted in 1962 (15 ares 55 centiares) and in 1972 (20 ares 52 centiares). Three-quarters of the wine is sold to the grower's private clients and the rest goes to the trade. Jean-Noël Gagnard is on the Commission of Five in charge of deciding the yields for the *Grands Crus*. "This producer's Bâtard-Montrachet has opened my eyes to Burgundy whites," confesses Serena Sutcliffe with her eyes lowered as if she had committed a sin. "I shall always be grateful to it."

Proprietor:
Domaine Jean-Noël Gagnard
Chassagne-Montrachet
21190 Meursault
Tel: 80 21 31 68

Production (in hectolitres):
1981: 13.68   1984: 11.40
1982: 25.96   1985: 15.96
1983: 18.24   1986: 18.24

Best vintages:
1955, 1969, 1979, 1983, 1985.

Tasting:

BM 1979. *Attractive to the eye although rather pale, this wine lacks character and appears to be suffering from slight oxidation. It seems younger in the mouth than its nose would suggest. Three or four years earlier, this Bâtard would doubtless have inspired very favourable comments. We should congratulate the grower for preserving already venerable vintages, for 79 was a great year though its wines will not all keep well.*

GAGNARD-DELAGRANGE
Domaine Gagnard-Delagrange

◊ *Montrachet* (M), *Bâtard-Montrachet* (BM)
Jacques Gagnard has chosen to give his daughters the vines they manage in Bâtard-Montrachet, firstly to mitigate death duties and secondly to allow them to manage their vines as best they think fit. Monsieur and Madame Gagnard are both growers and have vines in other appellations which they have both received as inheritances. They are even distantly related. On the deeds of sale of the Montrachet, the term Grand-Montrachet appears, indicating the Montrachet of today, which was confused with Bâtard-Montrachet before the creation of the AOCs.

The son-in-law of Edmond Delagrange-Bachelet and father of Laurence Fontaine-Gagnard and Claudine Blain-Gagnard (see above), Jacques Gagnard has the usufruct of 7 ares 83 centiares in Montrachet (owned without usufruct by Domaine Blain-Gagnard) and is owner of 26 ares 53 centiares in Bâtard-Montrachet. These vines, in Chassagne in Montrachet were bought in 1978 from the Fleurot family. The parcels in Bâtard-Montrachet come from a gift from Gagnard-Coffinet in 1960 (16 ares 23 centiares) and a purchase from the Barbot-Monnot family in 1969 (10 ares 30 centiares). All these vines are located in Chassagne. The vines in Bâtard were planted in 1971 and 1983 and also extend here over the *Premiers Crus* Clos Saint-Jean and Morgeot in red, Boudriotte and Morgeot in white, and Volnay (*Premier Cru* Champans).

Jacques Gagnard is increasingly marketing his wine in the bottle and always sells a proportion to wholesale suppliers.

Proprietor:
Domaine Gagnard-Delagrange
Chassagne-Montrachet
21190 Meursault
Tel: 80 21 31 40

Production (in hectolitres):
- **M**

1984:	2.56	1987:	3.65
1985:	4.69	1988:	3.94
1986:	4.56	1989:	3.75

- **BM**

1984:	4.84	1987:	12.83
1985:	6.18	1988:	13.37
1986:	15.39	1989:	12.73

Production started in 1986 of a parcel uprooted in 1982.

Best vintages:
1964, 1969, 1971, 1976, 1979, 1981, 1983, 1985.

Tasting:

M 1979. *A perfect 79 at the peak of its development. Bright to the eye, with aromas of vervain or vanilla approaching those of white truffle (to be found in the village!). This astounding Montrachet was praised time and time again: "Very good indeed." It deserves a place on a roll of honour.*

BM 1982. *Its richness does not melt sufficiently in the mouth. Its principal qualities are its vegetal aromas, fruity flavour and sturdy structure. By contrast, the attack remains rather dry and the alcohol should be more discreet.*

HOSPICES DE BEAUNE

◇ *Bâtard-Montrachet* (BM)
Much coveted, the Gailliot plot of 29 ares 7 centiares was acquired at the end of 1989 by the Hospices de Beaune, who wanted to extend their holdings of great white burgundies. Replanted in 1976, the vines belonged to Jean Gailliot, who in 1949 took over the family *domaine* and installed himself at Corpeau. His wine was sold to the firm of merchants-vintners Olivier Leflaive. Through the intermediary of the Société d'aménagement foncier of Burgundy, the Hospices de Beaune effected an exchange, disposing of nearly 2 hectares of Beaune *Premier Cru* to pay the 600.000 francs per *ouvrée* (approximately 12 million francs per hectare) for these vines. The cultivation has been entrusted to two vignerons, MM. Gossot and Milliard, in order to distribute the incomes of the "piece-workers" in the fairest possible way. This "cuvée" will probably be called "Dame de Flandre". The label presented here is an example supplied courtesy of the Hospices.

Proprietor:
Centre hospitalier
Avenue Guigone de Salins
21203 Beaune cedex
Tel: 80 24 45 00

JACQUIN
Madame Henri Jacquin

◇ *Bâtard-Montrachet* (BM)
This parcel of 32 ares 23 centiares of vines in Bâtard-Montrachet belongs to a *domaine* created by Henri Moroni and his wife between the wars and then completed by their daughter and their son-in-law Henri Jacquin. Since 1982 they have been run by Jacqueline Jomain, whose husband, Marc Jomain, is a merchant-vintner in Puligny-Montrachet. The vineyards also stretch into Referts, Combettes, Pucelles and Perrières (Puligny-Montrachet). The vines in Bâtard were planted in 1950. The wine is sold partly to merchants and partly to the firm's private clients.

Proprietor:	Tenant-farmer:	Production (in hectolitres):
Madame Henri Jacquin	Madame Jacqueline Jomain	1984: 15.45 1986: 19.20
Puligny-Montrachet	BP 3, Puligny-Montrachet	1985: 14.12 1987: 14.80
21190 Meursault	21190 Meursault	
	Tel: 80 21 30 48	Best vintage:
		1985.

JADOT
Domaine et Maison Louis Jadot

◊ *Chevalier-Montrachet* (CM)

A parcel of 52 ares situated in Cailleret and included in Chevalier-Montrachet in 1939 by the National Committee of the INAO, following the request of Louis Jadot who was acting in concert with Louis Latour, the owner of a neighbouring parcel. With Joseph Leflaive at their head, the growers of Puligny tried to block this classification, which was nevertheless allowed, after long discussion and much reflection. This vineyard came from the estate of Léonce Bocquet, a proprietor and merchant in Savigny-lès-Beaune, who was responsible for restoring the Château at Clos de Vougeot. When Louis Jadot and Louis Latour bought the vines in 1913, they were described as being "in Chevalier-Montrachet or in Cailleret". The publicity concerning the sale mentioned "in Chevalier-Montrachet" (*Le Bien public,* Dijon, September 22, 26 and 30, 1913). "So we have paid for the name," stated the two purchasers in 1938 in pleading their case. They explained that Léonce Bocquet had bought these vines under the same name as had Madame Leleu and Mademoiselle Coirier, the Moreau-Guillemot heirs, in May 1887. The deed of gift dated 1874 bears the words "in Chevalier-Montrachet". In 1857, there were two parcels, one in Montrachet and the other in Cailleret. The Moreau-Guillemot family had bought the Montrachet parcel in 1846 from two sisters in Beaune, Adèle and Julie Voillot, daughters of General Voillot, who had owned it under the name of Chevalier-Montrachet since the 1820s. Louis Jadot was the Moreau-Guillemots' son-in-law.

Without having formally received the right to do so, Louis Jadot and Louis Latour had adopted the habit of putting "Les Demoiselles" under the words Chevalier-Montrachet, "so renewing a tradition going back to the time when the vines were owned by Adèle and Julie Voillot, before 1846." No one could confirm or deny this assertion, which had the distinct commercial advantage of identifying the *climat* with Chevalier-Montrachet, even if historically these parcels were linked just as much to the neighbouring Cailleret.

The vines were planted in 1955. Marketing is assured of course through the firm of Louis Jadot, whose founder in the eighteenth century was a Belgian linen merchant who had come to Burgundy. As was often the case formerly, he also bought wines to sell in his own country. He became the owner of vines in the Côte by marriage. In the middle of the last century (1859), the Jadots adopted the profession of wine merchant. This widely respected firm now markets 50,000 hectolitres of wine annually throughout the world.

On Louis Jadot's death in 1962, André Gagey took over the management. Highly respected and a man whose opinions are carefully heeded, André Gagey has assumed a number of important positions in the vineyards of both Burgundy and the rest of France. He sits on the INAO national tribunal. He entered the firm in 1945 as assistant to Louis Jadot, who set him to all the different jobs within the firm, in order to teach him not only about wine but also about the men who work with it. André Gagey comes from Nuits-Saint-Georges and Vosne. He knows vines, for he has some (through his mother) which are run separately from those of Domaine Louis Jadot. The firm's offices are in the Jadot family house, which dates from the beginning of the century and is a perfect example of how to combine ancient and modern together with considerable finesse and intelligence. André Gagey's son, Pierre-Henri, has followed his father into the firm and has now worked with the Maison Jadot for a few years. Since 1984 the firm has had American shareholders linked to the excellent American firm of fine wine distributors, the Kobrand Corporation.

In the 1930s Louis Jadot enlarged his vineyards from 6 to 12 hectares (half in *Grands Crus*, half in *Premiers Crus*: Chambertin-Clos de Bèze, Clos de Vougeot). Today they cover 17 hectares, having grown with the addition of the Domaine Clair Daü. Apart from its own wines, vinified and aged in its cellars in Beaune, the firm of Louis Jadot vinifies and bottles almost all the great wines it markets. That has been the case for all the *Grands Crus* and white *Premiers Crus* since 1978. A new vat-house links tradition (wooden vats) with technological progress (vats with automatic punching of the cap). There are more than 4,000 oak casks in the cellars. An agreement was concluded a few years ago with the Domaine du Duc de Magenta in Chassagne-Montrachet, and Louis Jadot is now selling three of their wines under the label "Duc de Magenta, aged and bottled by Maison Louis Jadot". Traditionally orientated towards the international (mainly American) market, this firm is turning more towards a French clientèle, especially high-class restaurants.

André Gagey, a native of Burgundy and a remarkable taster.

Proprietor:
Domaine et Maison Louis Jadot
5, rue Samuel-Legay
21200 Beaune
Tel: 80 22 10 57

Production (in hectolitres):
1982: 21.66	1986: 21.66
1983: 13.68	1987: 13.68
1984: 15.96	1988: 21 66
1985: 17.10	1989: 18.24

Best vintages:
1962, 1966, 1971, 1973, 1979, 1982, 1983, 1985.

Tasting:

CM 1983. *This Chevalier has certainly not taken a vow of poverty. Open, half-fruit, half-flower, its aromas approach perfection. Rich and generous, it calls for foie gras.*

JOUARD
Gabriel Jouard

◊ *Bâtard-Montrachet* (BM)
This is the smallest parcel in Bâtard-Montrachet, covering 3 ares 70 centiares. As with part of Pierre Jouard's vines (see below) in this *Grand Cru*, it has been in the family a long time. Gabriel Jouard received it from his father Paul Jouard some thirty years ago. The vines extend over Chassagne-Montrachet and Santenay. The wine is generally sold to the trade.

Proprietor:
Gabriel Jouard
Chassagne-Montrachet
21190 Meursault
Tel: 80 21 30 30

Production:
Between 114 litres (one *feuillette)* and 228 litres (one *pièce)* per year.

Best vintage:
1947.

JOUARD
Domaine Pierre Jouard

◊ *Bâtard-Montrachet* (BM)

A parcel of 12 ares 70 centiares in Bâtard-Montrachet belonging for a very long time to this family: Pierre Jouard's parents and grandparents also owned it. The vines are old and the date of planting is not known. The wine is sold entirely to merchants This *domaine has Premiers Crus* in Chassagne: Clos Saint-Jean, Morgeot and Les Meix Goudard (reds); La Truffière, Chenevottes, Champs Gain, Morgeot and Maltroie (whites).

Proprietor: Domaine Pierre Jouard Chassagne-Montrachet 21190 Meursault Tel: 80 21 30 25	**Best vintage:** 1976.

LAFON
Domaine des Comtes Lafon

◊ *Montrachet* (M)

This domaine has been associated with the vines of Meursault and the wine of Burgundy for a century. Dominique and Bruno, both in their early thirties, have just taken over the administration. The first studied viticulture, the second management. They are determined to uphold the firm's formidable honour and reputation. Born in 1864 in Valence-d'Agen (Tarn-et-Garonne), Jules Lafon became a tax inspector in Dijon, where he was in charge of the registration of mortgages. In Meursault in 1867 he married Marie Boch. She was the only daughter of a family of the *cru* who owned vines in Santenots and Champans (Volnay), Gouttes d'Or, Charmes and Genevrières (Meursault) as well as Clos de la Barre. The present dwelling of the Comtes Lafon, constructed in 1869, and "Les Herbeux", the neighbouring property of the Prieur family (see below), were formerly one property, enhanced by magnificent trees. Here life is lived in a tranquil patrician manner, reminiscent of the southern states of America. Jules Lafon was an intransigent Roman Catholic. When Church and State separated, the authorities wanted him to go against his religion. It was the time of the Inventories when the State tried to force the doors of the Churches in order to catalogue their wealth. Jules Lafon resigned his post, unwilling to act against his conscience. The Holy Father showed his gratitude by raising him to the rank of Pontifical Count. He became a lawyer on the Boulevard Sévigné in Dijon, and played a very active role in the debates which enlivened Montrachet in the 1920s and 1930s.

Anxious that his Meursault *domaine* should flourish, he went to the Drapier auction on November 24, 1918. This was for the sale of nearly one hectare of Montrachet in Chassagne, the property of Charles Drapier, a grower and merchant in Puligny. The Drapier family had bought it in 1870 from the family of the Marquis de Courtivron. There were 97 ares 70 centiares of vines divided into two by the 1918 purchasers, each paying 16,250 francs – Auguste Fleurot in Santenay and Comte Jules Lafon in Meursault for his sons Pierre and Henri, then serving in the army. The asking price was 30,000 francs but the vines finally sold for 32,500 francs. As was of course his right, Léon Roizot decided to make a higher offer for the Montrachet. This would have entailed a new meeting for the sale and the purchasers thought it a better move to come to an agreement amongst themselves and divide the Montrachet into three equal parts. "I only want a small bit of Montrachet so as to have the complete range of whites," replied Comte Lafon as he accepted. Auguste Fleurot did the same and this is how the Drapier parcel was divided into three parts – Lafon/Fleurot/Roizot – on October 23, 1919. After discounting the walls, there are only 95 ares 28 centiares of vines, of which 30 ares 92 centiares belong to the Lafon family. Comte Lafon was to become one of the most flamboyant personalities of vine-growing Burgundy. In particular, he was in at the origin of the famous *Paulée de Meursault*, the last of the November *Trois Glorieuses* festivities. Comte Lafon died in Meursault in January 1940. Of his two sons, Pierre died in 1944, and Henri did not have any children and wanted to sell in 1946. His nephew René, Pierre's son, fought vigorously for ten years to avoid this sad fate. René, Comte Jules Lafon's grandson, did not receive his education at the prestigious Ecole Centrale like his father, but at another distinguished school. He had a brother Jacques, a sister Marie-Thérèse and four children. At all costs he wanted to prevent the disappearance of his grandfather's creation. In 1956 he managed to take on the Domaine, which was turned into a limited company. Altogether the vineyards covered nearly 13 hectares: Montrachet, of course (30 ares 92 centiares), but in addition, 1 hectares 71 centiares in Charmes in Meursault, 55 ares 55 centiares in Genevrières, 76 ares 81 centiares in Perrières, 39 ares 28 centiares in Gouttes d'Or and the monopoly of the Clos de la Barre over 2 hectares in Meursault-Village. So much for the whites. To this, the reds add 3 hectares 75 centiares in Volnay-Santenots, 52 ares in Champans, 38 ares 52 centiares in Clos des Chênes and one hectare in Monthélie.

All these vines were on *métayage* for half the yield. "When I took on the Domaine in 1956, I did not have the right to any loans," says Count René Lafon."For several years the wine was sold entirely to merchants without a single bottle under our name. Then we gradually got back on our feet again, invested and sold part of the production direct. And since 1961 we have given our label a new lease of life." The Domaine has been successively called "Lafon", then "Lafon et ses Enfants" and finally "Domaine des comtes Lafon". The new generation took up the torch a few years ago and gradually the vines on *métayage* will be run by Dominique and Bruno Lafon: 4 hectares 50 centiares since 1987 with nearly another hectare being replanted, and the rest over successive years. The Montrachet? Planted in 1953, it is on *métayage* to Pierre Morey. "He works very well," says René Lafon, "and we have entrusted him with a lot of vines. He could not lose everything overnight. As far as Montrachet goes, our contract with him lasts until 1994." Pierre Morey also has the vines of Maxence Poirier on *métayage* (see below) in Bâtard-Montrachet. There is likely to be a limited company owning the land of Domaine des comtes Lafon and another to look after the administration. This is a fine example, for this *domaine* could so easily have disappeared. Holding true to one's beliefs counts for everything in life... and for nearly everything in wine.

Proprietor:
Domaine des comtes Lafon
Clos de la Barre
21190 Meursault
Tel: 80 21 22 17

Métayer:
Pierre Morey
9, rue Comte-Lafon
21190 Meursault
Tel: 80 21 21 03

Bruno and Dominique Lafon in their cellars at Meursault.

Production (in hectolitres):	
1981: 2.85	1986: 4.76
1982: 9.12	1987: 3.44
1983: 2.85	1988: 5.10
1984: 3.42	1989: 5.70
1985: 4.56	

Best vintages:
1966, 1974, 1979, 1982, 1985.

Tasting:

M 1982. *Agreeable and well struc-tured, this 82 is holding itself in* *reserve. This vintage has not yet reached its peak. When it opens out, it will be like the awakening of China.*

LAGUICHE
Marquis Philibert et Jean de Laguiche

◊ *Montrachet* (M)

The firm of Joseph Drouhin is blessed with a peculiarly inappropriate address in Beaune (rue d'Enfer – Hell Street). For indeed this parcel of Montrachet is more evocative to wine lovers than the Garden of Eden or the Promised Land. It seems created for eternal harvests of divine nectar. Situated in Puligny, these vines covering 2 hectares 6 ares 25 centiares in one stretch represent the largest parcel in Montrachet. They have been in the same family for several centuries. Such continuity is quite exceptional in the vineyards of Burgundy.

In 1706 Charles de La Boutière married his only daughter to Jean-François-Antoine de Clermont-Montoison, whom he appointed residual legatee of his estate in 1710. By about 1740 the Clermont-Montoison family owned 4 hectares 28 ares in Montrachet, in a perfect quadrilateral. These lords of Chagny were loved and respected. They were also active in supporting of the vineyards of Puligny and Chassagne. In 1776 Marie-Jeanne de Clermont-Montoison married Charles-Amable de La Guiche. But the Revolution was to overturn this order of things.... The estate of the family, part of which had now emigrated, was sold for the nation on the second day of the month Germinal in Year Two of the Republic (March 22, 1794), in two lots to one Henri Pourtalès (for 35,000 and 37,100 francs respectively plus fees). After the conspiracy of Baron de Batz, Charles-Amable de La Guiche was condemned to death and guillotined in 1794. The sale of properties sequestered by the Revolutionary government is confused here for, unlike the majority of Burgundy vineyards which belonged wholly to religious communities or to noble families, Montrachet was already split up between proprietors whose goods were subject to sequestration and those entitled to retain their assets. In Montrachet purchases seem to have stopped at that. Vines were left abandoned and the authorities ordered the commune to find *métayers*, the nation taking half of the fruit. How did the La Guiche family (which changed its name to Laguiche under the Revolution, for the *sans-culottes* considered that a double-barrelled name was automatic proof of noble birth); how then did this family come to own two hectares of Montrachet? One story claims that the estate manager bought back the better part of the 4 ares 28 centiares and reconveyed them to his masters immediately after the Revolution. Improbable, for the Laguiche family has no details of such an honourable gesture.

By contrast, what is certain is the inventory drawn up after the death of Charles-Amable de La Guiche's widow on June 9, 1810. The total assets of the Laguiche and Mandelot families (also son-in-law and daughter of the Clermont-Montoison branch) were divided in two; so there were parcels of vines in Montrachet, in "Chevalier de Mon-trachet", in Vigne Blanche de Morgeot, in Grand Clos de Morgeot and so on, though the installations in Morgeot remained in a family trust. It seems that the Clermont-Montoison heirs (de Laguiche and de Mandelot) retained their property in Chassagne, Pourtalès having perhaps played the role of faithful estate manager. Moreover, if we are to believe A. Patriarche, who in his book, published in about 1910 makes reference to this family and its history, Bizouard, the postmaster at Rouvray, served a bottle of the Marquis de Laguiche's Montrachet to Napoleon I on his return from the island of Elba in April 1815. However, the legend of the good and faithful estate manager fails to stand

Prestigious wooden boxes of Montrachet from "Domaine de Laguiche".

up when we remember that on August 27, 1838, Bernard and Adolphe Bouchard, merchants in Beaune, bought 1 hectares 92 ares in Montrachet belonging to André-Adolphe, the Comte de Bataille de Mandelot in Autun. So this must be half of the parcel resulting from the breaking up of the family trust in 1810. The Clermont-Montoison heirs owned about 4 hectares at this time, within 30 ares of their holdings before the Revolution. For the rest, the parcels coming from the former Mandelot-Bouchard property represent 1 hectare 94 ares 82 centiares on the Land Register today: the equivalent of the land sold in 1838. The 1810 division into two halves then slightly favoured the Laguiche heirs who finally received 2 hectares 6 ares 25 centiares. The Montrachet of the Marquis de Laguiche belonged to Casimir de Laguiche (1777-1843) a *député* for the Saône-et-Loire, to Philibert de Laguiche (1815-1891), and to others. So often quoted, though in curtailed form, the Marquis de Cussy's declaration of love was addressed to this Montrachet: "O Montrachet! Divine Montrachet! The foremost, the finest of white wines which our rich France produces, you who have remained pure and unsullied in the hands of your honourable proprietor, the Marquis de Laguiche, I bow in admiration before you!" We should note that Cussy (sometimes referred to as "Comte" and therefore thought to have lived in the eighteenth century) was the author of *Art culinaire* (1855) and that he collaborated on a *Calendrier gastronomique* in the middle of the nineteenth century. The homage rendered to Montrachet by Alexandre Dumas was also said to have been inspired by the Marquis de Laguiche's wine.

The Laguiche family lived in Saône-et-Loire in the Château de Chaumont, near Saint-Bonnet-de-Joux. We have seen that they became owners of Montrachet through the 1776 marriage. Chaumont was bought by Girard, the lord of La Guiche in 1416. Like the family, the château is part of France's history. The stables constructed in the eighteenth century could take 99 horses, for only the King had the right to have stables for 100. The hundredth horse is here in Chaumont, however, in the form of a statue. On the eve of the Great War, General Pierre de Laguiche (1859-1940) was military attaché in Vienna,

Berlin and Saint Petersburg, and afterwards was in charge of liaison with the British army at the end of the war. His son, Comte Jean de Laguiche, born in 1889, died during deportation in 1945. The present proprietors are Philibert de Laguiche, born in 1921, Marquis and *Pair de France* (a title that has been in the family since 1815) and his son Jean.

Among the estate managers of the "Marquis de Laguiche" Montrachet, are a certain Moine, followed by Marcel Paquelin (from 1901), his nephew Jean-Baptiste Colin and his son, the priest Jean-Baptiste Colin, who died in 1987. All these managers were throughly conscientious. Such was not the case with one of their predecessors in the nineteenth century, who must have had a bad reputation, for a neighbour scrawled these lines on the lintel of the little door of Le Montrachet:

"Marquis de Laguiche Noble your title, high-sounding your name!
But soon, not a drop of your wine will remain."

Under a sole rights' contract, this wine, which was already marketed by the firm of Joseph Drouhin, is now vinified by this *domaine*. The parcel was planted in 1961, 1969 and 1984.

Created in 1880 by Joseph Drouhin, then directed by Maurice Drouhin, this very famous Beaune firm has been administered since 1957 by Robert J. Drouhin, a man with an international reputation. The firm specializes in AOC Burgundy and Beaujolais wines and has vines which today cover some 60 hectares. The installations have been designed for the ageing of several thousand casks and the oenologist, Laurence Jobard, the daughter of a grower from Pommard and the wife of a nurseryman, looks after vinification with scrupulous care. The Montrachet of the Marquis de Laguiche is obviously the jewel of this production. In February 1986 this firm took total control of its American importers, Dreyfus Ashby in New York (importers of Hugel wines from Alsace, Château Pétrus and so on). Jancis Robinson records her admiration for this Montrachet in her *Great Wine Book*. This wine was classed as the second best white wine in the world (behind Yquem) by *Cuisine et vins de France* at the "referendum" organized for the review's 40th anniversary in November 1986.

Laurence Jobard, oenologist for Joseph Drouhin. The Montrachet of the Domaine Marquis de Laguiche is her particular responsibility.

Proprietor:
Marquis Philibert and Jean de Laguiche
Château de Chaumont
71220 Saint-Bonnet-de-Joux

Vinification and marketing:
Maison Joseph Drouhin
7 rue d'Enfer – BP 29
21201 Beaune Cedex
Tel: 80 24 68 88

Production (in hectolitres):

1984: 58	1987: 86
1985: 104	1988: 101
1986: 117	1989: 91

Best vintages:
1959, 1962, 1969, 1978, 1979, 1983, 1985.

Tasting:
M 1985.

Fern and fresh almond, a marvellous sunny afternoon in the countryside. A pale colour without any particular brilliance. The overall impression is one of dominating finesse and elegance. A very great wine and a very great year which harmonizes all the refined qualities of Montrachet without excessive richness or power.

LATOUR
Domaine et Maison Louis Latour

◊ *Chevalier-Montrachet* (CM)

This vineyard of 50 ares 70 centiares also bears the name "Les Demoiselles". Domaine Louis Latour bought them in 1913 from the widow of Léonce Bocquet, née Bigot. A merchant in Savigny-lès-Beaune and proprietor of the Château du Clos de Vougeot, Léonce Bocquet (1839-1913) was one of the most flamboyant personalities in the Burgundy vineyards. For the history of these vines, see the article on Maison Jadot. Maison Louis Latour regularly buys the musts (unfermented wine) from Jean-Pierre Monnot (see below), a proprietor in Bâtard-Montrachet and Bienvenues-Bâtard-Montrachet. So it has sole rights on the marketing of this wine. In the middle of the nineteenth century Louis Latour (1835-1902) founded a firm of merchants at Aloxe-Corton. He was at once owner, cooper, broker and wine factor. An employee of the firm of Lamarosse, created in Beaune in the eighteenth century, he bought it up in 1866. His son Louis II (1874-1941) succeeded him. The family's vines gradually spread to cover 55 hectares, of which 36 are in Corton-Grancey, 1.6 in Chambertin, and 1.5 in Romanée-Saint-Vivant (these two lots were bought in 1898). "You are the sort of man who reflects your native region," Jacques Coupeau wrote to Louis Latour. "A man of tradition, the product of a region and a professional. A simple, honest man. When intelligence and honesty combine, they always create a sort of greatness. Péguy would have loved you." For fifteen years, Beaune's Hôtel-Dieu was his life and he directed the hospice and the vines at the same time. Among his children, Louis-Noël (Louis III), born in 1903, took on the merchant firm and Jean, born in 1905, looked after the vines, and in his turn became vice-president of the Board of Directors of the Hospice de Beaune. Now a new generation ensures the continuity of this great Burgundy firm. Who directs it? Another Louis Latour (Louis IV), who holds numerous professional posts in Burgundy. "Louis Latour is one of the names in Burgundy to reckon with," says Hugh Johnson. "He is particularly famous for his white wines, especially his Corton-Charlemagne. You could say that he literally wrote this name on the map at the end of the nineteenth century."

Louis Latour.

Proprietor:
Domaine et Maison Louis Latour
18 rue des Tonneliers
21204 Beaune
Tel: 80 22 31 20

Production (in hectolitres):

1982: 26.29	1986: 30.21
1983: 22.80	1987: 20.23
1984: 19.59	1988: 21.09
1985: 21.90	1989: 19.95

Tasting:
CM 1982.

An admirable wine, which deserves to be expected a little longer for it would be a pity to drink it now. More limpid than brilliant, it has wild, almost exotic aromas. All is luxury, calm and delight.

LEFLAIVE
Domaine Leflaive

◊ *Bâtard-Montrachet* (BM), *Chevalier-Montrachet* (CM), *Bienvenues-Bâtard-Montrachet* (BBM) – Here we have a veritable family saga against a background of Montrachet. From 1580 we find traces of a Marc Le Flayve in Gissey near Beaune. In 1717 Claude Leflaive, from the parish of Demigny, set up house in Puligny, having just married Nicole Vallée the widow of Claude Girardin. This house, in the present place du Monument, was to shelter eight generations of Leflaives in direct line, often christened Claude from father to son. Domaine Leflaive was originally the creation of Joseph Leflaive (1870-1953). A technician and naval construction engineer, who took part in the construction of the first French submarine, he went on to direct the factory of la Chaléassière, owned by his father-in-law, an ironmaster in Saint-Etienne. In 1926, he came back to his village to dedicate himself entirely to wine.

He was helped by his estate manager and friend, François Virot, born in 1890. The son of a grower from Chorey-lès-Beaune and a relative of the estate manager of Domaine Thénard, François Virot was an outstanding personality in the Burgundy vineyards up to 1964. Between 1905 and 1925 Joseph Leflaive developed the little vineyard which he had inherited. He acquired some 25 hectares in the best *climats,* and another 25 hectares of land and buildings which are now used for the business. The vineyards were restored from 1920, and replanted with chardonnay using high quality stock. Until 1933, the wine was essentially sold to merchants. Then marketing turned towards direct sales to private clients and restaurants, with the firm of Frederick Wildman in New York as distributors in the United States. The *domaine* was then divided up and given to Joseph Leflaive's children in 1930. Four of them, Jo Leflaive, Vicomtesse Louis de Noue (Jeanne Leflaive), Anne and Vincent Leflaive decided to retain the unity of the estate (1955), by creating a family trust. In 1973 a new phase began, with the vines being split up between the four proprietors, the creation of a limited company and another division – donation from the proprietors to their heirs (Joseph Leflaive's fourteen grandchildren).

From 1953, the *domaine* was run by the two Leflaives: Jo (an insurance man in Grenoble) and Vincent (an engineer in Paris). A flamboyant, keen and friendly person, Vincent has continued with this work since Jo's death in 1982, assisted by a board of directors whose members include a representative of the new generation from each of the families: Ludovic de Noue, Maria-Cruz de Suremain, *née* Malibran-Santibanez,

Vincent Leflaive (left) and François Virot (in 1960).

Anne-Claude and Olivier Leflaive, the joint manager of the *domaine* since 1986. In 1990 Vincent's eldest daughter Anne-Claude inherited his position of joint manager. Jean Virot, son of François, has taken over the position of estate manager.

Domaine Leflaive extends over Puligny-Montrachet (*Premiers Crus* Pucelles, Combettes) and Blagny (Dos d'Ane). It is also in Bâtard-Montrachet (1 hectare 91 ares 12 centiares), in Chevalier-Montrachet (1 hectare 91 ares 82 centiares) and in Bienvenues-Bâtard-Montrachet (1 hectare 15 ares 80 centiares). Three-quarters of the vines are over fifteen years old. The wine is sold principally to restaurants, 65% going for export. On September 15, 1977 it was drunk for the famous chef Alain Chapel's fortieth birthday. Claude Vrinat in *Taillevent* and many others swear only by Leflaive. The Chevalier-Montrachet 1983 was winner of the *Olympiades du vin* organized by Gault-Millau in 1986-1987 (17.6 points of out 20 – the best mark of all the 29 chardonnays from all over the world that were tasted on this occasion), beating a Californian chardonnay of Robert Mondavi. The "Leflaive style"is to let nature do its work, remain patient and insist on clinical cleanliness. The *domaine's* label has retained its original design, having lost only the words *"Mypont difficile à passer"*the family motto of the lords of the area, who used to ransom people passing through. But "difficult to pass" is hardly suitable to apply to a wine, it must be admitted. "Domaine Leflaive without doubt produces some of the world's greatest dry white wines,"Serena Sutcliffe rightly considers (*Great Vineyards and Winemakers*). "The immense breed and distinction of their wines come not only from the impeccable pedigree of the sites, but also from the skill and care of their wine making." Hugh Johnson also shares this view: "Perhaps the highly regarded white -wine specialist of the Côte d'Or (...), the sublimation of the chardonnay (*Wine Companion*)."

Proprietor:	Best vintages:	
Domaine Leflaive	1961, 1978, 1979, 1983, 1985.	**BBM 1983.** *It has lost its freshness and bouquet. Although it still has an attractive colour, the nose is disappointing and it has not much to say in the mouth.*
Puligny-Montrachet		
21190 Meursault	**Tasting:**	

Production (in hectolitres):

BM 1983. *Rather light in colour but satisfactory for a rich year. An original nose, grapefruit style. Full and rich, it has more fullness than depth. It is a good Bâtard 83 but not typical.*

These three 83s were tasted by the Revue du Vin de France (*April-May 1986*). Raoul Salama found the Chevalier superbly long in the mouth, the mark of a great success. He less enthusiastic about the Bâtard: "massive and far from being developed". For the Bienvenues, "a harmonious, clearly distinguished ensemble".

• CM

1982: 101	1986: 110
1983: 103	1987: 66
1984: 60	1988: 97
1985: 92	1989: 92

• BM

1982: 137	1986: 114
1983: 114	1987: 82
1984: 72	1988: 77
1985: 106	1989: 73

• BBM

1982: 83	1986: 68
1983: 68	1987: 41
1984: 39	1988: 58
1985: 48	1989: 55

CM 1983. *Green gold with a relatively discreet bouquet. It dazzles the palate. Finesse, elegance, roundness. It has all the power of the 83s balanced by a felicitous grace. General impression: excellent. It is the wine which won at Gault Millau's Olympiades du vin in 1986-1987 (1st in the two world chardonnay series).*

LEMONDE
Robert et Jean-Paul Lemonde

◊ *Bâtard-Montrachet* (BM)

Bought by Fernand Coffinet, a grower in Chassagne and the great-grandfather of Jean-Paul and Robert Lemonde, these vines were divided into two parcels of 13 ares 4 centiares. Each brother owns one. As neither is a grower, the vineyards are run by Pierre

Lacroix from Chassagne (tenant-farmer for one parcel, *métayer* for the other). who was also *métayer* for Jean-Paul and Robert Lemonde's father. He sells his wine to merchants.

Proprietors:	Production:	Best vintages:
• Robert Lemonde	1982: 12.40 hl1985: 14.79 hl	1982, 1983, 1985.
Chassagne-Montrachet	1983: 9.28 hl1986: 15.62 hl	
21190 Meursault	1984: 10.90 hl	
• Jean-Paul Lemonde	This is the total production of the	
Ozenay, 71700 Tournus	two parcels (26 ares 8 centiares	
	in all). From 1982 Pierre Lacroix	
Manager:	has taken two-thirds of the pro-	
Pierre Lacroix	duction, Jean-Paul Lemonde (*mé-*	
Chassagne-Montrachet	*tayage*), one-third. Robert Le-	
21190 Meursault	monde (tenant-farmer) receives a	
Tel: 80 21 33 83	lump sum.	

LEQUIN-ROUSSOT
Domaine Lequin-Roussot

BATARD-MONTRACHET

◊ *Bâtard-Montrachet* (BM)

This parcel of 24 ares 33 centiares situated in Bâtard-Montrachet in Chassagne was purchased by Jean Lequin in 1938. The previous proprietor had rented the vineyard out on an eighteen-year lease to Monsieur Mathey, a grower in Chassagne. He had planted "direct": that is, the grafts were not put into a nursery after coming out of the warmth but were planted directly. Jean Lequin has had the vines since 1946. They were partly replanted in 1974, 1979 and 1984. Domaine Lequin-Roussot produces Nuits-Saint-Georges, Corton, Pommard, Chassagne-Montrachet *Premier Cru* and white and red with the "Village" appellation, Santenay *Premier Cru* and "Village" and "Bourgogne" appellations.

At their father's side, René Lequin looks after marketing and management, while Louis takes care of orders and technical controls. Both of them work on the vines and in the cellars, for here everyone knows how to do everything. The Lequin-Roussot family has been in Santenay since 1869. Jean Lequin returned to the vines after postgraduate business studies in Paris, as he was the only one of his generation able to carry on with the family business. The family's house was constructed by Jean Lequin's grandfather in three stages. At that time, the grower built his cellar first, then the vat-house above it and the house wherever he could. The Lequins are particularly attentive vintners. They bottle 70% of their harvest themselves. Their first sizeable bottling was in 1969, then 1971 and has increased steadily ever since. About three-quarters goes for export. This wine also goes to private clients and restaurants.

Proprietors:	Best vintages:	Tasting:
Domaine Lequin-Roussot	"For sentimental reasons, 1946	**BM 1982.**
René and Louis Lequin Frères	and 1948", they reply. Why?	
Rue de la Gare	"They are the years in which we	*This is exactly the colour we would*
21590 Santenay	were born!" Otherwise? "1947,	*expect. A simple, elegant, slightly*
Tel: 80 20 61 46	1959, 1964, 1974, 1975, 1982	*grassy nose. Full, rich in the*
	and of course, 1985."	*mouth with a certain smokiness.*
Production (in hectolitres):		*Much acidity. What does it lack?*
1981: 6.84 1984: 5.13		*A certain fullness. Allowing for*
1982: 14.25 1985: 6.20		*the good and bad points of 82s,*
1983: 6.30 1986: 6.27		*we would expect it to be longer in*
		the mouth.

MONNOT
Jean-Pierre Monnot

◊ *Bâtard-Montrachet* (BM), *Bienvenues-Bâtard-Montrachet* (BBM)

A *domaine* very much in the style of Puligny, which does not sell by the bottle. Succeeding his father André Monnot, Jean-Pierre Monnot took over in 1977 together with his wife. Formerly the estate belonged to an uncle, Emile Monnot, who died in 1963. Their house, constructed in 1711 by a wine seller, is as charming as it is unusual. The architect certainly did not lack imagination.

Five and a half hectares of which 49 ares 72 centiares is in Bâtard-Montrachet and 50 ares 57 centiares in Bienvenues-Bâtard-Montrachet. The rest is in Folatières (10 *ouvrées*) and Referts (11 *ouvrées*) as well as in the "Village" appellation. These vines had to be completely replanted, for an ancestor more enthusiastic about music than about vines had utterly neglected them. *Métayage* turned into direct development. Originally from the region of Voudenay in the Auxois and Igornay in Saône-et-Loire, the two Monnots have courageously managed to give new life back to their *domaine.* All their white wine is sold in the form of must to the firm of Louis Latour (see above). Pressed and put in casks at the *domaine,* it leaves the following day by lorry for Pommard where Latour will see to the fermentation, ageing and marketing. Why not establish a private clientele? "Selling as must is a habit here and we did not want to change," replies Jean-Pierre Monnot's wife. "We have a good cellar. But we would have to take on staff. That is not easy... And then, we have a son studying history at Dijon University, and another son who wants to go into the police force. We keep the red here till the end of the malolactic fermentation; we like making wine but we have fewer problems like this." Jean-Pierre Monnot is on the Committee of Five in charge of establishing the yields for the *Grands Crus.*

Proprietor:
Jean-Pierre Monnot
Puligny-Montrachet
21190 Meursault
Tel: 80 21 30 45

Vinification, ageing and marketing (in part):
Maison Louis Latour
18 rue des Tonneliers
21200 Beaune
Tel: 80 22 31 20

Production (in hectolitres):
• BM

1984: 13.68	1987: 11.53
1985: 16.53	1988: 19.08
1986: 21.66	1989: 17.67

• BBM

1984: 11.40	1987: 23.94
1985: 24.51	1988: 26.12
1986: 30.21	1989: 23.94

This parcel was being replanted from 1980 to 1982.

The attractive home of the Monnot family in Puligny-Montrachet.

MOREY
Domaine Albert Morey

◊ *Bâtard-Montrachet* (BM)

A parcel of 14 ares 99 centiares which Albert Morey received from his parents in 1951. The vines were planted in 1964. He sells his wine to private customers.

Proprietor:
Domaine Albert Morey
Chassagne-Montrachet
21190 Meursault
Tel: 80 21 32 23

Production (in hectolitres):

1982:	10.26	1986:	9
1983:	7.40	1987:	7.12
1984:	5.10	1988:	7.56
1985:	9	1989:	7.20

Best vintages:
1959, 1971, 1976, 1978, 1982, 1985.

Tasting:

BM 1982. *This is voluptuous. In the old-fashioned style: full, corpulent, brimming with joy and spirit. Aromas of delicate complexity. Prolonged, almost endless harmony in the mouth with a background of honey and undergrowth.*

MOREY
Domaine Marc Morey et Fils

◊ *Bâtard-Montrachet* (BM)

Staunchly supported by his daughter Marie-Josèphe and his son-in-law Bernard Mollard, Marc Morey has 13 ares 60 centiares in Bâtard-Montrachet. Planted in 1956, this parcel has been in the family for a very long time. It comes from his father Fernand Morey who had it from his grandfather Jean-Marie Morey in December 1916. The latter had bought it in 1905 from M. and Mme George-Duvault for the sum of 650 francs with a small plot of vines in Macherelles. The family house used to be a posting inn before being turned into a restaurant, which closed its doors with the First World War.

Extending over some 10 hectares, Domaine Marc Morey et Fils produces wines with the Bourgogne appellation (Aligoté, Passe Tout Grain and red) as well as whites, Chassagne-Montrachet Village, *Premiers Crus* Chenevottes and Virondot, *Premier Cru* Pucelles in Puligny and Charmoy in Saint-Aubin. In reds: Chassagne-Montrachet Village, *Premiers Crus* Cailleret and Morgeot and a small plot of vines in Beaune Village. Among the firm's restaurant clients are some distinguished names: Georges Blanc in Vonnas, Haeberlin at the *Auberge de l'Ill* in Alsace, *Comme chez soi* in Brussels and more. A 1977 Bâtard-Montrachet was the winner at a tasting of wines from this *climat*, organized by Gault-Millau and the Impitoyables Club (*Gault-Millau*, suppl. Bourgogne, n° 188, Dec. 1984).

Proprietor:
Domaine Marc Morey et Fils
Chassagne-Montrachet
21190 Meursault
Tel: 80 21 30 11

Production (in hectolitres):

1982:	9.69	1986:	7.41
1983:	6.84	1987:	6.27
1984:	5.98	1988:	6.84
1985:	7.98	1989:	6.50

Best vintages:
1959, 1969, 1978, 1983, 1985.

Tasting:

BM 1985. *An intense colour for the year and a first fine nose of fruit. The second is more discreet. Its youth and its aromas are typical for the year. But the acidity seems too marked, which impairs the fullness and mellowness. A pretty wine, excellent Chassagne or Puligny. But it bears the name Montrachet, so it must be judged more severely.*

NIELLON
Domaine Michel Niellon

◊ *Bâtard-Montrachet* (BM) and *Chevalier-Montrachet* (CM)

A grower in Chassagne, Michel Niellon has 22 ares 73 centiares in Chevalier-Montrachet and 11 ares 90 centiares in Bâtard-Montrachet, planted respectively in 1962-1968 and 1926. His *domaine* also has Chassagne red and *Premier Cru* Clos Saint-Jean as well as Chassagne white and *Premier Cru* Vergers, Chenevottes and Maltroie. The wine is sold by the proprietor "by the bottle" and to merchants. Observations on Michel Niellon's wines include the following: "A choice of exemplary wines, all full, rich, with deep aromas and flavour" (Serena Sutcliffe); "a fine colour, clearly definable aromas, rich in alcohol, moderately long in the mouth and a dry finish" (tasting of a 1982 Bâtard-Montrachet in *Gault-Millau*, suppl. Bourgogne, n° 188, Dec. 1984).

Proprietor:
Domaine Michel Niellon
Chassagne-Montrachet
21190 Meursault
Tel: 80 21 30 95

Tasting:

CM 1985. *A very beautiful colour. A frank, floral intensity of aromas. Fine balance between richness and acidity with a rather excessive richness in alcohol. A good-quality bottle on a level with the best* Premiers Crus. *But it is an 85 and there is good reason to believe in its future balance.*

Harvesting at Domaine Niellon.

PERNOT
Domaine Paul Pernot et Fils

◊ *Bâtard-Montrachet* (BM), *Bienvenues-Bâtard-Montrachet* (BBM)

Paul Pernot owns 25 ares 96 centiares in Bâtard-Montrachet "in a shoulder round the Clos Poirier": these vines were bought around 1930 by Paul Latour, his maternal grandfather, from the Garnier family in Puligny. The vines were replanted in 1987. Paul Pernot also owns 8 ares 89 centiares in Bienvenues-Bâtard-Montrachet, a parcel which came to him through great-grandfather Latour. Formerly it had reds. The vines date from 1967. In the same *domaine:* GAEC Paul Pernot et Fils (Paul and Michel) has two parcels in Bâtard-Montrachet (22 ares 29 centiares and 11 ares 84 centiares) and 19 ares 47 centiares in Bienvenues. The parcel of 22 ares 29 centiares was bought in 1986 from Gisèle Bonneau who had it from her mother, *née* Brugnot, in Puligny. The other two were bought in 1980 from the Petitjean family (the merchant firm in Beaune taken over by the Jean-Claude Boisset group). The vines here were planted at the beginning of the 1950s. Two of these parcels (Petitjean and Marcilly) are run by Albert Joly-Charau, a grower in Puligny. A *métayer* for half the crop, Albert Joly-Charau has run these parcels since 1970. Formerly they belonged to the Bonneau daughters before being bought by Domaine Pernot. Apart from that this *domaine* has on *métayage* the parcel of 9 ares 36 centiares owned by Anne-Marie Rateau in Bienvenues (see below). The wine is sold to merchants and to the firm's private customers. It also includes the following appellations: Santenay, Beaune, Beaune-Teurons, Meursault-Blagny, Puligny-Montrachet, Puligny-Les Chalumaux, Puligny Clos de la Garenne, Puligny-Les Folatières and Puligny Les Pucelles: about of 12 hectares in all. Our panel was very enthusiastic about these two wines and praised them both highly.

Proprietor:
Domaine Paul Pernot et Fils
21190 Puligny-Montrachet
Tel: 80 21 32 35

Manager:
Albert Joly
21190 Puligny-Montrachet
Tel: 80 21 30 29

Production (in hectolitres):
Parcels run by Albert Loly.
• **BBM**
1981: 6.56	1984: 4.56
1982: 7.10	1985: 4.56
1983: 4.56	1986: 5.92

• **BBM**
1981: 6.56	1984: 4.56
1982: 11.40	1985: 6.84
1983: 6.84	1986: 9.72

Best vintages:
1970, 1973, 1982, 1983, 1985.

Paul Pernot and his sons: a tasting dynasty.

Tasting:

🍷 🍷 🍷

BM 1985. *Does it express its year? "Yes!" Does it express the qualities of Bâtard-Montrachet. "Yes!" three times over. This was the practically unanimous verdict of the members of the panel, though they thought that this wine was more agreeable to the palate than to the nose and eye, that a hint less alcohol would be preferable and that a final judgement could not be given because of its youth. Let us say simply that at this stage of its evolution it evoked only compliments.*

🍷 🍷 🍷

BBM 1985. *Rich, perfumed and well balanced, woody, this really is a "welcome" wine ("Bienvenu"). Completely clean and remarkably precocious. Its bouquet is rather closed up but develops in the glass. We feel it has more to say. A fine jewel from this domaine!*

PERROT
Marcelle Perrot

◊ *Criots-Bâtard-Montrachet* (CBM)
This tiny parcel of Criots-Bâtard-Montrachet belongs to Marcelle Perrot from Chassagne, the widow of André Perrot. It measures 4 ares 65 centiares: just enough to make one *pièce!*

Hubert Lamy has been Madame Perrot's tenant-farmer since 1955. A grower in Saint-Aubin from a long line of growers which has its earliest known roots in 1640, he runs a *domaine* of 13 hectares in Chassagne-Montrachet, Puligny-Montrachet, Santenay and Saint-Aubin. He has also been elected supplier to French expeditions in the Antarctic: doubtless polar expeditions warm up their bottles of Criots a little.

What is the difference between a tenant-farmer and a *métayer*? The *métayer* retains part of the harvest and delivers the rest to the proprietor in proportions agreed by contract (half and half, two-thirds and a third or conversely, etc.). The tenant-farmer keeps the harvest and pays the proprietor an annual sum which, unlike a simple rental agreement, is not fixed. This sum corresponds in fact to a third of the grape harvest and varies from year to year depending obviously on the abundance of the harvest and the price of the grapes. But is it possible to produce one single *pièce* of a *Grand Cru*? In reds, no. In whites, as fermentation takes place in the cask just a few hours after harvesting, it can be done. "As I produce both Chassagne and Puligny," explains Hubert Lamy, "I keep the dry solids in the press and I press the Criots on top." The vines were planted in 1975. This wine is sold entirely to the tenant-farmer's private customers.

Proprietor:
Marcelle Perrot
in Chassagne-Montrachet

Manager:
Hubert Lamy
Saint-Aubin
21190 Meursault
Tel: 80 21 32 55

Production:
An average of 228 litres per year. It is difficult to produce either more or less, for you have to round figures up or down. And vines do not have a mathematical turn of mind.

Best vintages:
1976, 1978, 1983.

Tasting:

CBM 1983. *Although of average limpidity without excessive brilliance, its nose is woody, with hints of vanilla, asking only to open up. Very full, it is more like Montrachet than Bâtard. Its youth makes it lively and anxious to please. But it should be left to age. It lacks that mellowness which characterizes the great crus among the dry whites. This may come with age.*

PETITJEAN
Jean Petitjean

◊ *Montrachet* (M)
Coming from a family holding, this parcel of 5 ares 42 centiares is situated in Chassagne in Dents de Chien, assimilated into Montrachet by the judgement of 1921. Its owner Jean Petitjean is not a grower; he has put it out on *métayage* to René Lamy-Pillot (see page 178) since November 1988. The previous *métayer* was Domaine Brenot in Santenay who sold his half of the crop in must to Reine Pédauque – SEDGV in Aloxe-Corton.

Proprietor:
Jean Petitjean
8 rue Xavier-Forneret
21200 Beaune
Tel: 80 22 14 10

Manager:
René Lamy-Pillot
Route de Santenay
21190 Chassagne
Tel: 80 21 30 52

Production:
Depending on the year, varies from one *feuillette* (114 litres) in 1983 and 1984 to one *pièce* (228 litres) in 1985 and 1986, and in 1982, one and a quarter *pièces.*

Tasting:

M 1985. *We say that a very great wine "has love". This one will certainly celebrate its golden wedding anniversary. Its heart speaks as much as its character, with the miracle of Montrachet – fine crystal under flawless armour. Joan of Arc must have appeared like this on her charger.*

PICARD-STOECKEL
GFA Picard-Stoeckel

◊ *Bâtard-Montrachet* (BM)
This little parcel of 8 ares 26 centiares in Bâtard was acquired in 1940 by M. and Mme Picard. Formerly it belonged to the Polignac family. Through inheritances, it became

the property of the Groupement Foncier Agricole of Picard-Stoeckel. Run by Château de la Maltroye in Chassagne, it is managed by André Cournut and his wife. The château, with its roof of attractive glazed tiles, has cellars dating from the fifteenth century.

A former pilot, André Cournut successfully converted himself into a grower. He is in charge of 15 hectares in Chassagne-Montrachet and Santenay, half white, half red: Morgeot, Grandes Ruchottes, Romanée, Clos du Château, Chenevottes, Maltroie, Boudriotte, Clos Saint-Jean, Santenay *Premier Cru* La Comme and Les Gravières, and others.

Production of Bâtard is slender (barely 500 bottles in 1987), made with a tiny press and a craftman's approach. The vines were planted in 1936. The wine is sold by the proprietor to his own customers, mainly abroad (United States and Great Britain).

Proprietor:
GFA Picard-Stoeckel
SCE Château de la Maltroye
Chassagne-Montrachet
21190 Meursault
Tel: 80 21 32 45 and 80 21 38 96

Production (in hectolitres):

1984: 3.96	1987: 3.96
1985: 4.56	1988: 3.96
1986: 4.95	1989: 3.96

Harvesting in front of Château de la Maltroye. The pilot André Cournut chose to land here permanently.

POIRIER
Claude-Maxence Poirier

◊ *Bâtard-Montrachet* (BM)

The Poirier family comes from Chassagne, and at the beginning of the century they were horticulturalists. Two of the four sons (Louis and Claude-Marius) acquired vines in Bâtard-Montrachet, whence we find two lines of Poiriers in this *Grand Cru* (see Vaudiaux-Poirier). Claude-Marius bought these vines in 1912 from the Barbier de La Serre family. They had been in the Ségault family since 1840. In 1873 Jeanne de Ségault married Gabriel Barbier de La Serre and kept this vineyard for herself. Her daughters, Vicomtesse Madeleine de Peyronnet, Marquise Mathilde de Montillet de Grenaud and Marie van Zeller d'Oosthove, inherited them, and sold them in 1912 for 9,000 francs (95 ares 76 centiares in Bâtard and 18 ares 60 centiares in Pucelles). The purchaser, Claude-Marius Poirier, an engineer in the farming industry, was then second in charge in the cellars of Pommery and Greno in Reims. This branch of the family then settled in Reims and Claude-Marius became director of Pommery and Greno, leaving his brother Louis, a grower in Pommard, to run the vines. Claude-Renaud Poirier, his son, was Moët-et-Chandon's technical adviser. Today Claude-Maxence Poirier, the latter's son and present owner of the vines, is an architect in Reims. Without going into details concerning the ownership with or without usufruct, these vines are in the hands of two *métayers*, Pierre Morey for 48 ares 51 centiares and Roger Caillot-Morey for 48 ares 52 centiares, a total of 97 ares 3 centiares. A grower in Meursault, Pierre Morey also cultivates the parcel in Montrachet belonging to Domaine des comtes Lafon (see above). Widely respected for his professional approach, he sells part of his wine direct to private clients. In 1983 Jon Winroth described him and his wines thus: "This extrovert but meticulous and highly analytical young man makes excellent wines with plenty of bouquet, well balanced and long in the mouth." His *domaine* stretches out over Meursault, Monthélie and Pommard (Epenots). He also produces white and red with the Bourgogne appellation, as well as Aligoté and Passe Tout Grain. The vines were planted in 1965. Claude-Maxence Poirier sells his wine in must to Domaine Louis Latour.

Proprietor:	Métayers:	Production (in hectolitres)	
Claude-Maxence Poirier	• Pierre Morey	(P. Morey's parcel):	
in Reims	9 rue Comte-Lafon	1982: 17	1986: 14
	21190 Meursault	1983: 12.50	1987: 11.40
	Tel: 80 21 21 03	1984: 9.50	1988: 12.22
	• Roger Caillot-Morey	1985: 12	1989: 11.40
	14 rue du Cronin		
	21190 Meursault	**Best vintages:**	
	Tel: 80 21 20 12	1978, 1979, 1981, 1983, 1985.	

PRIEUR
Domaine Jacques Prieur

◊ *Montrachet* (M), *Chevalier-Montrachet* (CM)

Successive purchases between 1890 and 1892 enabled Domaine Jacques Prieur in Meursault to acquire 58 ares 63 centiares in Montrachet: 38 ares 50 centiares from the Granger-Batault family and 6 ares 80 centiares, 6 ares 90 centiares, and 5 ares 93 centiares from the Collot-Girards, Collot-Collots and Jouard-Perrins. The last three parcels were just simple plots of land near Dents de Chien assimilated into Montrachet by the Beaune judgement of 1921. These vines were planted in 1957, 1979 and 1986 and are in Chassagne. Yet another property of this *domaine* is 13 ares 65 centiares in Chevalier-Montrachet in Puligny. Restored in 1967 and planted in the same year, this parcel had been partly purchased in 1907 (8 ares 56 centiares) from Benjamin Garnier and M. and Mme Derains. A distinguished member of the Brotherhood of the Chevaliers du Tastevin, Jacques Prieur (1893-1965) gave his name to the Domaine.

In 1956 Jacques Prieur created a limited company to guard against any division of the land on his death. Jean Prieur is the only one of the six children to run the *domaine*. His wife and son Martin, born in 1962, help him with the day-to-day management. The family, is in the business of vine-growing root and branch – and for them the expression has particular significance, for at the end of the last century Jean's great-uncle was one of the first to notice the appearance of phylloxera in Meursault. He reported it and four policemen were sent to mount guard round the contaminated vines to prevent any propagation by the devil's insect. Did the policemen fall asleep? For Jean, wine is not just a matter of finance. Much love and a sense of poetry are needed to appreciate it. His brother-in-law, the writer Pierre Poupon, shares this view and often takes part in tastings. For vinification, Jean Prieur has three pressings for his *Grands Crus,* then he leaves the new wine for twenty-four to forty-eight hours, followed by a careful racking. His fermentation temperatures are low and slow; he starts at 17° or 18°C (63° to 64°F) then cools down to 15°C (59°F) and puts the wine in cask, where they will come up to 20°C (68°F). He is not in favour of using too many new casks for the white wines, for he thinks that can provoke an undesirable yellowing. In 1987 he returned to the practice of fining with egg-whites. Five hundred were used.

The large Domaine Jacques Prieur holds a striking place in Burgundy. In fact it is one of the vineyard with the fullest complement of *Grands Crus*. Eighty-five per cent of production goes for export.

A group led by Bertrand Devillard (Antonin Rodet in Mercurey), made up of groups and families from Saône-et-Loire – Labruyère-Eberlé, Poch, Neyrat and Clayeux – acquired fifty per cent of Domaine Jacques Prieur in 1988. The joint managers are Jean Prieur and Bertrand Devillard. Bottling is carried out at the *domaine.*

Jean Prieur in front of the gateway of Le Grand Montrachet.

Proprietors:
• Domaine Jacques Prieur
Les Herbeux, 21190 Meursault
Tel: 80 21 23 85
• Bertrand Devillard and others
Maison Antonin Rodet
Mercurey, 71640 Givry
Tel: 85 45 22 22

Production (in hectolitres):
• **M**

1984:	18.24	1987:	14.82
1985:	23.94	1988:	22.80
1986:	22.80	1989:	19.38

• **CM**

1984:	2.28	1987:	3.42
1985:	5.70	1988:	6.84
1986:	4.56	1989:	4.56

Tasting:

• **M 1982.** *The shining gold colour brought only compliments. On the other hand, the aromas are too discreet. An agreeable, gentle, well-made wine. It lacks the mark of genius. It would be interesting to compare it with an 83.*

• **CM 1982.** *Fruity and supple, a good balance between richness and acidity. Brilliant for an 82 with a finesse which allows us to expect much more. You can fall in love with the Chevalier more quickly than with the Montrachet this became clear when we compared two of the same vintage.*

PRIEUR-BRUNET
Domaine Prieur-Brunet

◊ *Bâtard-Montrachet* (BM)

Guy Prieur, whose family settled in Santenay on 11 Ventôse in Year XII of the Republic (that is to say March 11, 1804) at the Château de Perruchot in upper Santenay, is the owner today of 7 ares 63 centiares of Bâtard-Montrachet which he has from his father. The vines were planted in 1945. His wife Elizabeth, née Brunet, comes from Meursault. Her family is one of the oldest stocks in Meursault which, she proudly says, cannot be uprooted! Guy Prieur sells all his wine to private customers and restaurants. The list of his clients reads like *L'Annuaire diplomatique*: apparently it is a tip passed discreetly from embassy to embassy! Domaine Prieur-Brunet also owns vines in Santenay (Maladière, Comme), Chassagne-Montrachet (Morgeot, Embazées), Meursault (Charmes, Chevalières, Forges), Volnay (Santenots), Pommard (Platière) and Beaune (Clos du Roi).

Proprietor:
Domaine Prieur-Brunet
21590 Santenay
Tel: 80 20 60 56

Production (in hectolitres):

1984:	3.62	1987:	3.60
1985:	4.56	1988:	3.70
1986:	4.56	1989:	3.62

Best vintages:
1959, 1978.

Tasting:

BM 1985. *Limpid and bright, a Bâtard with a clean, pleasing* nose, but small. Doubtless still closed up. Typical of its year. Well structured, but it lacks fruit and is not rich or, in a word, chic. *Its hardness comes perhaps from being bottled only recently. "To be drunk again later," as they say at the Tastevin.*

RAMONET
Domaine Ramonet

◊ *Montrachet* (M), *Bâtard-Montrachet* (BM), *Bienvenues-Bâtard-Montrachet* (BBM)
Many growers have succeeded in making a name for themselves, and some have gained a reputation. But Domaine Ramonet is a celebrity. The eldest of the family, Pierre Ramonet, 81 years of age, has a book of press-cuttings which might be the envy of many film stars or politicians. He has appeared on the cover of *Gault-Millau*, the American magazine *Connoisseur*, and more. It is an honour to enter his cellar. The family tree has its roots in Claude Ramonet, a grower in Chassagne at the beginning of the century. He had three children: a daughter who married Georges Bachelet (whence the present Domaine Bachelet-Ramonet – see above), and two sons, Claude and Pierre. Together they ran Domaine Ramonet. Claude did not marry and had no children. Pierre married Lucie Prudhon, the daughter of the vineyard manager at Domaine de l'abbaye de Morgeot (hence the double-barrelled name, traditional in Chassagne: Ramonet-Prudhon). They had one son, André who fathered two sons, Noël and Jean-Claude. Claude is now deceased and the present line has three generations: Pierre (grandfather), André (father) Noël and Jean-Claude (sons).

The *domaine* extends over 15 hectares: apart from the three *Grands Crus*, it produces Chassagne *Premiers Crus* whites (Ruchottes, Morgeot, Cailleret) and reds (Boudriotte, Clos Saint-Jean, Morgeot) as well as the "Village" appellation in this commune and some Aligoté. The Bienvenues-Bâtard-Montrachet (45 ares 8 centiares) and Bâtard-Montrachet (56 ares 9 centiares) were bought at the beginning of 1955 from Henri Coquet, who was the representative for the Havas Agency in Dijon and in charge of publicity for the *Le Bien public* newspaper. These two vineyards were next door to each other.

As for the Montrachet (25 ares 90 centiares) in Puligny, it was bought in 1978 from the Milan and Mathey (Dr. Blanchet) families. These vines were replanted some ten years ago and André Ramonet prefers not to replant them in stages. One day, fortune came Pierre Ramonet-Prudhon's way. It was at the Beaune viticultural exhibition of 1938. "Haven't you got anything I can rinse my mouth out with" asked Raymond Baudoin, one of the founders of the *Revue du Vin de France*. "That is how he spoke," says André Ramonet who, like all good growers, has another way of speaking. We gave him a bottle of Ruchottes to drink. "Ah! that's good," said Monsieur Baudoin. "Are you selling?" Yes, of course. It was the 34 we had not managed to sell well. "You'll be seeing me again," concluded Raymond Baudoin. Six months later he arrived in Chassagne in the company of an American who, just after the prohibition era, was to become one of the foremost wine importers in the United States. It was Frank M. Schoonmaker, and he was to reap great glory from the vineyards of Burgundy. "Have you still got that wine of yours?" Raymond Baudoin asked Pierre Ramonet. Yes. "Give us two bottles of white and two of red, and we'll bring you an order tomorrow." This was done. The next day Frank Schoonmaker bought 200 cases of 12 bottles of white and the same of red for the United States.

It was thus the 1934 vintage which arrived across the Atlantic some weeks before the war – and which moreover would not be paid for until 1945. So Domaine Ramonet became known and appreciated in the United States long before the rest, and was soon to go in for direct marketing.

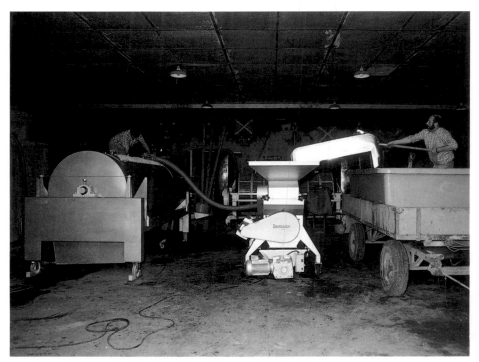

"One has only to see the family in the vat-house and cellar..."

These are vintners of outstanding ability. No one denies this in Chassagne and Puligny, and they have contributed greatly to the quality and fame of the wines of these communes. Prosperity has enabled them gradually to acquire *Grands Crus*. But it is true to say that the Montrachet is quite exceptional. Raymond Baudoin died in 1952, but already *Taillevent, la Pyramide, la Côte-d'Or, l'Oustau de Baumanière* and many other great restaurants were summoning the riches of Domaine Ramonet. Vrinat, Point, Dumaine, and Chapel have given this wine and this name dazzling fame. And the international press fell in love with Pierre Ramonet, fascinated by his ingenuous nature, his genius with wine and his unpolished cordiality. There is nothing artificial in this success. Furthermore, one has only to see the family in the vat-house and cellar, the yards and the secret stores to realize that vines and wines rule the Ramonets infinitely more than show or publicity.

They are, of course, a "clan" – the leading one in Chassagne. They work hard. They are conscientious and have style. They have earned their fame. The Burgundy journalist and novelist Fanny Deschamps recalled this fame in a chapter of her delightful *Croque-en-bouche* which appeared in 1976. An account of the wines and gastronomy of Burgundy, this book naturally covered Chassagne-Montrachet, where the famous chef Alain Chapel from Mionnay hoped to obtain a few bottles of Bâtard. "Among the vines, Ramonet seems to be at home," wrote Fanny Deschamps. "He never travels, apart from a short trip to a local customer who is a good cook (such as Chapel, Troisgros, Bocuse, Lameloise). Ramonet shuts himself up among his vines as in a world apart, a world which holds all he needs and all the love he can give. He lives almost motionless in the solitude of his vineyard. As patient and headstrong as a vine. Tending vines needs a lifetime of silent determination. So much so that a good vigneron is worth the price of his old bottles. Over the years, the man acquires as great a value as his wine. And his devotion is infectious: Dédé Ramonet's gaze rests on the grapes or a *tonneau* with the same tenderness as that of a father."

Fanny Deschamps is not quite right when she mentions, in the context of this family, the well-nigh eternal succession of growers from father to son who finish by belonging wholly to their vines. The first Ramonets were millers in Beaune. They settled in Chassagne at the end of the last century when their mill fell into disuse. But they worked hard. "They had guts,"as people say here, to the point of building a family empire in wine, less from the richness of their parcels of vines, extended little by little, than through their own qualities. But Fanny Deschamps tells the Ramonets' story wonderfully well. Mother scribbles her accounts in a school exercise book on the plastic tablecloth in the kitchen. "While you are about it," says Alain Chapel, "make my bill out. I have owed you quite a sum for nearly two years now..." "Could well be. Monsieur Alain, could well be, but with the banquet for the kid's confirmation, I'm a bit behind. But as soon as I have time, I'll see to it!" Keeper of the accounts of the *domaine,* grandmother Ramonet, dressed in black like her mother and grandmother before her, no longer bothers too much about the odd ten million centimes or so.

Father Ramonet is the person people come to see and hear as much as his wine. With his heavy old pullover, clogs and black velvet trousers, his cap screwed on to his head and his hands stained brown by grape juice, "he speaks of his wine with deep, intense poetry. The words do not come from his throat but his very bones." He left school at eight because he was needed in the vineyards. Among Pierre Ramonet's maxims are: "Mind you, you have to sell. I hold back and wait. And the wine which has not been made to be kept but to be sold does not hang on. It sells!"; "At one time here, all the growers used to select sets producing small berries, few but good. Now the youngsters choose large berries which give a high yield. But you never have the two together, quality and quantity"; "Either you go for money or you go for wine." But all that is legend now. Today it is difficult to meet father Ramonet. As for the generations who come after him, they have less time and inclination to chat.

No other *domaine* has contributed so much to the universal glory of Montrachet, will it be able to hold on to this standing?

Proprietor:	Tasting:	the mouth. Rich and heady. But
Domaine Ramonet		almost too much so, its warmth
Chassagne-Montrachet	**M 1982**. *Rich in aromas which*	*rather depriving it of that nuance*
21190 Meursault	*plunged our panel into an abyss*	*of freshness which makes up the*
Tel: 80 21 30 88	*of perplexity, this wine appeared*	*charm of the Montrachet. Account*
	rich and full; roasted hazelnut in	*should be taken of the vintage.*

RATEAU
Anne-Marie Rateau

◇ *Bienvenues-Bâtard-Montrachet* (BBM)
Formerly a schoolteacher, Anne-Marie (known as Denise locally) has a parcel of 9 ares 36 centiares in Bienvenues-Bâtard-Montrachet. It is a family property. The vines are on *métayage* to Domaine Paul Pernot et Fils (see above).

Proprietor:	Manager:
Anne-Marie Rateau	Paul Pernot et Fils
Puligny-Montrachet	21190 Puligny-Montrachet
21190 Meursault	Tel: 80 21 32 35

REGNAULT de BEAUCARON et GUILLAUME
Domaine Boillereault de Chauvigny

◊ *Montrachet* (M)

These four parallel and symmetrical parcels (26 ares 66 centiares, 13 ares 33 centiares, 13 ares 33 centiares and 26 ares 66 centiares) in Puligny belong to two families, the Guillaumes (the first two, to the east) and the Regnault de Beaucarons (the other two, to the west). Yet it is one concern, the *domaine* having been kept under one wing. With Domaines de Laguiche and Bouchard Père et Fils, it is one of the oldest family properties in Montrachet. Its origins go back to the early nineteenth century, when the vines made up part of Domaine Bouchard. Born in 1820, Anne-Marie Bouchard inherited part of the vineyard. The wife of Félix Cellard, a doctor in Meursanges, she had several children, one of whom Lucie, (born in 1851) married Ferdinand Boillerault in Volnay in 1875. Thus the Montrachet came into this family, Lazare Boillerault (1876-1930) marrying Geneviève de Chauvigny de Blot (1889-1969). They lived in the Château de Meursanges. With the most recent inheritance, the parcels were split up among the heirs of Geneviève Boillerault (or Boillereault as one side of the family spells it). Planted in 1970, 1975 and 1982, these vines are cultivated by Eugène and Bruno Rossignol from Volnay. The wine is sold to merchants under the aegis of the firm of Louis Latour. This *domaine* also extends over Volnay: en Chevret, Cailleret, en l'Ormeau, les Angles.

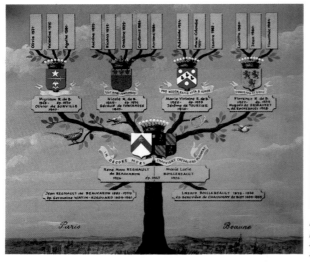

Proprietors:
• Comtesse Marie-Lucie Regnault de Beaucaron in Paris, and her daughters Myriam de Surville, Nicole de Fontanges, Marie-Violaine de Tourtier and Florence de Grimaudet de Rochebouët.
• Madame François Guillaume, in Menthon-Saint-Bernard and her children, Olivier, Anne, Lionel and Aleth Guillaume.

In charge of the domaine:
Comte René-Marc
Regnault de Beaucaron
49 rue Boissière, 75016 Paris

Production (in hectolitres):
1987: 34.20   1989: 38.34
1988: 39.72

Sleeve for a record made for the fortieth wedding anniversary of Marie-Lucie and René-Marc de Beaucaron in 1987: the family tree.

RENNER
René Renner

◊ *Criots-Bâtard-Montrachet* (CBM)

These two parcels of Criots (2 ares 67 centiares and 3 ares 70 centiares) belong to a physiotherapist, practising in Dakar for some forty years. He met the woman who was to become his wife during the Second World War, when he was in the medical service and she was a nurse at the front. So this Alsatian adopted Burgundy by marrying a girl from Chassagne, Suzanne Villien. He has an elegant house in the village and several rows of vines, notably these Criots, bought from one of his brothers-in-law, André Villien, a fighter-pilot and a member of the *Patrouille de France*. They are cultivated by another brother-in-law, Jacky Villien-Guyard, who owns 34 ares 40 centiares in the Clos Saint-Jean. He has some vines on *métayage* in Côte de Nuits, near Corgoloin and Villers-la-Faye, where his wife comes from. But he works mainly for Domaine Joseph Drouhin (see above), one of the finest viti-vinicultural businesses in Burgundy, which stretches from Montrachet to Chambertin-Clos de Bèze.

Métayage? Tenant-farming? "Neither one nor the other," replies Jacky Villien-Guyard. It is just the family helping out. The vines are very old in Criots, nearly fifty years. I generally declare this wine as Chassagne-Montrachet. There is only a slender yield, about 15 hectolitres. But it's good!"

Proprietor:	**Manager:**
René Renner	Jacky Villien-Guyard
BP 1227 Dakar	23 rue du Faubourg
Republic of Senegal	Saint-Jacques, 21200 Beaune
	Tel: 80 22 06 75

ROMANEE-CONTI
Domaine de la Romanée-Conti

◊ *Montrachet* (M), *Bâtard-Montrachet* (BM)
The sole proprietor of La Romanée-Conti and La Tâche, proprietor in Richebourg, Grands-Echézeaux and Echézeaux, manager and joint proprietor of La Romanée-Saint-Vivant Marey-Monge, Domaine de la Romaine-Conti is the *ne plus ultra* of Burgundy. Furthermore these are the only Burgundy wines whose auction prices are regularly published in the British review *Decanter*. Its two administrators (we might almost say "joint-princes", as in Andorra) are Lalou Bize-Leroy and Aubert de Villaine. They are the children of Henri Leroy and Edmond de Villaine, the creators of this exceptional *domaine*. The first, a remarkable woman from the vineyards of Burgundy, also directs the firm of Leroy in Auxey-Duresses, which has an extraordinary reserve of old vintages and a fantastic range of the most prestigious Gevrey-Chambertin appellations: in all, about 2.5 million bottles (the "national library" of great Burgundy wines). The Domaine's vineyards are in Auxey-Duresses, Meursault, Pommard, Vosne-Romanée, Vougeot, Chambolle-Musigny and Gevrey-Chambertin. In 1988, it acquired the 12 hectares of Domaine Charles Noëllat in Vosne-Romanée for a mere 65 million francs (with the buildings and a fine reserve stock). The private tasting which Lalou Bize-Leroy organizes every year in Auvenay brings together the "jet set" of the world of vines, wines and restaurants. Aubert de Villaine also has a personal vineyard in Bouzeron near Chagny, where he produces a remarkable Aligoté. With his wife Pamela, who comes from one an old Californian family, he gives a great deal of his attention to the vineyards in the Côte Chalonnaise. Both watch vigilantly over Domaine de la Romanée-Conti. Assisted by an estate manager (for a long time André Noblet, an outstanding figure in Burgundy, and today his son Bernard), they share administration and marketing equally between them (the United States and Great Britain for Aubert de Villaine and the rest of the world for Lalou Bize-Leroy).

The Domaine has three parcels in Montrachet located in Chassagne with a total size of 67 ares 59 centiares. The first parcel (34 ares 19 centiares) was bought in 1963 from

Comte de Moucheron in Meursault (the former Serre-Bernard property); the second in 1965 from Monsieur Roizot (16 ares 70 centiares – former Drapier property, acquired in 1870 from Monsieur de Courtivron), the third in 1980 from Roland Thévenin (16 ares 70 centiares). Two of these parcels were planted over fifty years ago; the third in the 1960s. In addition, the Domaine de la Romanée-Conti owns a parcel of 17 ares 46 centiares in Bâtard-Montrachet, planted more than fifty years ago, whose wine is sold exclusively in the cask to merchants.

The famous American wine specialist and journalist Terry Robards wrote of the Domaine's Montrachet 1985: "Rich, full and with generous aromas and hints of butter. A firm, powerful structure. A monumental Montrachet." Lalou Bize-Leroy replies: "It is completely closed up." Terry Robards then observes: "If that is true, we shall be dealing with a monster when it opens up." Lalou Bize-Leroy goes on: "It is not like in California. We do not make the wines. They make themselves" (*The Wine Spectator*, September 30, 1987). The retail price of this wine in New York at the end of 1980s: $315 per bottle.

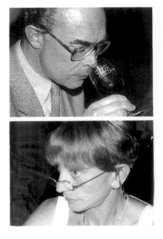

Proprietor:	Best vintages:
Domaine de la Romanée-Conti	1966, 1970, 1973, 1978, 1983,
Vosne-Romanée	1985.
21700 Nuits-Saint-Georges	
Tel: 80 61 04 57	**Tasting:**

Production (in hectolitres):
We here follow the Domaine's custom of indicating on the label the exact number of bottles produced and numbering each one.
• **M**
1984: 18.24 (2432 bottles)
1985: 20.35 (2174 bottles)
1986: 22.80 (2940 bottles)
1987: 15.96
1988: 28.38
1989: 26.22
• **BM**
1984: 4.56   1987: 4.56
1985: 4.56   1988: 7.33
1986: 4.56   1989: 2.28

M 1969. *The oldest vintage in this tasting. The panel spoke of rare emotions and classic flavours. It is impossible to compare such a bottle With the 83s or 85s. A handsome veteran, this wine was quite remarkable. We cannot reprove it for what it now lacks, and we have to admit that if everyone aged this well, old age would be blissful...*

"The two joint princes".

ROUX
Héritiers Roux (Collin et Picamelot)

◊ *Bâtard-Montrachet* (BM)
Not being growers, the heirs of Marie-Thérèse Roux in Chassagne-Montrachet gave their *domaine* on *métayage* in 1982 to vignerons from Remigny near Chagny. Apart from 70 ares in Clos Saint-Jean, there is notably 5 ares 36 centiares in Bâtard-Montrachet. The *métayers* press the grapes and sell the must immediately to the firm of Prosper Maufoux in Santenay.

Proprietors:	Métayers:	Vinification:
Famillies Collin and Picamelot in	GAEC des Vignerons	Prosper Maufoux
Chassagne-Montrachet	Guy Fontaine and Jacky Vion	21590 Santenay
	Remigny, 71150 Chagny	Tel: 80 20 60 40
	Tel: 85 87 14 01	

SAUZET
Domaine Etienne Sauzet

◊ *Bâtard-Montrachet* (BM), *Bienvenues-Bâtard-Montrachet* (BBM)

Born in 1903. Etienne Sauzet created in his village of Puligny a *domaine* of great renown. Thanks to him Combettes has attained a fascinating elegance. Etienne Sauzet died in 1975, and his grandchildren have now taken on the *domaine,* giving it the same careful attention. The firm of Domaine Etienne Sauzet has two parcels in Bâtard-Montrachet. The first (13 ares 77 centiares), in Puligny, was bought in 1936 by Etienne Sauzet. These vines were planted in 1956. The second (18 ares 31 centiares), in Chassagne, was bought in 1980 by his heirs. These vines were replanted in 1976. There is also a parcel of 11 ares 62 centiares in Bienvenues-Bâtard-Montrachet, planted in 1956. This large *domaine* extends over Puligny and Chassagne. There are several vineyards in the *Premiers Crus* of Puligny: Combettes (which often has all the qualities of a *Grand Cru*), Truffière, Champ Canet, Referts and Perrières. The *domaine* belongs to Etienne Sauzet's widow and to their daughter, Madame Colette Sauzet-Boillot, and is administered by the latter's daughter and son-in-law, Gérard Boudot. Originally from Creusot, this oenologist and one-time rugby player has been adopted by the Puligny growers since his marriage. The firm operates from the family house, constructed in the middle of the last century, and one of the rare few to look out over the *Grands Crus.* From his office window, Gérard Boudot can watch over the vines undisturbed. Since he arrived, he has carried out technical improvements and increased the proportion of new casks purchased for ageing the wines. He has no hard and fast rules for ageing his *Grands Crus* in the cask: one year, fourteen, fifteen months, sixteen months... "It is the wine itself which tells me," he says. His wife helps him with the administration but his three children are still too young to play a role in the business. He bottles ninety-five per cent of the production. Fifty per cent of the *Grands Crus* is exported, but he is presently expanding the French market. All his wines are as straightforward and open as he is

Gérard Boudot.

Proprietor:
Domaine Etienne Sauzet
Puligny-Montrachet
21190 Meursault
Tel: 80 21 32 10

Production (in hectolitres):
* **BM**

1981: 12.54		1986: 18.81	
1982: 22.80		1987: 15	
1983: 18.24		1988: 16	
1984: 13.68		1989: 15.40	
1985: 18.24			

* **BBM**

1981: 4.56		1986: 6.84	
1982: 6.84		1987: 5	
1983: 5.70		1988: 6	
1984: 4.56		1989: 5.50	
1985: 6.84			

Best vintages:
1962, 1964, 1966, 1969, 1970, 1973, 1979, 1982, 1983, 1985.

Tasting:

BM 1985. *Light, limpid and transparent, this Bâtard breathes new wood. Honey, hawthorn blossom or almond? It is charming. The attack is clean, the acidity clearly present, and fairly long in the mouth, but perhaps not quite sufficiently for this* climat. *It calls to mind a Meursault. But an 85 with a future. Give it time to live.*

BBM 1985. *Difficult to give a verdict. One of our panel thought the aromas were totally mute, the others found them extraordinarily fine. But the general opinion was very favourable: a wine with an exceptional future. Freshness does not rule out persistence. A wine of very high quality!*

THENARD
Domaine Thénard

◇ *Montrachet* (M)

If chemistry and wine agree on one point, it is that they revere the memory of the Barons Thénard. Closely linked with the history of Burgundy and that of the vine, this name features on Montrachet's roll of honour of illustrious names. It is part of the very walls. And indeed the property is over a century old.

This parcel of 1 hectare 83 ares 31 centiares was bought on February 25, 1873 from the Godard family of Saint-Aubin (1 hectare 7 ares) and the Simon family (72 ares 76 centiares) by Paul Thénard. Born in 1819, he was the son of the chemist Louis-Jacques Thénard (1777-1857), a member of the *Académie des sciences*, and created a baron by Charles X in 1825. His coat of arms was azure three crucibles argent. Azure? More precisely, the cobalt blue or "Thénard blue" invented for decorating Sèvres porcelain. Louis-Jacques Thénard was the *député* for Sens. When he came up for re-election, he was told he would have to make a profession of faith. In outrage he refused, doubtless considering that professions of faith were a matter for the church. He none the less became a peer of France and went back to his laboratory. We owe hydrogen peroxide to him. His son Paul, Baron Thénard, who acquired the Montrachet, was passionately fond of wine. Also a member of the *Académie des sciences*, an eminent chemist and distinguished agronomist (he created a model farm, and carried out studies of manures and fertilizers, among other work), he was to play a decisive role in the struggle against phylloxera in France. As early as 1869 he was the first to suggest using carbon disulphide to destroy the insect that was ravaging the vineyards. Although the first attempts were unsuccessful, Montpellier Agricultural College, and then the faculty of science of Marseilles University continued his work, perfecting the proportions and finally succeeding in producing a satisfactory treatment, though of limited efficacy. Later, it was grafting on to American stock which really saved French vines.

Paul Thénard, who owned the Château de La Ferté, married Philippine-Bonne Derrion-Duplan in Givry, also on the Côte Chalonnaise. They settled in Burgundy, where they created a fine large *domaine,* frequently spending time in the Château de Talmay near the hop fields of la Vingeanne (Côte-d'Or), which the Baron had inherited from an uncle, an ironmaster in Pesme. Up to his death in 1884 on the eve of harvesting, Paul Thénard kept careful records of his Montrachet, noting all his income and expenditure. The line of the Barons Thénard continued; they were administrators of Blanzy and Saint-Gobain, or newspapermen (when newspapers started writing about wine), and today Arnould Thénard directs Dijon's *Le Bien public.*

With considerable astuteness Paul Thénard's widow, who died in 1921 at the age of 98, took in hand the organization of the Domaine's succession. At 97, when the financial structure of the GFA (*groupement foncier agricole*) did not yet exist, she invented an equivalent formula. She created an SCA – a *société civile agricole.* Each of her six grandchildren was to receive 100 shares. This was not a family trust, but a limited company firm whose 600 shares remained in the family. This enabled the land of this remarkable entity to be solidly maintained.

Administered since 1960 by Jacques Bordeaux Montrieux, a member of the family from the Val de Loire who studied architecture ("I knew nothing about wine twenty-five years ago," he admits, "but you learn about wine just like anything else. It is simply a question of humility!"), Domaine Thénard has, apart from the Montrachet, 20 hectares in Givry red, 90 ares in Corton Clos du Roi, 85 ares in Pernand Ile des Vergelesses and 17 ares in Clos Saint-Jean in Chassagne. The Montrachet vines were replanted in stages in 1945, 1960, 1963, 1968, 1974, 1978 and 1981. They are cultivated by Denise Jusseau from Corpeau, who prunes and ties them. Her family and the helicopter help out when

Baron Paul Thénard was in the vanguard of the struggle against phylloxera in France.

necessary, and her grapes are transported very rapidly to the vat-house and cellars in Givry a few miles away.

A passionate and conscientious vintner, Jacques Bordeaux Montrieux sells part of his wine to the trade and part to direct customers. Until 1985 nearly all the production went to merchants, in particular the firm of Remoissenet in Beaune. Several bottles have always been held back for wine lovers, General de Gaulle or the Pope. To these must be added prestigious restaurants such as *La Tour d'Argent*. Why does Jacques Bordeaux Montrieux not sell more of his Montrachet "by the bottle"? He explains this quite simply: "Making wine is one profession; selling it is another. I have always considered that you should not mix the two. Each to his own job. Things are beginning to change now, but making wine, ageing it and making a success of it is enough to fill our days and nights, believe me! And then I like to hear the merchants saying: 'And it could have been so good.'" The firm of Remoissenet acts as brokers for everything. Other merchant-vintners have acquired Montrachet here in recent years: Louis Latour and Nicolas, for example. Over recent years – Louis Latour and Nicolas, for example.

In the style of former days, the old label used to mention the domaine's awards: first prize at the Chicago Universal Exhibition (1893), and in London (1908), non competitor (excellence acknowledged) at the Paris Universal Exhibitions of 1878, 1889 and 1900, gold medal in Paris in 1962. Foolishly, the authorities have erased these references which were prejudicial to no one, at least those pre-dating 1914: the feeling was that they might mislead the consumer. So the label has been changed, though retaining the soberly classic style: the decorative motive we see today was inspired by the seal of Charles the Bold. Aren't people now going to say that this great Duke's interest in Montrachet is without historical justification? The labels of the firm of Remoissenet are decorated with the family coat of arms and the famous "Thénard blue" created for the manufacture of Sèvres porcelain. An aristocratic wine? The aristocratic taste of today is rather democratic. "Read this," says Jacques Bordeaux Montrieux, holding out an article in *Libération*: "When you have drunk a Montrachet from Domaine du Baron Thénard with a simple *baguette* filled with a few whole truffles fresh from the oven, you fall hopelessly in love with wine," writes J.-P. Gene."This 1973 Montrachet is certainly an extreme example: with Baron Thénard, we are in the kingdom of the great French vineyards, in a year which, what is more, fully deserved its success" (August 26, 1986). For his hundredth article in the review *Decanter*, Michael Broadbent chose to evoke the memory of his best tasting: it was in the *Bordeaux Club* in Cambridge – a Montrachet 1978, Domaine Thénard.

An inscribed gateway.

Proprietor:
Domaine Thénard
7 rue de l'Hôtel-de-Ville
71640 Givry
Tel: 85 44 31 36

Production (in hectolitres):
1981: 51.87   1984: 70.88
1982: 75.44   1985: 77.72
1983: 68.97   1986: 72.60

Best vintage:
1973.

Tasting:

M 1985. *Bright and limpid, delicately woody with a slight hint of honey against a background of almond and vanilla, its structure is long rather than round. Attractive mellowness balanced by a sufficient level of acidity. This is a sure sign of a wine that is suitable for long keeping.*

URENA-MARTIN
now *COOMBE CASTLE FINE FOODS*

◊ *Bâtard-Montrachet* – Resulting from the division of the Domaine Louis Lancier-Brugnot, this plot of 15 ares 57 centiares belonging to Erick Urena-Martin of Meursault was sold in 1989 to Simon Oliver (Coombe Castle Fine Foods Ltd). This company is part of Mendip Foods, the largest retailer of farmhouse cheddar cheese in UK. The transaction was handled by Jean Saint-Arroman, European manager of the group and a Burgundian by origin. Simon Oliver owns no other vines and views this vineyard as a work of art. This Bâtard is cultivated on *métayage* by Dominique Piguet-Girardin (Auxey-Duresses), who sells his share in juice form to Louis Jadot.

Proprietors:
• Coombe Castle Fine Foods
19 Wolley Street

Bradford-on-Avon
BA15 1AB Wiltshire
Great Britain

• Jean Saint-Arroman
31, rue Maurice Ripoche
75014 Paris

VAUDIAUX-POIRIER
Jacqueline Vaudiaux-Poirier

◊ *Bâtard-Montrachet* (BM)

A doctor's wife from Nolay, Jacqueline Vaudiaux-Poirier has owned a parcel of 66 ares 95 centiares in Bâtard-Montrachet in her own right since 1987. Previously it was in a family trust with her sister, Marie-Rose Garnier. These vines were acquired at the beginning of the 1920s by Louis Poirier, the son of a nurseryman from Chagny, Joseph Poirier. According to family tradition, Louis Poirier found himself rather by chance at an auction sale in Santenay. No one wanted this Bâtard and he adopted it. And he was right. He died in 1972. His brother Claude-Marius (see Claude-Maxence Poirier) also established a vineyard in Bâtard-Montrachet. This vineyard, planted in 1921 is run on *métayage* for half the yield by Roger Caillot-Morey in Meursault. The proprietor's wine is sold entirely in must to the firm of Louis Jadot (see above), and that of the *métayer* to his private customers.

Jacqueline Vaudiaux-Poirier also has vines in Pommard (Arvelets and Croix Noires), while Roger Caillot-Morey is the owner of vines with the appellation Bourgogne Aligoté, Bourgogne blanc, Meursault Le Cromin (white), Puligny-Montrachet *Premier Cru* Les Folatières and in reds, Bourgogne Grand Ordinaire, Bourgogne rouge, Monthélie and Meursault (Côte de Beaune). He owns a large part of his vines through his wife Odile, née Morey. All together, he runs some 8.5 hectares of which 3 belong to him. Roger Caillot-Morey's two sons, Dominique and Michel are both growers. They have their own vines on *métayage* and by tenant-farming. They do not yet sell in the bottle. Roger Caillot does not want to expand his *domaine* by tenant-farming or *métayage*. He sells his wines in the bottle.

Proprietor:
Jacqueline Vaudiaux-Poirier
21340 Nolay
Tel: 80 21 78 47

Métayer:
Roger Caillot-Morey
14 rue de Cronin
21190 Meursault
Tel: 80 21 20 12

Production (in hectolitres):

1984: 29.64	1987: 22.80
1985: 63.84	1988: 16.52
1986: 57	1989: 12.54

Best vintage: 1959.

Proprietors, Managers and Merchant-Vintners

Amiot-Bonfils (Domaine)
Rue du Grand-Puits,
21190 Chassagne-Montrachet.
Tel: 80 21 38 62.
See page 125

Aufauvre, Jean
21290 Chassagne-Montrachet.
Tel: 80 21 31 04.

Bachelet, Anne-Marguerite
21190 Chassagne-Montrachet.
Tel: 80 21 32 49.

Bachelet, Bernard (et Fils)
71150 Dezize-lès-Maranges.
Tel: 85 91 16 11 and 80 21 37 27.
This grower from Dezize has acquired Domaine de la Connière in Chassagne, formerly in the hands of the Beaune firm of Marcilly.

Bachelet, Jean-Claude (Domaine)
Gamay, 21190 Saint-Aubin.
Tel: 80 21 31 01.
See page 126

Bachelet-Ramonet Père et Fils (Domaine)
21190 Chassagne-Montrachet.
Tel: 80 21 32 49.
See page 126

Harvesting at the château.

Bader-Mimeur
Château de Chassagne,
21190 Chassagne-Montrachet.
Tel: 80 21 30 22.
Merchant-vintner and proprietor. An old Chassagne family long resident in the château.

Barolet-Pernot Père et Fils
21190 Saint-Romain.
Tel: 80 21 20 88.
See page 127

Baudrand-Gaudet et Fils
71150 Remigny.
Tel: 85 87 18 26.

Bavard, Charles et Paul
21190 Puligny-Montrachet.
Tel: 80 21 31 48
See page 127

Bavard, Jean-Paul
4 rue Derrière le Château,
21190 Puligny-Montrachet.
Tel: 80 21 38 17.
See page 127

Belicard, Bernard
Rue du Meix-Pelletier,
21190 Puligny-Montrachet.
Tel: 80 21 31 25.

Belland, Joseph (Domaine)
Rue de la Chapelle,
21590 Santenay.
Tel: 80 20 61 13.
See page 128

Bernard, Jean-Claude
Rue du Chêne,
21190 Chassagne-Montrachet.
Tel: 80 21 30 56.

Bidault, Jean-Claude
Place du Monument,
21190 Puligny-Montrachet.
Tel: 80 21 36 32.

Blain-Gagnard (Domaine)
Route de Santenay,
21190 Chassagne.
Tel: 80 21 34 07.
See page 128

Blonde, Albert
Morgeot,
21190 Chassagne-Montrachet.
Tel: 80 21 34 07

Blondeau-Danne (Domaine)
Château, 21190 Saint-Aubin.
Tel: 80 21 31 46.
See page 129

Boissard, Michel
21190 Puligny-Montrachet.

Bonnardeau, Fernand
21190 Chassagne-Montrachet.
Tel: 80 21 31 05.

Bonneau, Gisèle
6 rue de la Mairie,
21190 Puligny-Montrachet.
Tel: 80 21 30 85.

Bonnefoy, Charles
21190 Chassagne-Montrachet.
Tel: 80 21 30 89.
See page 130

Henri Bonnefoy.

Bonnefoy, Henri
Route de Santenay,
21190 Chassagne-Montrachet.
Tel: 80 21 36 90.
He is said to be the most hardworking man in Chassagne. He does not count the hours he puts in and he always wears a smile. Henri Bonnefoy has hardly any vines of his own but he works those of the Marquis de Laguiche; that is noble enough. He also figures in the first part of this book.

Bonnefoy, Pierre
Route de Santenay,
21190 Chassagne-Montrachet.
Tel: 80 21 33 04.

Bouchard Père et Fils
Au château, 21200 Beaune
Tel: 80 22 14 41.
See page 130

Bouzereau, Hubert
22 A, rue Velle,
21190 Meursault.
Tel: 80 21 20 05.

Bouzereau, Michel
3 rue Planche-Meunière,
21190 Meursault.
Tel: 80 21 20 74.

Bouzereau, Philippe
15 place de l'Europe,
21190 Meursault.
Tel: 80 21 20 32.

Bouzereau, Pierre
7 rue Labbé, 21190 Meursault.
Tel: 80 21 23 74.

Brenot (Domaine)
21590 Santenay.
Tel: 80 20 61 27.
See page 132

Bzikot, Stanislas
Rue de Poiseul,
21190 Puligny-Montrachet.
Tel: 80 21 33 39.

Caillot-Morey, Roger
14 rue de Cronin,
21190 Meursault.
Tel: 80 21 20 12.
See page 175

Carillon, Louis (et Fils)
Rue Drouhin,
21190 Puligny-Montrachet.
Tel: 80 21 30 34.
See page 133

Chartron, Jean (Domaine)
Grande-Rue,
21190 Puligny-Montrachet.
Tel: 80 21 32 85.
See page 133

Chartron et Trébuchet
13 Grande-Rue,
21190 Puligny-Montrachet.
Tel: 80 21 36 91.
Merchant-vintner. See page 133

Château de Puligny-Montrachet (Domaine du)
Château, 21190 Puligny-Montrachet. Tel: 80 21 38 38.
Sold in 1985 to Domaine Laroche (Chablis) by Roland Thévenin, the vine-growing poet, Domaine du Château de Puligny Montrachet was acquired in 1988 by Crédit Foncier de France for 35 million francs. The Japanese group Suntory were also among the bidders. In addition to the 18th century château being restored, the buildings have just been renovated and enlarged (the cuverie). The domaine covers 21 hectares (Puligny Montrachet, Meursault, Pommard, Monthélie, Côte de Nuits – 4 hectares at Comblanchien in the Côte de Nuits bought in 1989 from a South African). Claude Schneider manages the estate and Jacques Montagnon takes care of the vines.

Chauve, Marie-Anne
Rue du Chêne,
21190 Chassagne-Montrachet.
Tel: 80 21 35 17.

Chauve, Marie-Thérèse
21190 Chassagne-Montrachet
Tel: 80 21 32 89.

Chavy, Anne-Marie
Rue de Poiseul,
21190 Puligny-Montrachet.
Tel: 80 21 33 99.
See page 135

Chavy, Gérard
Rue du Vieux-Château,
21190 Puligny-Montrachet.
Tel: 80 21 31 47.

Chavy, Marie-France
Ets Louis Chavy
Place des Marronniers,
21190 Puligny-Montrachet.
Tel: 80 21 31 39.
This firm of merchants founded in 1950, has been directed by Marie-France Chavy since 1985. It primarily serves restaurateurs and private clients. The domaine is run separately.

Chavy, Pierre
Rue du Vieux-Château,
21190 Puligny-Montrachet.
Tel: 80 21 32 88.

Chavy-Chouet, Hubert
29 rue Mazeray,
21190 Meursault.
Tel: 80 21 61 74.

Chavy-Ropiteau, Albert
10 rue Moulin-Landin,
21190 Meursault.
Tel: 80 21 28 01.

Chifflot, Rémy
21190 Puligny-Montrachet.

Clerc, Henri (et Fils)
Place des Marronniers,
21190 Puligny-Montrachet.
Tel: 80 21 32 74.
See page 135

Coffinet, Fernand
21190 Chassagne-Montrachet.
Tel: 80 21 31 22.
See page 136

Colin, Bernard
21190 Chassagne-Montrachet.
Tel: 80 21 32 78.

Colin, François (Madame)
Place de la Bascule,
21190 Chassagne-Montrachet.
Tel: 80 21 85 03.
Two of the three Colin brothers (François and Louis) are dead. There remains Pierre for this generation. Jeanne Colin is François' widow, Michel Colin-Deléger their son. Bernard is Louis' son Marguerite, Marc's mother. The wine of Domaine François Colin has had moments of great glory. At

a private tasting on their estate in the Napa valley, Robert Mondavi's wife used a bottle of this domaine as a reference for judging their whites. Jeanne Colin has superb Demoiselles in Puligny.

Colin, Marc (Domaine)
Garnay, 21190 Saint-Aubin.
Tel: 80 21 30 43.
See page 137

Colin, Marguerite
21190 Chassagne-Montrachet.

Colin, Pierre
21190 Chassagne-Montrachet.

Colin-Deléger, Michel (Dne)
21190 Chassagne-Montrachet.
Tel: 80 21 32 72.

Cotessat, Jean
21190 Chassagne-Montrachet.

Courreaux, Bernard
RN 74, 21190 Puligny-Montrachet. Tel: 80 21 32 02.

Crépeau, André
Route de Santenay,
21190 Chassagne-Montrachet.
Tel: 80 21 35 78.
André Crépeau is Gaston's son; Marcel, his cousin.

Crépeau, Gaston
Route de Santenay,
21190 Chassagne-Montrachet.
Tel: 80 21 30 37.

Crépeau-Roulot, Marcel
21190 Chassagne-Montrachet.
Tel: 80 21 33 33.
The only person in the area to have other crops, he is a farmer and grower. One more difference which he does not hide: he is a Communist, and holds this flame aloft in Chassagne.

David, Camille
21190 Puligny-Montrachet.
Tel: 80 21 30 18.

Delagrange-Bachelet (Domaine)
21190 Chassagne-Montrachet.
Tel: 80 21 32 67.
See page 138

Deléger, Georges
21190 Chassagne-Montrachet.
Tel: 80 21 32 56.
See page 139

Deléger, Joseph
21190 Chassagne-Montrachet.
Tel: 80 21 31 26.

Deléger, Robert
Merceuil, 21190 Meursault.
Tel: 80 21 47 24.
See page 139

Deveze, Bernard
21190 Puligny-Montrachet.

Drouhin (Maison et Domaine Joseph Drouhin)
7 rue d'Enfer, BP 29,
21102 Beaune Cedex.
Tel: 80 24 68 88.
See page 140

Dubuisson, Jean-Michel
Grande-Rue,
21190 Puligny-Montrachet.
Tel: 80 21 33 74.

Dupard Aîné
Grande-Rue,
21190 Puligny-Montrachet.
Tel: 80 21 33 38.
Grower and merchant-vintner.
See page 134

Duperrier-Adam, Roger
21190 Chassagne-Montrachet.
Tel: 80 21 31 10.

Dury-Millot, François
23 rue Velle, 21190 Meursault.
Tel: 80 21 25 55.

Fagot, Bernard
21190 Corpeau.
Tel: 80 21 30 24.

Fleurot, René (Domaine)
Château du Passe Temps,
21590 Santenay.
Tel: 80 20 61 15.
See page 140

Fontaine-Gagnard (Domaine)
Place de l'Eglise,
21190 Chassagne-Montrachet.
Tel: 80 21 35 01 and 80 21 35 50.
See page 142

Fontaine-Vion (GAEC)
71150 Remigny.
Tel: 85 91 21 72.

Gacon-Moingeon, Yveline
Rue du Vieux-Château,
21190 Puligny-Montrachet.
Tel: 80 21 33 22.

Gagnard, Jean-Noël (Domaine)
21190 Chassagne-Montrachet.
Tel: 80 21 31 68.
See page 143

Gagnard-Delagrange (Domaine)
21190 Chassagne-Montrachet.
Tel: 80 21 31 40.
See page 144

Gailliot, Jean
21190 Corpeau.
Tel: 80 21 32 32.
See page 145

Garaudet, Philippe
21190 Puligny-Montrachet.
Tel: 80 21 30 18.

Girardin, Jacques and Vincent
21590 Santenay.
Tel: 80 20 60 12.

Gonet, Albert
21190 Chassagne-Montrachet.
Tel: 80 21 36 29.

Guérin, Gérard
Rue Derrière-le-Château,
21190 Puligny-Montrachet.
Tel: 80 21 30 90.

Guérin, Renée
21190 Puligny-Montrachet.
Tel: 80 21 32 25.

Henry, Etienne
21190 Puligny-Montrachet.

Henry, Marcel
Petite-Rue,
21190 Puligny-Montrachet.
Tel: 80 21 36 39.

Jacquin, Henri (Madame)
21190 Puligny-Montrachet.
See page 145

Jadot, Louis (Domaine & Maison)
5 rue Samuel-Legay,
21200 Beaune.
Tel: 80 22 10 57.
See page 146

Jelic, Stéphane
Grande-Rue,
21190 Puligny-Montrachet.
Tel: 80 21 35 30.

Joly, Daniel
21190 Puligny-Montrachet.
Tel: 80 20 62 53.

Joly-Charau, Albert
21190 Puligny-Montrachet.
Tel: 80 21 30 29.
See page 160

Jomain, Marc
Ets Vve Henri Moroni
Rue de l'Abreuvoir.
21190 Puligny-Montrachet.
Tel: 80 21 30 48.
Marc Jomain is a grower. Jacqueline manages the firm of merchant vintners founded in 1922 by Henri Moroni to augment a vineyard of

René Lamy's treasure-house.

7 hectares (Combettes, Pucelles, Perrières, Referts, Puligny Montrachet white and red "Village" appellation). The merchant side is more concerned with the Côtes de Nuits and de Beaune. A tasting cellar.

Jouard, Gabriel
21190 Chassagne-Montrachet.
Tel: 80 21 30 30.
See page 147.

Jouard, Pierre (Domaine)
21190 Chassagne-Montrachet.
Tel: 80 21 30 25.
See page 148

Lacroix, Pierre
Place de la Bascule,
21190 Chassagne-Montrachet.
Tel: 80 21 33 83.
See page 156

Lamy, Hubert
21190 Saint-Aubin.
Tel: 80 21 32 55.
See page 161

Lamy-Pillot, René
Route de Santenay,
21190 Chassagne-Montrachet.
Tel: 80 21 30 52.
René Lamy, former president of the Federation of Viticulturalists of Chassagne-Montrachet for four years and originally from Saint-Aubin, has been a proprietor in Chassagne for twenty years. He worked on the Duc de Magenta's vines for five years before setting up himself. Today he runs 16 hectares of vines, a third of which he owns and two-thirds of which

Purchased by Domaine Laroche in Chablis in September 1985 from Roland Thévenin, the Château de Puligny, together with its vineyard, have belonged to the Crédit Foncier de France since 1988. See Château de Puligny-Montrachet.

he leases with the following appellations: reds, Bourgogne, Saint-Aubin Les Argilliers, Saint-Aubin Premier Cru Les Castets, Chassagne Montrachet, Chassagne Montrachet Premier Cru (Morgeot, Clos Saint-Jean, Boudriotte) Santenay Les Charrons, Blagny Premier Cru La Pièce sous le Bois and in whites: Bourgogne Aligoté, Saint-Aubin Les Pucelles, Chassagne Montrachet Premier Cru, Chassagne Montrachet Premier Cru Morgeot.

From a family of seven children of whom two brothers and two sisters are growers, René Lamy exports 40% of his production. The rest is sold to private customers. There is a considerable volume of sales direct from the cellar. He has a highly original cellar for tasting decorated with a splendid collection of corkscrews. René Lamy has had Petitjean's parcel in Montrachet on métayage since 1988.

Latour, Louis (Domaine et Maison)
18 rue des Tonneliers,
21204 Beaune.
Tel: 80 22 31 20.
See page 153

Leflaive (Domaine)
Place des Marronniers,
21190 Puligny-Montrachet.
Tel: 80 21 30 13.
See page 154

Leflaive, Olivier (Frères)
Place du Monument,
21190 Puligny-Montrachet.
Tel: 80 21 37 65.
Created in 1985 and separate from Domaine Leflaive, this firm of merchant-vintners specializes in Burgundy appellations and retains a "human dimension". Ageing of the wines is in the hands of Franck Grux.

Lequin-Roussot (Domaine)
Rue de la Gare,
21590 Santenay.
Tel: 80 20 61 46.
See page 156

Llorca, François
Cour du Vieux-Château,
21190 Puligny-Montrachet.
Tel: 80 21 32 61.

Llorca, Gérard
21190 Puligny-Montrachet.

Magenta (Domaine du Duc Philippe de)
Château de Sully, 71360 Epinac
et Abbaye de Morgeot,
21190 Chassagne-Montrachet.
Tel: 80 21 30 77.
Marketing: Maison Louis Jadot,
5 rue Samuel-Legay, Beaune.
Tel: 80 22 10 57.
The great grandson of Edme Patrice de MacMahon, Duc de Magenta, Field Marshal of France and President of the Republic, Philippe de Magenta has owned the beautiful old Domaine de la Chapelle de l'Abbaye de Morgeot between Chassagne and Santenay since 1967 (the Abbaye de Morgeot belongs to René Fleurot of Santenay). He has invited all the "jet set" there. Production and marketing of the wines of Domaine du Duc de Magenta has recently been entrusted to the firm of Louis Jadot for a pe-

riod of twenty years. Altogether there are 12 hectares of vines: 4 ha 40 a Clos de la Chapelle, 2 ha Premier Cru Clos de la Garenne in Puligny, 3 ha 20 a in Auxey-Duresses and 80 a in Meix Chavaux in Meursault. The Clos de la Chapelle, near Abbaye de Morgeot, is a monopoly.

Maltroye (Château de la)
21190 Chassagne-Montrachet.
Tel: 80 21 32 45 and 80 21 38 96.
See page 162

Maroslavac-Kovacevic, Stephan
Vieux-Château,
21190 Puligny-Montrachet.
Tel: 80 21 33 01.
A Yugoslavian émigré, Stephan Maroslavac came to France in 1930 to find work. After being a plasterer, then a farmer in Puligny, he became métayer of a farm belonging to Harorf (former proprietors of Domaine Thévenin) in Puligny-Montrachet. When the Thévenins bought the farm back, Stephan Maroslavac was given a house. He then took the vines of Comtesse de Montlivault on métayage. He has expanded since, and is the present owner of the old Château de Puligny-Montrachet. Since his retirement, his vines have been run by his son, Stephan, a great success; and a story of love and determination.

Stephan Maroslavac.

Maroslavac-Léger, Roland
43 Grande-Rue,
21190 Puligny-Montrachet.
Tel: 80 21 31 23.
Stephan Maroslavac's grandson, 36-year-old Roland Maroslavac started on his own sixteen years ago. He is tenant-farmer of his grandfather's vines (through his mother Jeanine Tremeau) - 2 hectares in Puligny, Puligny Montrachet Premier Cru Les Combettes, Chassagne Montrachet white and

red, Bourgogne Aligoté, Bourgogne; tenant-farmer of one hectare (of the late Monsieur Patin) in Puligny Montrachet; and his own vines in Saint-Aubin red, Puligny Montrachet, Bourgogne white and Aligoté, Meursault and Auxey-Duresses: altogether about 9 hectares. Recently he has started to market 20 - 25% of his production in the bottle, which he sells to private clients and restaurants.

Maroslavac-Tremeau, Stephan
21190 Puligny-Montrachet.
Tel: 80 21 30 19.
Stephan Maroslavac-Tremeau runs his father's 4 hectares, his own 13 and 7 hectares on métayage.

Matrot, Michel
Moulin aux Moines,
21190 Auxey-Duresses.
Tel: 80 21 22 19.

Maufoux, Prosper
21590 Santenay.
Tel: 80 20 60 40.
See page 170

Maurice, Gérard
Place de la Bascule,
21190 Chassagne-Montrachet.
Tel: 80 21 31 21.

Meney, Georges
Rue du Vieux-Château,
21190 Puligny-Montrachet.
Tel: 80 21 33 21.

Mignot, Gaston
21190 Puligny-Montrachet.
Tel: 80 21 33 93.

Mollard-Morey, Bernard
21190 Chassagne-Montrachet.
Tel: 80 21 33 52.

Monnot, Jean-Pierre
Place des Marronniers,
21190 Puligny-Montrachet.
Tel: 80 21 30 45.
See page 157

Montlivault, Madame de
Blagny, 21190 Puligny-Montrachet.
Tel: 80 21 30 35.
On the death of Madame Louise de Montlivault, the domaine was divided out by her son Richard d'Ivry-Montlivault between his children Anne de Cherisey, Jacques and Jean-Louis de Montlivault (Premiers Crus Hameau de Blagny, La Garenne and Chalumeau), Richard himself retaining the usufruct on the greater part of the property both in Puligny-Montrachet and in Meursault Premier Cru. The property has belonged to the Montlivault family since 1811 (bought from Monsieur Villard of Beaune). The chapel of the Maizières monks which belongs to it was acquired in 1913 from Léonce Bocquet who had mutilated it.

J.-M. Morey in his cellar.

Moreau, Bernard
Route de Chagny,
21190 Chassagne-Montrachet.
Tel: 80 21 33 70.

Morey, Albert
21190 Chassagne-Montrachet.
Tel: 80 21 32 23.
See page 158

Morey, Jean-Marc
21190 Chassagne-Montrachet.
Tel: 80 21 32 62.
Named in 1987 as "grower of the year" by Gault Millau, on whose cover he featured, Jean-Marc still has his feet on the ground and his head on his shoulders. He is a marvellous vintner and his bottles are to be found in the restaurants of Bocuse, Troisgros and Chapel, in Australia and Japan. The son of Albert and brother of Bernard, Jean-Marc Morey studied at Beaune Agricultural College and took finishing courses with Max Léglise. In 1964, he started working with his father. After the latter split his vines up among his children (with the exception, of course, of the Bâtard), Jean-Marc worked on his own. That was in 1981 and he quickly became one of the most brilliant "rising stars" of the young generation. He owns, or has on métayage, 8 hectares of whites (Les Caillerets, Chassagne Montrachet and Saint-Aubin) and reds (Beaune Grèves, Santenay, and Chassagne-Montrachet). His Champs Gains are stupendous. He is now President of the Syndicat viticole of Chassagne Montrachet.

Morey, Marc (et Fils)
21190 Chassagne-Montrachet.
Tel: 80 21 30 11.
See page 158

Morey-Coffinet, Michel
Rue du Clos-Saint-Jean,
21190 Chassagne-Montrachet.
Tel: 80 21 31 71.

Morey-Perrin, Bernard
21190 Chassagne-Montrachet.
Tel: 80 21 32 13.

Morin, Henri
21190 Puligny-Montrachet.

Morin, Roland
Rue du Château,
21190 Puligny-Montrachet.
Tel: 80 21 35 20.

Moroni, Henri (Madame)
See Jomain, Marc

Muretta, Francisco
10 rue Clous,
21190 Chassagne-Montrachet.
Tel: 80 21 37 25.
The daughter of the family and her sister Marie-France are the only two women in the area to do all the work on the vines. They even drive the tractor.

Muretta, Marie-France
21190 Chassagne-Montrachet.

A now-famous nurseryman.

Niellon, Michel (Domaine)
21190 Chassagne-Montrachet.
Tel: 80 21 30 95.
See page 159

Nouhaud, Pierre
Rue Poiseul,
21190 Puligny-Montrachet.
Tel: 80 21 36 92.

Pascal, Jean-Luc
Grande-Rue,
21190 Puligny-Montrachet.
Tel: 80 21 34 57 and 80 21 32 07.
A native of Puligny-Montrachet by his grandmother, Jean-Luc Pascal created a limited company with his father in 1978. They work both on their vines (6 hectares owned by them and 9 hectares on métayage) and in their nursery. Their wines have the appellation: Bourgogne red and white, Bourgogne Aligoté, Puligny Village red and white, Puligny Mon-

trachet Premier Cru (Chalumaux, Folatières, Hameau de Blagny, Champ Gain white), and in red Blagny Premier Cru, Volnay Cailleret, Volnay and Pommard.
Jean-Luc Pascal loves both professions. His father, Jean Pascal, was one of Domaine Leflaive's many métayers, but when the inheritors took it in hand in 1955, he was unable to continue. As Jean was an excellent worker, Domaine Leflaive proposed that he should look after the young plantations to compensate him. That is how he and his son became nurserymen. He has made a great success as a grower, and his reputation was quickly established. Among others, he supplies Domaine Leflaive, the firm of Patriarche and Domaine Sauzet. Their turnover figure has increased by 40 % thanks to the nurseries. From 1967, they decided to sell three-quarters of their production in the bottle (between 40,000 and 50,000 bottles per year). On average, they sell 300,000 vines per year, not counting years of frost such as 1986, when they produced 600,000. Losses can be enormous. Grafts do not always take because of poor weather conditions. In 1985, 45% were successful, in 1986 52%, but in 1987 only 30% on account of bad weather in spring. A single vine costs between 6 and 7 francs depending on the variety and graft.

Pernot, Paul (et Fils)
Place du Monument,
21190 Puligny-Montrachet.
Tel: 80 21 32 35.
See page 159

Pillot, Fernand
Les Champs-Gains,
21190 Chassagne-Montrachet.
Tel: 80 21 33 64.

Pillot, Jean
21190 Chassagne-Montrachet.
Tel: 80 21 33 35.

Pillot, Paul
21190 Chassagne-Montrachet.
Tel: 80 21 31 91.

Poinot, Marcel
21230 Voudenay

Ponelle, Daniel
Rue du Creux-de-Chagny,
21190 Puligny-Montrachet.
Tel: 80 21 36 26.

Ponelle, Jean
Rue Poiseul,
21190 Puligny-Montrachet.
Tel: 80 21 35 98.

Ponelle, Jean-François
Rue Poiseul,
21190 Puligny-Montrachet.
Tel: 80 21 32 33.

Pouleau, Georges
Place de la Bascule,
21190 Chassagne-Montrachet.
Tel: 80 21 33 71.

Prieur, Jacques (Domaine)
Les Herbeux, 21190 Meursault.
Tel: 80 21 23 85.
See page 163

Prieur-Brunet (Domaine)
21590 Santenay.
Tel: 80 20 60 56.
See page 164

Ramonet (Domaine)
21190 Chassagne-Montrachet.
Tel: 80 21 30 88.
See page 165

Ramonet, Noël
21190 Chassagne-Montrachet.

Reine Pédauque
Aloxe-Corton,
21420 Savigny-lès-Beaune.
Tel: 80 26 40 00.
See page 161

Reynold de Seresin, Olivier
21200 Beaune.

Riger, Jacky
21190 Puligny-Montrachet.
Tel: 80 21 31 16.

Rodet, Antonin
Mercurey, 71640 Givry.
Tel: 85 45 22 22.
See page 164

Roux, Roger
21190 Chassagne-Montrachet.
Tel: 80 21 33 90.

Roux père et Fils (Domaine)
21190 Saint-Aubin.
Tel: 80 21 32 92 and 80 21 34 09.
In 1960, Fernand Roux left his son Marcel the little vineyard on which he had lived a hand-to-mouth existence. Five hectares of vines (the wine being sold to the trade), a few cows and two horses. After three catastrophic harvests (frost in 1956 and hail in 1957 and 1958), the cellar was almost empty. For Marcel Roux, the choice was simple: either leave for the city or hold on with determination. He decided to stay. He borrowed, rented vines and bought a tractor. Profits were small and the more inadequate because his two sons were interested in the business. Marcel

PULIGNY-MONTRACHET
1er Cru - La Garenne
Appellation Puligny-Montrachet Contrôlée

Mis en bouteille par
ROUX PÈRE & FILS   5d
Négociants à Saint-Aubin par Meursault (Côte-d'Or)
France

Roux then took a big decision. He was going to take full advantage of appellations contrôlées, sell bottles directly to private clients and extend the domaine into the neighbouring communes of Santenay and Puligny-Montrachet... It worked. Customers gave their friends this reliable name. In 1975, his eldest son Christian (who had just finished studying oenology in Beaune) joined him, bringing the backing of his technology. In 1980, Régis finished college in Beaune and also came to work on the domaine. The situation was clearly better. Demand exceeded supply. But three households had to live from the 20 hectares being worked. And Emmanuel, the youngest, had just gone to agricultural college. So Marcel, Christian and Régis founded a small merchant business, anxious to provide high quality. From then on, they bought wines which they matured themselves – wines from neighbouring communes from growers whom they had known for a long time, but only in the Côte de Beaune.
Still surprised that his family can be taken as a model of how to expand a small domaine in Burgundy, Marcel Roux, whom his friends affectionately call "le père Roux", explains: "There is no secret. We simply tried always to make the best possible wine with the slender yields at our disposal. The first customers were satisfied and told their friends, and so on. The children have brought an up-to-date approach to the business and to the oenology side of things too."
The domaine has Burgundy whites: Bourgogne Aligoté (2 hectares), Bourgogne (2 ha 50 a), Saint-Aubin La Pucelle (4 ha 25 a), Saint-Aubin Premier Cru La Chatenière (1 hectare), Chassagne Montrachet (1 hectare), Pu-

ligny Montrachet Les Enseignières (35 a), Meursault Premier Cru Clos des Poruzots 25 ha) and reds: Bourgogne Passe Tout Grains 1 ha 15 a), Bourgogne Les Grands Charmeaux (2 ha 75 a), Saint-Aubin (6 ha), Chassagne Montrachet (1 ha), Santenay Premier Cru (2 ha), Chassagne Montrachet Premier Cru (75 a).

Sauzet, Etienne (Domaine)
21190 Puligny-Montrachet.
Tel: 80 21 32 10.
See page 171

Savry, Marcel
21190 Puligny-Montrachet.
Tel: 80 21 33 69.

Thénard (Domaine)
7 rue de l'Hôtel-de-Ville,
71640 Givry.
Tel: 85 44 31 36.
See page 172

Thevenot, Jacques
13 rue des Forges,
21190 Meursault.
Tel: 80 21 21 77.

Thomas, Pierre
Rue Drouhin,
21190 Puligny-Montrachet.
Tel: 80 21 33 75.

Thusseau, Michel
Rue Drouhin,
21190 Puligny-Montrachet.
Tel: 80 21 33 13.

Toinet, Marcel
21190 Chassagne-Montrachet.

Urena-Martin, Erick
27 rue des Forges,
21190 Meursault.
Tel: 80 21 24 03.

Vallot, Guy
Grande-Rue,
21190 Puligny-Montrachet.
Tel: 80 21 33 31

Verjus, Bernard
Place de l'Eglise,
21190 Puligny-Montrachet.
Tel: 80 21 34 64

Villien-Guyard, Jacky
23 rue du Faubourg-
Saint-Jacques, 21200 Beaune.
Tel: 80 22 06 75.
See page 168

The Vintages

Year	Production in hectolitres					Observations
	M	**CM**	**BM**	**BBM**	**CBM**	
1945	nd	nd	nd	nd	nd	The vintage of the Liberation shared in the general rejoicing.
1946	340	6	nd	nd	nd	Nothing remarkable.
1947	108	56	530	nd	nd	A great vintage.
1948	26	16	165	nd	nd	Although the Bordeaux reds of this vintage were outstanding, the white Burgundies can only just be called "passable". They quickly disappeared.
1949	79	25	307	nd	nd	Very great vintage; the best since 1934. One of the "years of the century".
1950	169	107	625	nd	nd	Abundant harvest. The whites which escaped rot have breeding and are agreeable, sometimes excellent.
1951	122	107	384	nd	nd	Late harvest. Quality not up to standard.
1952	102	87	449	nd	nd	Great hopes had been placed on this vintage but it was ruined by a dull September. Passable but no more.
1953	91	95	433	nd	nd	A wait of four years was needed before wine of the quality of the 1949s was seen once again.
1954	116	261	358	nd	nd	Large harvest and wines of very differing quality. Generally mediocre.
1955	115	46	316	82	40	Excellent white wines with the required body and finesse. The abundant quantity did no harm.
1956	90	81	287	70	36	Light wines from a late and ungenerous harvest.
1957	74	59	188	26	22	Another slender harvest but some whites were very successful.
1958	123	81	242	56	40	Generally the whites are better than the reds. Large production.
1959	121	149	428	91	50	Record year for quantity, christened "year of the century" rather too hastily, for its development is very variable.
1960	150	180	370	81	53	Wines of feeble structure with no great charm.
1961	97	117	264	83	35	Excellent bottles were born of this abundant vintage.
1962	115	106	330	119	50	Fruity wines lacking body. Simple and fine. An elegant year.
1963	163	155	374	178	64	Large harvest with varying results, often mediocre.
1964	173	175	341	142	49	A very great vintage.
1965	146	103	223	85	27	Late harvest giving light wines of no great character, destined for early drinking.
1966	186	138	360	135	53	Remarkable wine and generous yields.
1967	154	135	230	59	23	Average quality but no more.
1968	133	101	285	81	24	The grapes were sodden with constant rain. Although the whites are better than the reds, this eventful year left no pleasant memories for the people of Burgundy.
1969	151	91	310	100	26	A great vintage, which has now aged for 20 years but will perhaps not last much longer.
1970	238	208	457	118	25	If they did not suffer from hail, the whites were better than the reds - light and elegant, but lacking body.
1971	103	123	305	83	19	The over-ripe whites quickly turned gold and suffered from their insufficient acidity and very high alcohol level. Today those that were laid down have a "taste of Sauternes" which gives them a curiosity value.
1972	211	166	441	121	50	Although the reds needed ten years to develop, the whites rapidly disappeared from memory and cellars. Their acidity is overpowering and their grassy taste is surprising without being charming.

Year	Production in hectolitres					Observations
	M	CM	BM	BBM	CBM	
1973	225	276	496	135	52	Very good year after a hot, dry summer, with particularly long wines, supple and elegant. It was also the last year of the old "cascade" system which, in cases of high yields (as in 1973), allowed wines to be declassified in successive tranches (e.g. 35 hectares as Chassagne, 15 as Burgundy, the rest as table wine).
1974	226	139	360	96	34	Resembles the 1972, with frost and rather "unripe" wines produced by two fruitings; fairly round, they are already over the hill.
1975	156	138	284	99	48	Better in whites than reds; a rather poor year both in quality and quantity as a result of unfavourable weather conditions.
1976	220	140	239	144	54	Reds hard, whites too dry. This year of drought had an exceptional amount of sunshine. An early harvest. Historic wines were hoped for which more often than not are still austere and closed up. Will they ever open up?
1977	166	181	452	127	66	A single month of fine weather is not enough to make a great vintage (a sunny autumn after a summer of rain). The wines are astringent and of no lasting virtue. More vigour than fullness: in short, thin.
1978	137	153	398	119	52	Small harvest, excellent quality. Remarkable wines which have not yet reached their peak. A classic vintage thanks to clear, warm and entirely typical aromas (undoubtedly the best since 1929).
1979	214	233	519	131	58	Wines which were finally successful despite initial fears. Sometimes perfect, often very "white" (new-style Burgundy).
1980	233	194	485	135	71	Cold, wet June, late vegetation, thin harvest. This vintage, saved at the eleventh hour, has been greatly decried but has produced some good wines. The whites often have much perfume but are sinewy and thin.
1981	174	149	458	135	32	Very good whites, rather lively with a hint of acidity. More successful than the reds. Autumn saved the day.
1982	442	305	713	223	61	Like 1973, this could be called the year of the grower; very satisfactory quality (supple, agreeable wines) and a phenomenal quantity.
1983	377	144	557	189	41	Successful though hard wines with predominant astringency, typical of a vintage for long keeping. The natural degree of alcohol was very high and the wines have often evolved in the same way as the 1971s.
1984	107	195	396	138	60	Whites fairly good; overall satisfactory, despite difficult weather conditions and generous chaptalization.
1985	118	298	521	164	89	Great vintage with all the qualities expected of the great Burgundies. Perfectly balanced.
1986	165	319	608	216	82	Generally the whites are more successful that the reds.
1987	257	217	473	155	79	The weather situation was the opposite of 1984: after a very rainy summer, the sun saved everything in September. Difficult harvesting because of the return of the bad weather. Modest quantity but sometimes dazzling wines, more brilliant in reds than whites.
1988	356	346	508	183	136	A model of regularity in the vegetative cycle of the vine led to an exceptional vintage for the reds, with deep concentration and for long keeping. Abundant harvest for the whites. Quite fresh, more slender than fat.
1989	276	285	528	174	71	The vintage of the Bicentenary. Another great year with a 9. Maximum sunshine and early harvest. The whites are rich and fat, sweet and generous, a great success. In ten years'time, will it be the 88s or the 89s that come out top? A real conundrum.

Abbreviations: M (Montrachet), CM (Chevalier-Montrachet), BM (Bâtard-Montrachet), BBM (Bienvenues-Bâtard-Montrachet), CBM (Criots-Bâtard-Montrachet), nd (not declared).

Size: *Montrachet,* 8 ha 7 a 51 ca according to the Land Register, 7 ha 99 a 80 ca according to the INAO, *Chevalier-Montrachet:* 7 ha 14 a 50 ca (decree of June 13 1939), 6 ha 95 a 72 ca (present Land Register), *Bâtard-Montrachet:* 5 ha 81 a 80 ca in Chassagne-Montrachet, 3 ha 71 a 47 ca in Puligny-Montrachet, i.e. 9 ha 53 a 27 ca (decree of June 13 1939). *Bienvenues-Bâtard-Montrachet:* 3 ha 68 a 60 ca. *Criots-Bâtard-Montrachet:* 1 ha 57 a 20 ca.

Curiosities

Under the evocative name of John Bourgoyne, Laurence Clark Powell relates his amorous adventures when he was a student in Dijon and Burgundy (*Le Train bleu*, Buchet-Chastel, 1978). One of the heroines of the book is called Madeleine Montrechet – obviously a thinly disguised homage to this famous *cru*... "Madeleine Montrechet warms the body with her soul," wrote Henry Miller in his preface. The same might be said of the wine.

*

Sir Francis Chichester was making his solo voyage round the world in his *Gipsy Moth*. On February 24, 1967, a tempest was raging round Cape Horn. But the navigator continued his log. That day he wrote: "I drink a toast to the health of my wife Sheila with a delicious Montrachet which she has put on board for me... What a wonderful, quite exceptional wife Sheila is! I shed a tear for her. But let us not be sentimental; let us get back to the delicious Montrachet and enjoy it to the full..." (published in *Life*, June 1967, then issued in one volume).

*

W. Somerset Maugham adored Montrachet. In his novel *The Razor's Edge*, published in France in 1947, he mentions this wine several times. In connection with a picnic, one of his characters says:
"I had told them it would be a flop. I had begged Louisa to include a bottle of Montrachet which I had sent her just before the war, but she would not listen. They took a flask of hot coffee and nothing else. What can you expect in such conditions?" And then at table: "Mellowed by the generous Montrachet served at the beginning of lunch and by the delicate Bordeaux which had followed, Elliott considered with blissful satisfaction the various possibilities which sprang to mind..."

*

A number of towns have streets called Montrachet: Creusot, for example, or Dijon.

*

The heroes of Paul-Loup Sulitzer's novel *Popov* drink a Bienvenues-Bâtard-Montrachet 1978 from Ramonet-Prudhon. This dinner took place at Chapel's restaurant in Mionnay.

*

Recent auctions of Montrachet at *Christie's* in London: 1,050 francs for a bottle of Domaine de Laguiche 1953, 7,800 francs for a jeroboam of Domaine de Laguiche 1959, 44,000 francs for a case (12 bottles) of Domaine de la Romanée-Conti 1969. Same Domaine: 27,000 francs for a case of 1970, 55,000 francs a case of 1971, 25,000 francs a case of 1978. Domaine Thénard: 7,200 francs a case of 1978, 6,000 francs a case of 1983. Domaine de Laguiche: 8,600 francs a case of 1983. At *Nouveau Drouot*, 3 bottles of Montrachet 1971: 2,500 francs (November 21, 1986).

*

The other Montrachet and its cheese
Just as from long-standing practice there are vines called La Romanée, several *crus* called Musigny, a Morey in the canton of Givry which is etymologically the brother of the Morey from Côte de Nuits, another Montrachet has the right to this name.
Not far away from the first, it is generally known as the name of a cheese – *Montrachet*. The Château de Montrachet is in the hamlet of Messeugne, a commune of Savigny-sur-Grosne in Saône-et-Loire and has always been known by this name. Mont-Rachet, the origin of the name's is etymologically identical. The monks of Cluny had a sort of convalescent home here.
The grandparents of Michel Marmorat, the present managing director of the cheese factory Montrachet SA now situated in the château, were poulterers, selling poultry round Lyons. "René Marmorat, my father, created the cheese factory which, thanks to a trade secret, can

make cheeses all year round. At first they were farmhouse cheeses in the Charolais style. Then we specialized in traditional goat cheese, obtaining the milk from the centre of France. There was a wide range of products, 60% of which was exported to the United States. *Montrachet* was a name we registered in 1956 as a dairy product. In 1986, the firm of Bresse-Bleu – an agricultural co-operative whose head office is in Servas in the *département* of Ain – decided to start making goat cheeses. It was interested in our factory and our brand name. That is how Bresse-Bleu came to take over Montrachet SA."

A collector, finisher and seller of cheeses, René Marmorat died in 1971, and now his son Michel markets one million cheeses per year, of which 600,000 go to the United States. Expansion is in the offing, for Bresse-Bleu plans to produce its own Montrachet and is currently enlarging its American factory in Wisconsin to manufacture it in the United States. Beside the château, two small places called La Garenne and Les Clos formerly produced a great deal of wine. People nostalgically remember rows nearly three-quarters of a mile long along the hillside. Poor harvesters! There are still a few vines up at the top, belonging to the growers of the *cave coopérative* of Saint-Gengoux-le-National. The Montrachet press is in the Caveau of Viré. All this land which today produces maize and colza is classified as Bourgogne AOC. Furthermore, trace has been found of a wine of Montrachet (Savigny-sur-Grosne) which was awarded a gold medal at an exhibition in Brussels at the beginning of the century.

It is claimed that the monks of Cluny learned and perfected their work here and then transplanted their vines to Chassagne and Puligny to create a second Montrachet. It is even claimed that the name Montrachet was sold to the two villages in the Côte de Beaune. Pure fable...

According to Androuet, the great cheese expert, Montrachet made with goat's milk is a soft paste with a thin crust, drained for several days. It spends a week in a ventilated cellar. It is generally in the shape of a cylinder 10 cm high and 5 to 6 cm in diameter. It weighs about 100 g and is sometimes wrapped in vine or chestnut leaves.

*

Chassagne stone

Chassagne has fine quarries of stone which is as hard as that of Comblanchien (only Dijon spiced bread is denser), as pink as that of Premeaux or beige like the limestone of Burgundy, and which was used for the Trocadéro or the *Café de Paris*. The Ministry of Finance, a recent extension of the Louvre, used stone from Chassagne. These quarries have been worked industrially since the middle of the nineteenth century (today by Rocamat and Gabriel Lardet): they produce some 4000 cubic metres of blocks yearly, sold primarily in France, Switzerland and Belgium.

Huge underground quarries in Puligny were once worked for vitrifiable sand and friable rock, crushed by a millstone and used in Chalon-sur-Saône for glassmaking. Found to be potentially dangerous, they were closed in 1873 and are now no more than a memory. Between the two world wars these quarries served for mushroom-growing. One of them is now a wine cellar.

*

One of the best restaurants in New York is called *Le Montrachet* (235 W Broadway).

And I quote...

Morachet *(sic)* is a little area between Chassagne and Puligny on the plain with a vein of earth which makes this terrain the only one of its kind; it produces a white wine, the most curious and most delicious in France; there is no other wine its equal, be it a wine from the Côte Rôtie, a Muscat, or a Frontignan. It is made in very small quantities, and accordingly it sells at a very high price; and to obtain some, you have to order it a year in advance, it being always reserved before it is even made. But take care not to be deceived, for vines which are neighbours to this vineyard somewhat resemble it in quality and sometimes pass for Montrachet. That is why you should be sure of having a trustworthy agent if you wish to procure some. This wine has qualities whose finesse can be expressed neither by the Latin nor the French tongue. I have drunk six or seven casks and am unable to express its delicacy and excellence.

> Abbé Claude Arnoux
> *Dissertation sur la situation de la Bourgogne,*
> *sur les vins qu'elle produit, etc.* (1728)

The most excellent white wine in Europe.

> Abbé Claude Courtépée
> *Description générale et particulière*
> *du duché de Bourgogne* (1775-1785)

It combines all the qualities which go to make a perfect wine. It has body, a high alcohol content and great finesse, a very agreeable flavour of hazelnut, unique and distinctive, and in particular a vitality and bouquet whose intensity and smoothness distinguish it from the other white wines of Burgundy.

> André Jullien
> *Topographie de tous les vignobles connus*
> (1822 and successive editions until 1866)

In good years its lightness, its perfume, its finesse, its extreme delicacy, its liveliness without being dry, its sweetness without being insipid, make it one of the best white wines you can drink.

> Dr Denis Morelot
> *Statistiques de la vigne dans le*
> *département de la Côte-d'Or*

So the wine of Montrachet should be considered as one of those rare marvels of which the chance of appreciating its perfection is granted to only a chosen few. Let the man who is able to buy a few bottles of the best vintages consider himself fortunate, whatever the price; he will never have paid too much.

> Dr Jules Lavalle
> *Histoire et statistique de la vigne*
> *et des grands vins de la Côte-d'Or* (1855)

It is an acknowledged fact that the wine of Montrachet as such is the best of all French wines.

> Alexandre Dumas
> *Grand Dictionnaire de Cuisine*

This admirable white wine is the foremost of the white wines of Burgundy, just as Château Yquem is the foremost white wine of Bordeaux. Leave them to fight it out between them, say the enthusiasts; but let us simply observe that they are both the foremost white wines of the whole world... After admiring this Montrachet, this jewel, which is one of the brightest if not the most brilliant of the jewels in the Côte-d'Or, what more can I add?

> Bertall
> *La vigne* (1878)

It is the *extravagance of perfection*, as the people of Bordeaux say of their Château Yquem in its great years. These kings of wine – Château Lafite, Romanée, Montrachet – defy hyperbole.

Adrien Berget
Les vins de France (1900)

White wines are rare in the Côte-d'Or; but one of them has a reputation comparable to that of Yquem in Gironde: it is the Montrachet.

Paul Jamain
La Vigne et le Vin (1901)

The pearl of Burgundy white wines... full-bodied, mellow, a rich bouquet, halfway between Meursault and Chablis; taste of hazelnut. Can be kept for a very long time.

Ali-Bab (Babinsky)

The sumptuous slope of the vineyard sweeps down from this cheerless solitude; and from this association of robust soil and fiery atmosphere is born the precious wine blending the energy of iron ore and the sunbeams' flame.

Camille Rodier
LE vin de Bourgogne (1920)

Very great. The best makes your veins stand out like whipcord.

George Saintsbury
Notes on a Cellar-Book (1920)

The amber colour of Montrachet is of a unique liveliness. You would think that it has absorbed more sun than all the others. Its mellowness caresses your palate and then its bouquet develops with an extraordinary power and unctuousness, like a *Magnificat* reverberating in the vaults of some Gothic cathedral.

Maurice des Ombiaux
Le Gotha des vins de France (1925)

A great, loyal and powerful lord which dominates all other Burgundies by its vitality virility and, by the majesty of its concentrated aroma. which perfumes the whole of the room in which it has been uncorked, shedding its solar beads in a vast crystal glass, and by its colours of amber and topaz; by its truly personal flavour of ripe grapes and almond which thrills the palate and slips like a sunbeam into the crannies of the larynx, smoothing its honey along the insid of your mouth to finish by lining your throat, then gradually fading away slowly, like the vibrations of a bell... like a superb twilight.

Dr Paul Ramain
Les grands vins de France (1931)

Montrachet. There can be no greater name on a wine list. It is splendid in its isolation.

Pierre Léon-Gauthier
Les Clos de Bourgogne (1931)

... and finally the divine Montrachet. The apotheosis of the great Burgundies, this liquid gold with its green-gleaming beams of magic.

Gaston Roupnel
La Bourgogne (1936)

My walk came to an end at Montrachet, that land of miracles; that scrap of land which, with every visit, seems to diminish, so narrow is it and sparse. Yet what grandeur, what splendour in its wine! When I drink it, at home or with friends, this wine surprises me by its superiority, placing it clearly way above all the others. Whenever I come across it I am amazed by it, and I hope it will never cease to astonish me.

Pierre Poupon
Vignes et jours (1963)

It is not a wine; it is an event.

Frank M. Schoonmaker
Encyclopaedia of Wine (1967)

The Montrachet vineyard is the *great lord*. Like Yquem in Sauternes or Romanée-Conti in the Côte de Nuits, it cannot be classified: it is above and beyond any system of classification... When I drink it, I have the same impression as when I first heard the *Eroica Symphony*.

Frederick S. Wildman Jr.
A Wine Tour of France (1967)

Montrachet? It is so full that you recognize it with the first sip.

Raymond Dumay
Guide du Vin(1967)

These white wines, with their green-gold colour and perfume resembling hazelnut, are both unctuous and dry, that is to say that they have no sugar, are supple and as soft as velvet.

Edouard Kressmann
Le Guide des vins et vignobles de France (1975)

The greatest white table wines produced anywhere in the world come from the vineyards of Puligny-Montrachet in the heart of the Côte de Beaune in the French Burgundy country.

Terry Robards
The New York Times Book of Wine (1977)

The *grand cru* – THE *grand cru* – is Le Montrachet, indisputably the greatest dry white table wine (...). It is a great, round, deep wine, with a lovely bouquet, and its fullness contains delicate undertones...

H.W. Yoxall
The Wines of Burgundy (1968 and 1974)

It is almost impossible to find the words to do justice to this wine, and words alone can often do little more than convey vague impressions or sensations (...) My own very first tasting was a revelation: the wine was masterly and so exquisite that it almost seemed decadent .

Hubrecht Duijker
The Great Wines of Burgundy (1983)

A wine of exceptional elegance and breeding.

Alexis Lichine
Encyclopaedia of Wines and Spirits (1979)

The *Grand Cru* Montrachet earns its fame by an almost unbelievable concentration of the qualities of white Burgundy. It has more scent, a brighter gold, a longer flavour, more succulence and yet more definition; everything about it is intensified – the mark of truly great wine.

Hugh Johnson
World Atlas of Wine (1977)

The best dry white wine in France... An exquisite wine, golden with shades of green; an unforgettable perfume blending ripe grapes, honey and almonds.

Jon Winroth
Cuisine et Vins de France (November 1982)

In it all the properties that the mouth water in memory and anticipation are brought to a resounding climax.

Hugh Johnson
Wine Companion (1983)

A star!

Revue du Vin de France (December 1986)

Honey, almonds, hawthorn and great textured richness are all found in Le Montrachet.

Serena Sutcliffe
Pocket Guide to the Wines of Burgundy (1986)

Magnificent!

Harvey Steiman
The Wine Spectator (February 1988)

Bibliography

Alexandre (Jean-Louis), *Le Village de Puligny, la grange de Blagny et leur finage à la fin du Moyen Age*, Ecole pratique des hautes études, 1987.

Arnoux, *Dissertation sur la situation de Bourgogne, sur les vins qu'elle produit, etc.*, London, 1728 (re-edited by Daniel Morcrette in Luzarches, 1973).

Bazin (Jean-François), *Le Clos de Vougeot*, Paris. Jacques Legrand, 1987.

Berger (Adrien), *Les Vins de France*, Paris, F. Alcan, 1900.

Bertall, *La Vigne, voyage autour des vins de France*, Paris, Plon, 1878.

Blanchet (Suzanne), *Les Vins de Bourgogne*, Jema, 1985.

Cannard (Henri), *Puligny-Montrachet et son vignoble*, from the author, BP 11, 21021 Dijon-Lac, 1986.

Courtépée (abbé Claude) and Beguillet, *Description historique et topographique du duché de Bourgogne*, Dijon, 1775-1788, re-edited several times (notably by Horvath in Roanne, 1986).

Danguy (R.) and Aubertin (Ch.), *Les Grands Vins de Bourgogne (la Côte-d'Or)*, 1892 (re-edited by Laffitte Reprints in Marseilles, 1978).

Deschamps (Fanny), *Croque-en-bouche*, Albin Michel, 1976 and in the Livre de Poche series. A delightful portrait of the Ramonet family, visited by Alain Chapel, an old friend.

Doutrelant (Pierre-Marie), *Le Prince de Bourgogne* in *L'Express*, February 28, 1986.

Dubrion (Roger), *Contribution climatique à l'étude du milieu d'implantation des plantes à affinités méditerranéennes en Bourgogne orientale*, Dijon University Press, 1973 (and different studies on the climatography of Montrachet).

Dumay (Raymond) *et al. Le Vin de Bourgogne*, Montalba, 1976.

Dumay (Raymond), *La Mort du vin*, Stock, 1976.

Duijker (Hubrecht), *Grands Vins de Bourgogne*, Fernand Nathan, 1980.

Fèvre (Danielle), *Histoire de la seigneurie de Chassagne au Moyen Age*, Dijon University Press, 1962.

Gadille (Roland), *Le Vignoble de la Côte bourguignonne*, Les Belles Lettres, Paris, 1967.

Galtier (Gaston), *La Viticulture de l'Europe occidentale à la veille de la Révolution française, d'après les notes de voyage de Thomas Jefferson*, Société languedocienne de géographie, n° 3, June-Septmeber 1968, Montpellier University Press.

Grivot (Françoise), *Le Commerce des vins de Bourgogne*, Sabri, Paris, 1964.

Hanson (Anthony), *Burgundy*, Faber and Faber, London, 1982.

Jamain (Paul), *La Vigne et le vin*, O. Doin - Librairie agricole, Paris, 1901.

Jefferson and Wine, The Vinifera Growers Association, The Plains, Virginia, 1976. Thomas Jefferson's Burgundy travel-notes were published by Princeton University Press (1955-1956).

Johnson (Hugh), *The World Atlas of Wine*, Mitchell Beazley, 1977; *Wine Companion*, Mitchell Beazley.

Jullien (André) *Topographie de tous les vignobles connus*, Lacroix et Baudry, Paris, 1832, several editions from 1816 to 1848 (re-edited by Champion-Slatkine, Paris-Geneva, 1985).

Landrieu-Lussigny (Marie-Hélène), *Le Vignoble bourguignon, ses lieux-dits*, Jeanne Laffitte, Marseilles, 1983.

Laurent (Robert), *Les Vignerons de la Côte-d'Or au XIXe siècle*, Les Belles Lettres, Paris, 1958.

Lavalle (Dr Jules). *Histoire et statistique des grands vins de la Côte-d'Or*, Dusacq, Paris, 1855 (re-edited by the Geisweiler Foundation, 1972).

Léon-Gauthier (Pierre), *Les Clos de Bourgogne*, Librairie de la Renaissance, Beaune, 1931.

Levine (Jonathan), *Le Montrachet* in *The Friends of Wine*, August-September 1988.

Leygnier (Alain), *Montrachet: Petit vignoble pour Vin immense* in *Cuisine et Vins de France*, September 1988.

Lichine (Alexis), *Encyclopaedia of Wines and Spirits*, Weidenfield and Nicholson 1979.

Luchet (Auguste), *La Côte-d'Or à vol d'oiseau*, Michel Lévy, Paris, 1858.

Manuel des vignerons-associés de Chassagne, suivi d'une notice historique et très intéressante sur ce village, Beaune, 1844.

Montorgueil (Georges), *Le Vin de Bourgogne*, edited by Ets. Nicolas in the series *Monseigneur le Vin*, 1926.

Morelot (Dr Denis), *Statistique œnologique de l'arrondissement de Beaune*, Paris, 1825; *Statistique de la vigne dans le département de la Côte-d'Or*, Dijon-Paris, 1831.

Patriarche (A.), *La Famille royale des vins de France*, Paris, circa 1910.

Pitiot (Sylvain) and Poupon (Pierre), *Atlas des grands vignobles de Bourgogne*, Jacques Legrand, Paris, 1985.

Poupon (Pierre), *Vignes et jours*, 1963. A few pages on the wine of Montrachet.

Poupon (Pierre) and Forgeot (Pierre), *Les Vins de Bourgogne*, P.U.F., 1985.

Pouteau (Jean-Luc) and De Rabaudy (Nicolas), *Le Mariage des mets et des vins*, J.-C. Lattès, 1986.

Quittanson (Charles), *Connaissance des vins et eaux-de-vie*, Borelli, 1984.

Ramain (Paul), *Les Grands Vins de France*, La Vie technique et industrielle, Paris, 1931 (re-edited by Laffitte Reprints, Marseilles, 1980). This work includes an article on the wine of Montrachet.

Renoy (Georges), *Les Mémoires du Bourgogne*, B.A.V., 1985.

Rodier (Camille), *Le Vin de Bourgogne*, Damidot, Dijon, 1920, 1937 and 1948 (re-edited by Laffitte Reprints and Damidot, 1981).

Roupnel (Gaston), *La Bourgogne*, Horizons de France, Paris, 1936.

Rozet (Georges), *La Bourgogne tastevin en main*, Horizons de France, Paris, 1949.

Schoonmaker (Frank M.), *Encyclopaedia of Wine*, London, 1967.

Steiman (Harvey), *Magnificent Montrachet*, in *The Wine Spectator*, February 29, 1988.

Sutcliffe (Serena) *et al. Great Vineyards and Winemakers*, QED, London, 1981.

Sutcliffe (Serena), *Guide to the Wines of Burgundy*, Flammarion, 1987.

Vialay (Amadée), *La Vente des Biens nationaux pendant la Révolution française*, Perrin et Cie, Paris, 1908.

Yoxall (H.W.), *The Wines of Burgundy*, Stein and Day, New York, 1970 and 1978.

The Municipal Libraries of Beaune, Dijon and Autun.

The Archives of the Côte-d'Or and ancient Province of Burgundy.

The Archives of Saône-et-Loire.

Index

Picture acknowledgements:

Jean-François Bazin (18, 86 133, 134, 143, 174, 176 right); Bernuy (170 bottom); Christian Chesnais (14, 22, 24, 26, 30, 33, 42, 46, 50, 64, 67, 68, 83, 84, 86 bottom left, 90, 93, 95, 111 left, 113, 120, 124, 125, 130, 131, 132, 137, 141, 149, 151, 152, 153, 154, 157, 160, 164, 166, 171); Jean-Pierre Coqueau (170 top); Maison Louis Jadot (Jean-Pierre Muzard: 147); Domaine Laroche (178 right); Domaine Leflaive (58 right, 61); Laurie Matheson (136, 178 left, 180 right); Michel Plassart (cover, 35, 38, 56, 72, 74, 78, 81, 98, 100, 103, 106, 108, 109, 122, 159, 162, 176 left, 179, 180 left); Photo X (111, 138).